Crane Brinton, Professor of History at Harvard University, has now been at his alma mater for almost fifty years, although he received his Dr. Phil. from Oxford in 1923. A Fellow of the National Institute of Arts and Letters, the American Philosophical Society, and the American Academy of Arts and Sciences, he is also a Chevalier of the Légion d'Honneur and President of the American Historical Association. His fifteen books include *English Political Thought in the Nineteenth Century* (1933, 1949), *The Anatomy of Revolution* (1938, 1952), *A History of Western Morals* (1959), *The Fate of Man* (1961), and *Ideas and Men* (1950, 1963), of which this book is a part.

Dr. Brinton claims that his Age of Reason began at Harvard under Harold Laski and Irving Babbitt, whose contrary influences he has been trying to reconcile ever since. "My earlier optimistic rationalism," he says, "has been tempered by an awareness of the place of prejudices, sentiments, the unconscious, and the subconcious in human life." And yet, he adds, "I think I have kept to the basic belief of my youth in the rightness . . . of human reason."

The Shaping of Modern Thought consists of chapters 7-14 and the Introduction of *Ideas and Men,* second edition. The original edition was published by New American Library as *The Shaping of the Modern Mind.*

THE SHAPING OF
MODERN THOUGHT

CRANE BRINTON

Prentice-Hall, Inc., *Englewood Cliffs, N. J.*

To my wife

Current printing (last digit):

15 14 13 12 11 10 9 8 7

TABLE OF CONTENTS

INTRODUCTION

Scope and Purpose

This is a book about the world-views of men in our Western tradition, the ideas they have held and still hold on the Big Questions—cosmological questions, which ask whether the universe makes sense in terms of human capacity to comprehend and, if so, what kind of sense; theological and metaphysical questions, which ask further questions about purpose and design of the universe, and about man's place in it; and ethical and aesthetic questions, which ask whether what we do and what we want to do make sense, ask what we *really* mean by good and bad, by beautiful and ugly. The recorded answers to these and similar questions—that is, most of our Western philosophy, art, literature, and in some senses, natural science—fill millions of volumes. Any account of them, therefore, must omit vastly more than it can include.

There are many possible schemes for guiding the historian of these ideas and attitudes, for what we may call figuratively the cartography of ideas. The figure is more apt than such analogies often are, for neither the historian nor the cartographer can ever reproduce the reality they are trying to communicate to the reader of books or of maps; they can but give a plan, a series of indications, of this reality. There are contrasting schemes for choosing from enormous numbers of geographic details. You may have a map in which every feature that can be named, every hill, brook, crossroads, is crowded in; or you may have a map in which many details are omitted in the effort to show the reader the lay of the land, the shape of the mountain systems, the relations of drainage, relief, communications, and so on. Both kinds are useful, depending on the needs of the user. In mapping the history of ideas, this book will definitely attempt to follow the second scheme. It will try to show the lay of the cultural and intellectual land; it will omit many famous names, and perhaps even a few landmarks, in an effort to make clear what large groups of men and women in the West have felt about the answers to the great questions of human destiny.

There is, however, another important, contrasting set of schemes for guiding the intellectual historian. This may be put as the contrast between picking out the ideas and attitudes the historian thinks are right, or true, and setting forth a fair selection of ideas and attitudes for the reader to exercise his own judgment upon. The first, translated into educational terms, is based on the principle "To teach is to affirm"; the second is based on the principle "To teach is to put problems." In the real world, these two are by no means mutually exclusive. The most dogmatic approach—at least in the West—hardly means that the learner repeats by rote exactly what he hears or reads; and the most tentative and open-minded approach hardly means that no one takes anything on authority, that everybody works out his own ideas in his own private world. Both poles are as bleak and as uninhabited as the poles of this earth. Nevertheless, this book will try to keep to the hemisphere of the second pole, to the principle that the individual should do a great deal of his own thinking and choosing—that, to use Alfred North Whitehead's expressive phrase, intellectual history is an "adventure of ideas" for anyone who will embark on it. But all adventure implies uncertainty.

These two choices—for the broad lines instead of the details, and for independent thinking instead of absorbing "correct" information and interpretation—are in accord with a growing feeling in the United States that in the past we have absorbed too many facts and have thought about them too little.

This feeling is clear in the movement for general education, by whatever name it may be called. Like most such movements, that for general education may well go too far. Folk wisdom recognizes the danger of throwing the baby out with the bath. The "baby" of good sound command of the necessary facts is one that no sensible person wants to throw out. On the whole, however, our culture is admirably organized to permit the rapid and accurate accumulation of and ready access to the facts necessary to useful thinking about a given problem. Libraries, encyclopedias, textbooks that are really reference books, all abound.

The "baby" of sound generalizations, or theories, is also one that no sensible person wants to throw out. But there is a difficulty here, that of determining which generalizations are sound and which are not. In fields such as natural science, there exists a core of theories that are known by all competent persons and must be accepted by all who work in the field. This, as we shall shortly see, is simply not so in the fields of theology, philosophy, literature, and art, where it is plain that men of education and taste do differ widely. For in these fields we are not just asking ourselves *what is,* but rather we all feel, more or less strongly, that *something else ought to be.*

Now in a democratic society it is believed that each member of the society has a part to play in the complex process by which *ought*—that is, men's wants and the communicable forms they give those wants—slowly, imperfectly, unpredictably perhaps, alters *is*. (The problems we meet trying to understand and control this process, indeed the problem as to whether such human control of this process is possible—that is, the old question of determinism or freedom of the will—are good examples of the insoluble but persistent and by no means unimportant problems that have vexed the Western mind for millennia.) In a democratic society, the individual must exercise his judgment on questions like this, for if he does not, they may be answered by authoritarian enemies of democracy in a way he will not like. The word "exercise" was chosen deliberately; it means mental as well as physical effort. But mental effort means making decisions, trying to solve problems not decided in advance, trying to balance and choose among conflicting generalizations. This book should give the serious reader ample opportunity for such exercise.

It is not a book designed primarily to impart information, not a book that will help the reader to shine very brightly in quiz programs. It is not a history of any one of the great disciplines, theology, philosophy, scholarship, science, literature, art. A brief book that covered all these fields would be no more than a list of names and a few more or less appropriate labels, like the "ethereal Shelley" and the "sweet-voiced Keats." More especially, this book is not a history of philosophy; it is not written by a professional philosopher and it treats no philosopher fully and in the round. It makes an effort to deal with that part of a philosopher's work that went into the climate of opinion of the intellectual classes. It is, to use D. C. Somervell's distinction, rather a history of opinion than a history of thought. It is no substitute, for those who wish to undergo such discipline, for a thorough study of the history of formal philosophy.

One final word of explanation. The serious reader may find our approach to many of these problems the reverse of serious, may find it light, undignified. This is a genuine difficulty. It seems to the writer that many of the grand questions about the beautiful and the good have commonly been approached, especially among English-speaking peoples, with so much reverence that *ought* has been disastrously confused with *is*. Americans like to think they are idealists, and many of them are. But foreigners often accuse us of keeping our ideals and our actions in separate compartments. They are unfair, but their position has a base in fact. We tend as a people to revere certain abstract ideas so much that we are likely to fall into the error of thinking that once we have got the ideas on paper, once we have legal and verbal acceptance of a goal as virtuous, then we have attained the goal. Witness many plans for world government, now, right away, by getting a world constitutional convention to work. Witness the Eighteenth Amendment. In this book an attempt is made at a clinician's attitude toward these matters, an attitude that demands working over a good deal of the petty and the undignified in order to understand what we are really dealing with when we study ideas at work among living human beings. It is an attitude not of *irreverence,* but of *nonreverence* while the clinical work is being done. In no sense does it involve a denial of the existence—and desirability—of the beautiful and the good, any more than the attitude of the medical clinician involves a denial of the existence and the desirability of the healthy and the sane.

The Limits of Intellectual History

The field of study known as intellectual history or history of ideas is not a clear-cut and simple one. Under some such labels there can be found a wide range of actual subject matter, from the writings of very abstract philosophers to expressions of popular superstition like triskaidekaphobia, which in simpler language is excessive fear of the number thirteen. Intellectual historians have dealt with the ideas of the philosopher and with those of the man in the street. Their main job, however, is to try to find *the relations between the ideas of the philosophers, the intellectuals, the thinkers, and the actual way of living of the millions who carry the tasks of civilization.*

It is a job that should chiefly differentiate intellectual history from such old, established disciplines as the history of philosophy, the history of science, and the history of literature. The intellctual historian is interested in ideas wherever he find them, in wild ideas as well as in sensible ideas, in refined speculation and in common prejudices; but he is interested in these products of men's mental activity as they influence, and are influenced by, men's whole existence. He will not, then, deal solely with abstract ideas that breed more abstract ideas; he will not deal, for instance, with that very abstract political theory known as the social contract as though it were just a bit of legal reasoning. But he will treat even the most abstract ideas as these ideas filter into the heads and hearts of ordinary men and women; he will try to explain what the social contract meant to those eighteenth-century rebels who held that their rulers had violated it.

This is a difficult task. The intellectual historian is trying to work out a very complex set of relations between what a few men write or say and what many men actually do. He finds it very easy, at least for the last twenty-five hundred years of our Western society, to discover and analyze what the few have written and said. That record is not perfect, but it is extraordinarily good, even for ancient Greece and Rome, thanks to the labors of generations of scholars. But, until the printing press and popular education gave the historian in newspapers, periodicals, pamphlets, and the like a record of what ordinary men thought and felt, the rest of the intellectual historian's task was very difficult. The historian can describe pretty clearly how all sorts of people in Germany and outside Germany regarded Adolf Hitler; he can never know just how the common, unheard millions of people in the Graeco-Roman world regarded Julius Caesar. There were no Gallup polls in those days, no letters to the editor, no popular magazines. Nevertheless, if he is not to limit himself to analyzing ideas in terms of still more ideas, the intellectual historian must make an effort to piece together from scattered sources some notion of how ideas got to work among the crowd.

There is, indeed, some justification for limiting intellectual history to what the late J. H. Robinson called the "intellectual classes." Professor Baumer of Yale has defined the intellectual class as "not only the comparatively small group of really profound and original thinkers, not only the professional philosophers, scientists, theologians, and scholars in general, but also creative literary men and artists, the popularizers, and the intelligent reading public." In a way, it would seem sensible that intellectual history should be confined to the doings, sayings, and writings of intellectuals; and yet Professor Baumer's definition seems a bit too narrow. Not until the eighteenth century was there anything like a reading public. Moreover, quite unintellectual, even, in a scholarly, bookish, verbal sense, quite unintelligent, human beings do entertain ideas about right and wrong, have purposes that can be, and are, stated in words, and are moved by all sorts of beliefs, creeds, superstitions, traditions, and sentiments. The history of the intellectual classes is worth writing, but it is not the whole of intellectual history; or if it is, some other name must be found for what this book is concerned with.

Sources for the study of the ideas (in the broadest sense) of ordinary men and women are, in fact, many. Literature is obviously less purely intellectual, less highbrow, than formal philosophy or science. What has survived from the days before printing is, of course, relatively highbrow. From Greek, Roman, medieval, and even Renaissance times we have more of the equivalent of *The New York Times* and less of the equivalent of the tabloids, more of the equivalent of T. S. Eliot or Alfred North Whitehead and less of the equivalent of *Little Orphan Annie*. Still, we have a great deal that is obviously nearer to earth than philosophy. We can check on the philosopher Socrates as he appeared to his disciple Plato by reading Aristophanes' *Clouds,* in which a popular and successful playwright makes fun of Socrates. We can see medieval men and women, not only as the theologians and philosophers described them, but as men of the world—like Chaucer in his *Canterbury Tales*—described them.

The ordinary man has, indeed, left many traces other than those left in what we call literature. Of religions we have not only the theologies—

that is, the more obviously intellectual elements corresponding to what in secular matters is called philosophy—but also the rituals, the daily practices, and even what, if we feel patronizing, we call the superstitions of ancient and medieval men. A great deal of what the intellectual historian must draw on has been amassed by specialists called social historians, who have set themselves the task of finding how men and women of all classes actually lived. These social historians have often been interested, not only in what men and women ate, and wore, and did to earn a living, but also in what they believed true or false, right or wrong, in what they wanted from life on this earth and in the next world. Many social historians became, in a sense, intellectual historians, focusing on what went on in the heart and head of the man in the street.

The full task of the intellectual historian, then, is to gather into an intelligible whole materials ranging from abstract philosophic concepts to concrete acts of men. At one end of his spectrum, he comes close to being a philosopher, or at least a historian of philosophy, and at the other end he comes close to being a social historian, or just a plain historian, concerned with the daily lives of human beings. But his special task is to bring the two ends together, to follow ideas in their often tortuous path from study or laboratory to the market, the club, the home, the legislative chamber, the law court, the conference table, and the battlefield.

In carrying out this ambitious task, the intellectual historian may find himself invading still another field of study long cultivated by scholars. This is the vague, all-embracing field traditionally known as the philosophy of history. The philosopher of history tries to use his knowledge of what has happened in the past to unlock all the mysteries of man's fate. A complete philosophy of history (like any and all philosophies) seeks to give final answers to all the Big Questions: What is the good life? How can human beings lead the good life? What are the prospects that human beings will be able to lead the good life? In short, where are we, and where are we going?

In a later chapter, we shall try to see how it comes about that in this mid-twentieth century some of the most popular philosophical systems are in fact philosophies of history, and that names like Spengler, Sorokin, and Toynbee are known wherever high intellectual matters are discussed. For the present we need only note that the intellectual historian, though he may well be tempted to put on the mantle of the prophet and philosopher of history, ought to resist the temptation to do so. He will work more profitably if he confines himself to the more modest but still arduous task of tracing the ways in which the answers men have given to the Big Questions—Life, Destiny, Right, Truth, God—have apparently affected their conduct. He may—and indeed if he is a normal human being he will—have his own answers to some, at least, of the Big Questions.

But if he is true to the traditions of science and scholarship as they have matured for the historian of today, he will do his best to keep his own answers from affecting his report of other men's answers. Again, we shall in later chapters have more to say about this whole matter of scientific method and objectivity and its relation to the study of human behavior. Here it should be sufficient to note that intellectual history as interpreted in this book is not offered as an answer to all the problems that beset modern men, but rather as a help toward putting some of those problems more clearly and, perhaps, toward indicating what consequences are likely to follow upon various attempts to solve them.

Indeed, the reader should be warned that the task of tracing the work ideas have done and still do among the great masses of human beings in Western society can be but imperfectly done. It is not merely that the historical sources before modern times are lacking or difficult to assemble; competent specialists, once their attention is turned to this problem, can over the next few generations do something to supplement our lack of materials. There is a graver difficulty. We do not yet understand sufficiently well, despite the work of psychologists, sociologists, and philosophers, just what goes on in men's minds and hearts, just how they are moved to action—or to inaction. Above all, men who have long studied these problems are by no means agreed concerning the part played in human behavior by reason, logic, ideas, knowledge, in contrast with emotion, sentiment, drives, urges. There is among such men a by no means complete agreement that there is to be found in concrete human behavior some such components as the rational and the nonrational, but there is no universally accepted set of effective working definitions of these terms.

The reader must not expect from the study of the history of ideas the kind of answers to problems the engineer, for instance, expects to get to his problems. The fact is that we are dealing in this book mostly with what must be called imprecise thinking, a term used here descriptively, not scornfully. It is true that thinkers in the Western tradition we may call scientific and rationalist are doing their best to devise ways to rendering more precise the great vague terms that mean so much to all of us— terms like "beauty" and "truth" we have already used often in this introduction. For example, W. T. Jones in his interesting recent *The Romantic Syndrome: Toward a New Method in Cultural Anthropology and History of Ideas* (1961), though he is rather harsh toward his predecessors who have grappled in terms he calls "regrettably vague" (and varied) with "romanticism," does work out a system of roughly measurable coordinates to enable us to use more exactly that old chestnut of literary history and criticism, indeed, of philosophy, Romanticism. Yet not even Professor Jones has quite managed to isolate all the variables in his romantic syndrome with even the degree of success the pathologist can achieve for a syndrome such as "epilepsy." Most of us will have for some time to make merely rough and ready, imprecise and controversial, use of such great emotion-charged words as "democracy," "freedom," "God" (or "god"), and "nature" (or "Nature").

The Role of Ideas

There remain, therefore, a few bothersome questions of methods, perhaps even of philosophy, before we can begin the study of our Western intellectual heritage at its major Greek and Hebraic sources. The intellectual historian will try to see how ideas work in this world, will study the relation between what men say and what men actually do: What does he mean by ideas and what does he mean by saying that ideas do work in this world? Now these are themselves philosophical questions, about which men debate without agreeing. This fact alone should make it clear that these are not questions that can be answered as any American boy could answer such questions as: What does the automotive engineer mean by carburetor? and what does he mean when he says a carburetor does work?

Ideas are clearly different from carburetors, but one should not make the mistake of thinking they are less real than carburetors, less important in our lives, or that they are mere words and not important at all. We shall here take "ideas" in a very broad sense indeed as almost any coherent example of the workings of the human mind expressed in words. Thus, the word "ouch" uttered by a man who hits his finger with a hammer is probably not an idea at all. His statement "I hit my finger with a hammer" is a very simple proposition, and therefore an idea. A further statement, "My finger hurts because I hit it with a hammer," begins to involve more complicated ideas. Statements such as "My finger hurts because the hammer blow affected certain nerves which carried to my central nervous system a kind of stimulus we call pain" and "My finger hurts because God is punishing me for my sins" are both very complex propositions, taking us into two important realms of human thought, the scientific and the theological.

Now the classification of all the kinds of ideas that go to make up what we commonly call knowledge is in itself the major task of several disciplines, among them logic, epistemology, and semantics. And then there follows the task of deciding what knowledge is true, or how far given knowledge is true, and many other tasks that we cannot here undertake. In our own day, the study of semantics, the analysis of the complicated ways in which words get interpreted as they are used in communication among human beings, has aroused widespread interest. For our present purposes, it will be sufficient to make a basic but very controversial distinction between two kinds of knowledge, cumulative and noncumulative.

Cumulative knowledge is best exemplified by the knowledge we call commonly natural science, or just science. From the beginnings of the study of astronomy and physics several thousand years ago in the eastern Mediterranean, our astronomical and physical ideas have *accumulated,* have gradually built up into the astronomy and physics we study in school and college. The process of building up has not been regular, but on the whole it has been steady. Some of the ideas or theories of the very beginning, such as the ideas of the ancient Greek Archimedes on specific gravity are still held true, but many, many others have been added to the original stock. Many have been discarded as false. The result is a discipline, a science, with a solid and universally accepted core of accumulated knowledge and a growing outer edge of new knowledge. Dispute —and scientists dispute quite as much as do philosophers and private persons—centers on this growing outer edge, not in the core. This core all scientists accept as true.

New knowledge can, of course, be reflected back through the whole core, and cause what may not unfairly be called a "revolution" in the science. Thus quantum mechanics and relativity theories have been reflected back into the core of Newtonian physics; but the work of twentieth-century physicists has not proved Newton's work "wrong," at any rate not in the sense the convinced Christian must hold that the mission of Jesus proved the Graeco-Roman faith in the gods of Olympus (polytheism) to be "wrong."

Noncumulative knowledge can here be illustrated best from the field of literature. Men of letters make certain propositions, entertain certain ideas, about men, about right and wrong action, about beautiful and ugly things. Over two thousand years ago, men of letters were writing in Greek on these matters; at the same time others were writing in Greek about the movements of the stars or about the displacement of solids in water. But our contemporary men of letters are today writing about the very same things the Greek men of letters wrote about, in much the same way and with no clear and certain increase in knowledge. Our men of science, on the other hand, have about astronomy and physics far more knowledge, far more ideas and propositions, than the Greeks had.

To put the matter most simply: A Greek man of letters like Aristophanes, a Greek philosopher like Plato, if miraculously brought to earth in the mid-twentieth century and given speech with us (but no knowledge since his death) could talk fairly soon about literature or philosophy with a G. B. Shaw or a John Dewey, and feel quite at home; a Greek scientist like Archimedes in the same position would, even though he were a genius, need to spend a good many days grinding over elementary and advanced textbooks of physics and acquiring enough mathematics before he could begin to talk shop with a modern physicist like Bohr or Einstein. To put it another way: A modern American college student is not wiser than one of the sages of antiquity, has no better taste than an artist of antiquity, but he knows a lot more physics than the greatest Greek scientist ever knew. He knows more *facts* about literature and philosophy than the wisest Greek of 400 B.C. could know; but in physics he not only knows more facts—he understands the relations between facts, that is, the theories and the laws.

This distinction between cumulative and noncumulative knowledge is useful and obvious, which is about all one need expect from a distinction. *Such a distinction does not mean that science is good and useful, and that art, literature, and philosophy are bad and useless, but merely that in respect to the attribute of cumulativeness they are different.* Many people do take this distinction as a statement that art is somehow inferior to science, and are offended by it to the point of rejecting any truth or usefulness the distinction may have. This is a common habit of men, and one the intellectual historian must reckon with.

Perhaps it is merely that in the last three hundred years science has accumulated very *rapidly,* while art, literature, and philosophy have accumulated *slowly* for several thousand years. Our great men may in some senses be wiser than the great men of old; and the average wisdom, or good sense, of American citizens may be greater than that of Athenian citizens. But these matters are very hard to measure, very hard to get agreement on; and the cumulative character of scientific knowledge is well-nigh indisputable. The most hopeful defender of progress in art and philosophy would hardly maintain as a formula: Shakespeare is to Sophocles as Einstein is to Archimedes or that Greek drama is to American drama as the horse-drawn chariot is to the rocket-propelled space vehicle.

The foregoing necessarily oversimplifies the distinction between cumulative and noncumulative knowledge. Notably, for generations of Western thinkers, as for many thinkers today, that part of human knowledge not subsumed under "science" is given less than justice by the tag "noncumulative." It can be argued that what are commonly called the social sciences have in their own right, not just as rather feeble imitations of the natural sciences, an accumulated body of knowledge about the interrelations of human beings. This knowledge is an accumulation not merely of facts, but also of valid interpretations of the facts. Thus economists, in the century and a half from Adam Smith to Lord Keynes, have come to *understand* more about economic activity. It can be argued that philosophers, though they still face some of the questions that faced Plato and Aristotle, have over the centuries improved their methods of analysis, and have refined into greater precision the questions they ask themselves. Finally, though the cynic may say that all we learn from history is that we never learn from history, most of us would hold that over the centuries Western men have built up a body of wisdom and good taste that was not available to the Greeks. How widely such wisdom and taste are spread in our society is another question.

Indeed, for both cumulative and noncumulative knowledge the problem of *dissemination,* the problem of correcting common errors in public thinking, is at least as important as, and in a democratic society perhaps more important than, the problem of getting the experts to agree. This should be evident, save to the most determined scorners of economic thought, in a field like economics. Of course the economists disagree. So do the doctors. Even in modern America, where medicine has a very high prestige among all classes, it is by no means easy to educate the public to act intelligently in medical matters. In economic matters, the public remains even in mid-twentieth century largely unable to make use of the accumulated knowledge the experts possess.

The intellectual historian clearly must concern himself with *both* cumulative and noncumulative knowledge, and must do his best to distinguish one kind of knowledge from another, to trace their mutual relations, and to study their effect on human behavior. Both kinds of knowledge are important, and each does its own work.

We thus come to the second of our questions: How do ideas work? Any answer must take into account the fact that often *ideas* are really *ideals*—expressions of hopes and aspirations, goals of human desire and effort. We say, for instance, that "all men are created equal," or, with the poet Keats,

> "Beauty is truth, truth beauty,"—that is all
> Ye know on earth, and all ye need to know.

What can statements like these mean? If you assert that a heavy weight and a lighter weight will drop through the air at different rates, you can drop them from a height and see. Galileo did this, though not, we now know, from the Leaning Tower of Pisa. Witnesses can also see, and should agree after they have checked what they saw. But you cannot possibly test the assertion of human equality or the identity of truth and beauty in any such fashion, and you can be very sure that after argument on such propositions, a random sample of human beings will not in fact agree about them.

In a general way, the kind of knowledge we have called cumulative, that is, scientific knowledge, is subject to the kind of test that makes it possible for all sane, properly trained men to agree upon its truth or falsehood; and the kind of knowledge we have called noncumulative is not subject to such a test, nor capable of producing such an agreement. Hence, as stated earlier, some have concluded that noncumulative knowledge is of no use, is not really knowledge, has no meaning, and, above all, has no real effect on human behavior. These people often fancy themselves as hard-boiled realists, as sensible people who know what the world really is like. They are actually very mistaken people, as narrow-minded as the most innocent of the idealists they condemn.

For, at the very least, a proposition like "all men are created equal" means that somebody *wants* all men to be equal in some respects. In the form "all men ought to be equal" the proposition would be frankly what we call an ideal. This confusion of "ought" and "is" turns out for the intellectual historian to be another of the abiding habits of men's thinking. Moreover, he will realize that "ought" and "is" influence one another mutually, are parts of a whole process, not independent, and not—at least not often—mutually contradictory. Indeed, he will know that the effort to close the gap between ideal and real, between "ought" and "is," supplies one of the main interests of intellectual history. The gap has never been closed, certainly not by idealists who deny the "is," nor by realists who deny the "ought." Men do not consistently act in logical (rational) accordance with their professed ideals; here the realist scores. But their professed ideals are not meaningless, and thinking about ideals is not a silly and ineffective activity that has no effect on their lives. Ideals, as well as appetites, push men into action; here the idealist scores.

Today in the United States we are perhaps more liable to be led astray by the realist's than by the idealist's error, though throughout our history we have been lured by many ideals. Again, the study of intellectual history ought to help us understand why. But for the moment we can content ourselves with the observation that in human history there are no important facts unrelated to ideas, no important ideas unrelated to facts. The debate, a favorite one between Marxists and their opponents, whether economic changes are more basic than other changes, is logically pointless. No automotive engineer would dream of debating whether the gasoline or the spark makes an internal-combustion engine run, let alone which came first, the gasoline or the spark. No intellectual historian need debate whether ideas OR interests move men in their relations in society, nor which comes first. Without BOTH gasoline and spark, no working gasoline-powered internal-combustion engine; without BOTH ideas and interests (or appetites, or drives, or material factors) no working human society, and no human history.

Contemporary Importance of Intellectual History

The study of intellectual history is especially important in our time, for such study should contribute to clearer thinking on one of the main issues of our day. This issue has been put before us all by many forms of education and propaganda. It is sometimes put temperately, some-times quite hysterically. The columnists like to put it something like this: Science and technology have made possible weapons that can destroy the human race in the next war. Political and moral wisdom, on the other hand, seem not to have devised any way of preventing the next war. We must, they say, find a way to bring our political and moral wisdom (hitherto noncumulative, or at best very slowly cumulative) and its application up to a level with our scientific knowledge and its application in technology (both rapidly cumulative), and we must find it quickly, so that there will be no next war.

The matter can be put in the less excited terms we have already used. What we have called cumulative knowledge has, especially within the last three centuries, enabled human beings to attain an extraordinary mastery over their nonhuman environment. Not only do men manipulate inorganic matter, but they can do a great deal to shape living organisms. They can breed animals for maximum use of mankind. They can control many microorganisms, and have prolonged human life in advanced countries far beyond what seemed possible only a few generations ago.

But men have not yet won comparable triumphs in the control of the human environment at the highest levels of conscious human behavior. Knowledge of why men want certain things, of why they will kill other men to get those things, of how their desires can be changed or satisfied, of much of the whole range of human behavior, seems to belong rather to noncumulative than to cumulative knowledge. Now this noncumulative knowledge, whether philosophy, theology, practical wisdom, or plain horse sense, has never yet been sufficient to preserve peace on earth, let alone to banish all kinds of evil in human relations. Unless we get another kind of knowledge of human behavior, say the alarmists, cumulative knowledge of the sort the physicist or biologist has, we shall get affairs in such a mess that our civilization, and possibly even the human race, will be destroyed.

In short, one of the great problems of our day is this: Can the so-called *social or behavioral sciences* (including applied human genetics) enable man to control his human environment to anything like the extent the natural sciences have enabled him to control his nonhuman environment? An intellectual historian today is almost bound to focus his work on this problem, and to concentrate primarily on the way men in the past have dealt with the basic problems of human relations. He will write, in a sense, a history of the social sciences.

Intellectual history will not, it should be noted very clearly, in itself give the anwsers to the problems that are worrying us all today. Those problems will be answered only by the collective effort of us all, and in ways that the wisest philosopher or scientist—even the wisest columnist— cannot predict. If the social sciences follow the course the natural sciences have taken, the answers to the great problems will be given by the kind of people we call geniuses; but the geniuses will be able to get their answers only because of the full, patient work of thousands of workers in research and in practical life. Still more important, the answers can be translated into effective social action in a democratic society only if the citizens of that society have some basic understanding of what is going on. Both for those engaged in active work on problems of human relations and for those whose main work lies in other fields, the study of intellectual history can be useful.

For those engaged directly in the field of human relations, either as social scientists or as practical workers, a knowledge of how men have behaved in the past is of major importance. We shall see in a later chapter that the problem of the uses and limitations of historical study has been a much-debated topic at certain stages of our Western civilization. There have always been individuals to whom the study of history seems unprofitable, even vicious, a limitation on the possibilities of soaring that the human spirit not dragged down by history might have. But the general verdict of Western civilization has been that a knowledge of history is at the very least a kind of extension of individual experience, and therefore of value to the human intelligence that makes use of experience. And certainly the kind of knowledge we have called cumulative— natural science—is committed to the view that valid generalizations must depend on wide experience, including what is commonly called history. Thus, the historical or genetic sciences, such as historical geology or paleontology, are as essential as analytical sciences like chemistry in the achievement of the natural sciences. History is quite as essential in the social sciences.

History should, in fact, supplement field work and experimentation if the social sciences are to advance. The record of what men have done in the past is essential to save us today from wasting our time in blind alleys. UNESCO, the United Nations Educational, Scientific, and Cultural Organization, is engaged on a vast cooperative study of the tensions that threaten to break out into violent conflict. None of these tensions can be understood without some attention to their histories—their *case histories*. History thus provides some of the essential data, the raw material of facts, the record of trial and error, necessary to an understanding of human behavior today.

But more important is the use a knowledge of history, and especially of intellectual history, can have for those of us who do the many important tasks of our civilization that do not call for specialized knowledge of the social sciences, or for creative work in them. One can imagine a society in which a few experts manage the masses of men skillfully and efficiently; indeed, Aldous Huxley in his *Brave New World* has imagined just such a society, and B. F. Skinner has devised a most ingenious one in his *Walden Two*. It is an ideal that often tempts the engineering temperament. But this product of "cultural engineering" would not be a *democratic* society, and, even were it attainable, which is most doubtful, Americans brought up in our national traditions could not possibly bring themselves to work for it. We are committed to the democratic, widespread, voluntary solutions of our problems, to solutions arrived at by free and extensive discussions and decisions made by some form of counting individual decisions. The scientists, the creative minority, will of course initiate solutions; but solutions will not be attained until we all understand them and put them into practice because we understand, approve, and want them ourselves.

Here again we can get light from what has happened in the natural sciences. Pathologists, immunologists, practicing physicians have done the creative work that has all but stamped out certain diseases, typhoid and diphtheria for instance. But in our society this progress in public health has been possible only because the great majority of the people have in the last few decades had some understanding, however imperfect, of the germ theory of disease, have wished to eradicate disease, and have collaborated freely and intelligently, for the most part, in the work of the experts.

Some progress in the eradication of such diseases as typhoid and diphtheria has indeed been made by experts working with an ignorant population, a population holding ideas about disease quite different from those we hold. Even in India and Africa public health has been improved. But this improvement has been slower than with us, and less secure, just because the experts could not really share their knowledge with the rest of the populations, but had to use authority, prestige, persuasion, and tricks to put their prescriptions across.

The process of successful innovation, from the idea in the mind of the genius to its widespread working out among human beings—the subject of the last few paragraphs—is one of the many important problems we still know relatively little about. We can be sure there is a problem, and that the catchy phrase attributed to Emerson, "if a man make a better mouse-trap, the world will beat a path to his door," is at the least misleading. There will be a confusing criss-cross of paths, or perhaps no path. Vaccination had first to win the medical profession, and then the public, though on the whole its course was relatively simple. But how about the ideas Marx had? What is the tortuous set of paths that led from the British Museum to the Kremlin? Note that here, even among the experts, there is nowhere near the general agreement on the truth and value of Marx's ideas that holds for vaccination.

If our experts do find ways of curing, or at least palliating, such social ills as war, depressions, unemployment, inflation, delinquency, crime, and all the long tale of evil, they will not succeed in making those ways effective unless the rest of us have some knowledge of what they are about. And if in our own time the progress of the social sciences is not very great, if we have to rely on the kind of leaders and the kind of ideas about human beings that our predecessors had to rely on—why then, it is still more important that all citizens of a democratic society should have some knowledge of intellectual history. If the experts fail us in our time and we have to fall back on common sense, it is important that that common sense be really common. History, like all forms of experience, is a most useful guide in the formation of common sense. It is a guide, not an infallible Leader, not a worker of miracles. If you want miracles—certainly a very human want—you must look elsewhere than to history. Clio is a very limited goddess.

Some Patterns of Intellectual History

In this mid-twentieth century we possess in printed form so complete a record of what human beings have said and done in the past, both original records and the comments of successive generations of historians and critics, that no one person could ever read everything pertaining to any considerable part of the record. One life would not be sufficient to read every word we possess written by the ancient Greeks and every word written about them. Writers and readers of history alike must pick and choose from this immense body of writings. This is commonplace, but none the less important.

The critical problem we must all face is how we choose, how we sort out the important from the unimportant, how we know the important when we run up against it. A full answer to such questions would demand a whole book on the methodology of the historian; here we can only attempt to justify in broad lines the choices exercised in this book. But first we may examine some other possible choices that have been rejected.

A plausible principle of choice, and one very popular in America nowadays, is to choose what is said to be "living" for us today and reject what is said to be "dead." The former is held to be important, the latter of no interest save to the pedant and the specialist. Hence, we are told, let us by all odds have the "living thought" of Plato, but not the part of his thought that was applicable only to the Greeks of his own day.

The difficulty lies in knowing what you mean by *living* in such a context. You may mean "accepted as true by the great majority of men." Now in this sense it may be argued that all the physicist needs to know about Greek physics is the part that is still accepted as true. Yet even the scientist can learn much from the history of science; he can learn how easily mistakes can be made, how difficult, even in a field like this, sound innovation is. And he can learn that science is no ivory tower, but a part of full human life.

Physics, however, is clearly an example of cumulative knowledge.

Plato was not a physicist, but a philosopher, whose main concern was problems of right living and wrong living, the existence of God, the immortality of the soul, the relations between permanence and change, and many more of the sort. These are matters of noncumulative knowledge, about which it is by no means easy to decide what is true and alive today, and what is false and dead. It is a fact of experience that twentieth-century readers of what Plato himself wrote range from those who think it all sublime wisdom to those who think it all nonsense, with many variants between these extremes.

Sometimes those who talk about choosing only what of the past is alive today seem to mean by alive what is familiar, and by dead what is strange. Take, for instance, a classic Greek tragedy, the *Antigone* of Sophocles. The play deals with the efforts of Antigone to secure the proper funeral rights for the corpse of her brother Polyneices, who has been slain in rebellion against Creon, lawful ruler of Thebes. Creon, holding that the fate of Polyneices must be held up as an example of what happens to rebels and lawbreakers, refuses proper burial and, when Antigone makes a pathetic attempt to perform ritual burial for her brother, condemns her to death.

Now the universality, the applicability to human beings like ourselves, of the struggle between Antigone and Creon is clear enough. Antigone sets her own sense of right and wrong against the commands of the legal system she lives under. There are those who maintain, however, that what stirs her sense of right and wrong—the treatment of her brother's corpse—is so strange, almost so trivial, to modern Americans that they miss the whole point of the drama unless they are carefully told what it is. According to these critics and teachers, the masterpiece of Sophocles can only be made alive for us if it is made clear that Antigone was really a kind of Thoreau or Gandhi, indulging in "civil disobedience."

Of course she was not these, but a Greek maiden of the great age of Greece, moved profoundly by notions of human dignity in part alien to us. Now what is alien in Antigone is most important to us. History—even intellectual history—is above all useful because it takes us out of the narrow and limited range of our own lives, and makes us aware of how wide human experience has been, how complicated what we carelessly label "human nature" is, how much men are alike and predictable, how much unlike and unpredictable.

If we take the familiar, the things we find least difficult to accept as human, as our principle of choice in the welter of historical facts, we shall vastly lessen the value of any study of the past. Were our knowledge of men and women truly and simply cumulative, like our knowledge of physics, we could keep the living parts and reject the dead parts of the record of the past. But our knowledge of men and women is not cumulative, and we cannot exercise sensibly any *simple* principle of choice between alive and dead, valid and invalid, important and unimportant. Some choice there must be, and everyone who writes or reads history makes a choice. But it should be a wide choice, as good a sampling as possible, and not a choice determined by any closed system of ideas. A history of democratic thought should not pass over antidemocratic thought.

Still another principle of choice, in intellectual history at least, might be to take the figures the general opinion of cultivated people today has marked out as classics, as the great thinkers and writers, and outline as clearly and as succinctly as possible what they wrote. Now this is worth doing, and has been well done. It is not, however, what we mean in this book by intellectual history. It is rather the history of philosophy, or the history of literature, or the history of political theory. What we mean by intellectual history is something more and less than a record of the achievements of the great minds in the fields of noncumulative knowledge. It is more in that it seeks to find how quite ordinary men and women, not the geniuses, not the great, felt and thought and acted; it is less in that it cannot, without reaching interminable lengths, analyze thoroughly the formal thought of the great and near-great thinkers as this thought is analyzed professionally, technically, in the standard manuals of philosophy, art, and literature. We are not here interested so much in Plato's thought in and of itself as in how far that thought is part of the Greek way of life, how far it rejects that way of life, how far it was accepted by ordinary educated men in later societies; in short, we are interested less in Plato-in-himself than in what men have made of Plato, or Kant, or Nietzsche.

Finally—and this is the thorniest problem of all—there is the kind of choosing among the almost infinite details of the past which arranges them with a view to proving something. All historians do, in fact, arrange their materials in such a way as to lead the reader to believe that some propositions—often very big and very philosophical propositions— about men and their destiny are true. St. Augustine in his *City of God* used the facts of history as he collected them to prove that Christianity had not weakened the Roman Empire, that the Empire fell because God punishes the wicked. George Bancroft in his history of the United States used his selected facts to show that we Americans are the real chosen people of a truly democratic God, that our Manifest Destiny is to lead the world to better living. The nineteenth-century English philosopher Herbert Spencer found that history clearly showed men progressing from warlike competitive societies to peaceful, collaborating, industrial societies.

History is still, and may always remain, a part of noncumulative rather than of cumulative knowledge. Some of its research methods, its ways of deciding reliability of evidence, are indeed scientific or cumulative. But sooner or later the historian comes up against the problem of what his evidence means in terms of human loves and hates, hopes and fears; sooner or later he makes judgments of value, decides about good and bad, brings in purpose. Science *as science* itself does none of these things, but confines itself to establishing uniformities or laws at bottom descriptive, not normative.

This book has a pattern of values, a thesis, an explanation of the course of human events, which should come out definitely enough for those who pursue it to the end. Briefly, this book will try to show that in the course of the last two thousand years Western intellectuals have helped build up very high standards of the good life and rational conduct; that in the last three hundred years, especially through the doctrines of progress and democracy, the notion has been widespread that everybody here and now on this earth can, or ought to, live up to these standards and be "happy"; that the two world wars of our day and their attendant evils, the Great Depression, and much else have made the postponement of this good democratic life, if not its abandonment, seem likely to many thoughtful people; that the most plausible explanation of the comparative failure of the ideals of democracy and progress lies in the overestimation their holders made of the reasonableness, the powers of analytical thought, of the average man today; that therefore all interested in man's fate should study with great care the way men actually behave, the relation between their ideals and their acts, their words and their deeds; finally, that this relation is not the simple, direct, causal relation most of us were brought up to believe it is.

Throughout this book, there runs a very great problem indeed, one that is today much in the minds of all concerned with human relations. It is a problem that you will find very early in Western intellectual history, among the Greeks of the fifth century B.C. It is a problem implicit in our distinction between cumulative and noncumulative knowledge. Let it be granted that science, cumulative knowledge, can tell us in many concrete cases what is true and what false, even what will "work" and what will not. Is there any reliable knowledge that will tell us what is good and what is bad? Is there a science, a knowledge, of *norms?* Or are what are usually called value-judgments (we cannot here go into all the depths a rigorous treatment of these terms would demand) incapable, at bottom, of being rated by the instrument of thought?

Now clearly in matters of right and wrong, beautiful and ugly, Western men have not in fact attained the kind of agreement they have attained in matters of natural science. But there is a very strong current in the Western tradition that refuses to accept the thesis, which has cropped up every now and then in Western history from the sophists to the logical positivists, that there is no use reasoning about men's morals and tastes, about their *wants*. In spite of popular sayings like "there's no use disputing about tastes" and assertions like "might makes right," many, probably most Western men and women reject the belief that values are the mere random outcome of conflicting human desires. This rejection is in itself a major fact.

In this book we shall attempt, not to dodge this great question of the existence of a normative knowledge of values, but to stimulate the reader to do his own thinking on this question. The writer must confess that in his own thinking he has gone rather far toward the position that value-judgments cannot for Western men be given a solid ranking order save by the intervention of a human activity commonly called *faith*. Men can and do believe that Bach is a better composer than Offenbach as firmly as they believe that Mt. Everest is higher than Mt. Washington. They can think about the Bach-Offenbach relationship and their judgment on that relationship; they can communicate much of what they think (*and feel*) about that relationship to their fellows; they can even persuade their fellows to accept their own views of that relationship.

We cannot here do more than touch the surface of the question of normative judgments. Clearly one does not use the same criteria in judging the relation between the music of Bach and the music of Offenbach that one uses in judging the relation between the height of Mt. Everest and the height of Mt. Washington. To decide the latter problem, most of us would go to· a good reference book and accept its authority, rather than try to measure the mountains ourselves. Such use of an appeal to authority in a question of fact (in a sense, of "science") is often pounced upon by defenders of the validity of normative judgments in ethics, aesthetics, and other fields, who then urge us to accept the authority of, say, the Church concerning the existence of God. There really is, however, a difference between the use of authority in the two instances. Any properly trained person can go through the steps, accepted as valid by all geographers, that ended in the measurement of the two mountains. Such an operation is impossible for the existence of God. Properly trained persons can indeed follow the reasoning by which theologians prove the existence of God; but they will find many conflicting reasonings, including some that end by proving that God does *not* exist.

Properly trained persons can also follow the reasoning by which a music critic shows that the music of Bach is better than that of Offenbach. Here he will find differences enough, but much more agreement than on the existence of God. He will find the argument from authority—that the most competent judges agree that Bach's music is better than Offenbach's. He will find complex arguments, edging into the field of ethics, to show that Bach was a more elevated musician than Offenbach, that he wrote music more exacting and more satisfying by aesthetic standards. He will find very technical explanations based on the mathematics and physics of music. Finally, and happily, he will find the explanation that Bach writes serious music very well, and that Offenbach writes light music very well, and that a man may well enjoy both in their proper places.

Reason is thus by no means helpless in problems of value. It can do much; above all it can persuade men and teach men. But it cannot achieve the impossible task of eliminating what to the pure rationalist is the perverseness of men—each man's conviction that beyond some irreducible point he is not like other men, that he has a will, a personality of his own. That will, at some point, must bolster itself with faith, "the evidence of things not seen."

CHAPTER ONE

MAKING THE MODERN WORLD

I. HUMANISM

Origins of the Modern Mind

Men have always lived in "modern" times but they have not always been so much impressed with the fact. Our own time, conventionally considered as beginning about 1500 A.D., is the first to coin so neat a term and apply it so consistently. *Modern* derives from a late Latin adverb meaning *just now,* and in English is found in its current sense, contrasted with *ancient,* as early as the sixteenth century. This awareness of a shared newness, of a way of life different from that of one's forebears— and by 1700 awareness of a way of life felt by many to be much *better* than that of their forebears—this is in itself one of the clearest marks of our modern culture.

This culture is a most complex one. We cannot define *modern* neatly here, but must hope to build up a definition slowly in the following chapters. At this point we face the problem of disentangling *modern* from *medieval.* It is a very difficult problem, for the millions of concrete situations we try to sum up in these general terms are not related in the simple way our rhetorical habit of thinking conveys. Medieval does not stop, and modern begin, at any one point in space-time. The modern is not a sunrise ending the medieval night. The modern is not the child of the medieval, nor even the medieval grown to manhood.

Indeed, the distinction between medieval and modern has bothered professional historians greatly in the last fifty years or so, as research has dimmed the clearer distinctions our grandfathers drew. In the late nineteenth century the periodization of medieval and modern was clear in all the textbooks: Renaissance and Reformation, humanism, the geographical discoveries, the invention of printing, and the breaking down of medieval religious unity all come neatly between 1453 and 1517. Americans, particularly, found for modern history a very convenient starting point: 1492. This has all been changed. The Renaissance, in particular, has been pushed back so far into what was once considered the unadulterated Middle Ages that the distinction between medieval and modern seems to vanish; the two are telescoped, like a train wreck in time.

Is your criterion the "revival of learning," a truer appreciation of pagan Latin culture? Charles H. Haskins in his *The Renaissance of the Twelfth Century* pushed this back well into medieval times. Is your criterion achievement in science and technology? Historians now hold that the last few centuries of the Middle Ages are centuries of marked scientific advancement. Indeed, as George Sarton liked to point out, the humanists proper of the Renaissance, the men of letters, theologians, moralists, were at least as contemptuous of grubbing natural science, at least as "deductive" and as respectful of written authority, as were the Schoolmen. It is even possible, though a bit extreme, to defend the thesis that the Renaissance proper means a *regression* in the growth of modern science. Is your criterion economic, the growth of a money economy, banking, extensive trade? Modern research pushes most of these back to the Crusades, to the high Middle Ages, and especially to the late medieval Italian city-states, Florence, Venice, Genoa, and the rest. Is your criterion the establishment of the territorial state in the place of the feudal congeries of holdings? Surely France and England are both territorial states by the time they begin their Hundred Years' War in the fourteenth century.

But the reverse approach is possible. When did the Middle Ages end? Apparently, for purposes of controversy, never. Any editorial can use pejoratively today "medieval" or "feudal"—"Boston's medieval streets," "our feudal officeholders in Washington." More seriously, if you take concrete examples in various fields of human culture, you will find medieval ways persisting quite clearly in western Europe as late as the seventeenth century—the legal system in England, the landholding system in France, medieval weights and measures everywhere, and everywhere much, in Protestant as well as in Catholic Europe, of the "Christian way of life." The seventeenth-century British colonists who came to Virginia and New England brought with them a surprising amount of the Middle Ages—commons, stocks and pillories, belief in witches, traces of medieval domestic architecture. The colonists of New France even brought with them *seigneurs* and the manorial system, the impress of which still remains in the province of Quebec.

The Middle Ages, then, *grows into* the Modern Age in a way that the life of no single organism really illustrates. Nor can conventional narrative history really embrace the complexities of cultural change. We shall here not by any means abandon the historical approach, but attempt to combine it with an analytical approach. In the next three chapters we shall deal with the building up of the modern way of life in the late fifteenth, the sixteenth, and the seventeenth centuries; and

for purposes of analysis we shall consider separately art and letters, religion, and science and technology, trying not to forget that in the
real life of our society they were inseparably combined.

By so doing, we shall go contrary to the established canon of historical
writing, which accepts a periodization roughly by centuries—though the
Renaissance has to be pushed back into the fifteenth and even the
fourteenth century. We shall treat humanism, Protestantism, and rationalism as constituent parts of Western intellectual life that can for
purposes of analysis be separated from the whole and treated as a
unit over the centuries, roughly from 1450 to 1700, which separate the
Middle Ages from the Age of Enlightenment. Our central theme is
how the medieval view of life was altered into the eighteenth-century
view of life. This eighteenth-century view of life, though modified in the
last two centuries, is still at bottom *our* view of life, especially in the
United States. The late fifteenth, the sixteenth, and the seventeenth
centuries are from this point of view essentially *transitional,* essentially
the years of preparation for the Enlightenment. In this transition humanism, Protestantism, and rationalism (and natural science) do their work of
undermining the medieval, and preparing the modern, cosmology.

They work, as ideas always do, through the hearts and heads of men
and women who are by no means pure intellectuals. They do not explain
all modern history. They are even, in a sense, abstractions that we build
up in our own minds in our effort to make sense of the past. But they
do make sense. We believe what we believe today, behave as we do,
in part because of what the men we label humanists, Protestants, rationalists, scientists, or inventors wrote and did several centuries ago.

The Terms "Renaissance" and "Reformation"

Once upon a time a pair of fair-haired twins named Renaissance and
Reformation, persecuted and abused, turned against their wicked but
doddering stepmother, the Catholic Church of the Middle Ages. . . .
Of course, our history books never came to such a simple and undignified
way of putting the matter; they couldn't quite begin like a fairy tale.
But, except for Roman Catholics, most Americans who have had to learn
some European history have come out with the notion that the movements we call the Protestant Reformation and the Renaissance were
somehow the same in inspiration and purpose. One was directed toward
religious freedom, the other toward artistic freedom, and both together
worked for moral freedom, and, of course, for what became in the
nineteenth century democracy. Both worked to *emancipate* ordinary
men and women from restraints that custom and superstition had combined to lay upon them in the Middle Ages.

Now even this very misleading view is not *wholly* mistaken. Many a follower of Luther must have felt a kind of exaltation, a sense of being freed from routine obligations that confined him, a new confidence in his own powers. We know well that artists and men of letters, scientists and explorers, all felt the lift of new worlds to conquer, new opportunities to do things—all sorts of things—in ways no one had ever yet made use of, ways therefore of *being themselves,* of being striking personalities. Vague, loose though the terms are, there is some sense in equating the Middle Ages with *authority,* and both Renaissance and Reformation with *liberty.* But not much sense, if you stop there.

For the facts are too complex for the formula that seeks to explain them. Luther used his authority to help suppress the Peasants' Revolt. Many of the emancipated humanists of the Renaissance set up the masters of Greek literature as authorities beyond their questioning, as models for everything they wrote. Cicero and Plato were worshiped as blindly as any literary masters have ever been worshiped. In politics the Renaissance tyrant, the Renaissance despot are common figures. Neither Renaissance nor Reformation worked consciously toward individual freedom of a democratic sort.

Even less true is it that Renaissance and Reformation always worked harmoniously together for the same ends. A good Calvinist had to hold in horror the Renaissance artist who sculptured from nude models, lived recklessly and prodigally, took no thought of the morrow. Luther came to hate the humanist Erasmus, and the feeling was reciprocated. Here we have no simple antithesis between the religious ascetic and the frankly sensuous artist. Erasmus loved Christianity, he loved flawless Greek and the after-dinner conversation of scholars, and in a rather academic way he loved common sense; he made a very poor rebel. The career and personality of Erasmus, indeed, fits in poorly with a cut-and-dried formula for either Renaissance or Reformation.

Humanism, indeed, is an attitude toward life that is fundamentally out of harmony with that side of democracy that is concerned with the common man, with the welfare of the masses. The artist, the man of letters of the Renaissance, believed in a privileged class—not the old feudal nobility, but the new privileged class of talent and intellect. He was indifferent to, or even contemptuous of, the undistinguished many not concerned with art or philosophy or gracious living. From this humanist attitude toward life has come, in part, such a familiar and undemocratic modern attitude as the contempt of artists and intellectuals for the philistines, the Babbitts, the middlebrows. Most modern defenses of an aristocracy—or, since "aristocracy" suggests the old European *noblesse* hardly anyone cares to defend, one might better say, of an elite—have gone back to Renaissance sources for patterns. Nietzsche, following his fellow professor at Basel, Jakob Burckhardt, found in the bright, fierce life of these Renaissance masters of art and man the nearest earthly realization of his master-men, the Supermen.

There is indeed at least one element in the complex of humanist attitudes that has been taken over into democratic tradition—the notion of the career open to talent, to innovating, daring, individual talent. Yet on the whole our modern democrats have not held quite the same notion of talents to be encouraged that the Renaissance held. Obviously the important point about the doctrine of freedom of opportunity is the simple question, Opportunity for what? The eighteenth and the sixteenth centuries, the men of the Enlightenment and the men of the Renaissance, answered this, as we shall see, very differently.

The facts, then, show that the simple view of the Renaissance and Reformation as joint heralds of modern democracy is not accurate. Had modern civilization followed strictly and carefully down the paths blazed for it by humanists or Protestants, we might never have heard the phrase "the century of the common man."

Some of our democratic heritage is very old indeed, as old as the civilization of the Greeks and the Hebrews. Some of it is relatively new, as new as the steam engine. Some of it we owe to the humanists, but not nearly so much as the conventional textbooks of the last few generations usually made out. We must beware of exaggerating the age of our democracy. It is still, in the balance, young, still a growing, striving force in a world long used to other ways of life.

The Range of Humanism

The mere fact of their rebellion against the Catholic Church gave the Protestants at least a common name, no matter how great the differences between an Anglican (Episcopalian) and an antinomian (from the Greek, *against law*—almost our *anarchist*) or an Anabaptist. There is no such single name for those who in art, letters, and philosophy were in a sense united by the fact that they didn't like medieval art, letters, or philosophy. The best we have is the term *humanists,* a term that has had much wider and much narrower uses than are altogether convenient for the intellectual historian. Especially today, a humanist can be a theologian trying to do without a personal God, an educational reformer who thinks we have too much of natural science and not enough of the humanities, a philosopher who holds that humans are rather more than animals if less than gods, and no doubt much else. Even if we limit ourselves in this chapter to those Renaissance admirers—yes, imitators— of Greece and Rome who are usually classed as humanists, we shall miss much that we ought not to miss.

Let us, then, accept humanism as a kind of cover-all under which may be grouped all men whose world-view is neither primarily theological nor primarily rationalistic. In this use, humanism is not at all necessarily to be taken as a sort of halfway house between the supernatural of religion and the natural of science, though in many cases humanism was just such a halfway house. Humanism tends, in these early modern centuries, to reject medieval habits of mind, medieval ideals, especially as embodied in Scholasticism, but not to accept Protestantism, nor the rationalist view of the universe as an efficiently functioning, regular arrangement (almost a machine). The humanist is a great rebel against medieval cosmology, but he has no very clear cosmology of his own. The humanist is a great individualist—he wants to be himself. But he is not very clear about what to make of himself. He is much more in debt to the Middle Ages than he will admit, notably in what he most prides himself on, his learning. And he is not, Leonardo da Vinci and a few others excepted, a scientist. Even Leonardo, perhaps, is better described as an inventor than as a scientist.

Of course, certain of the concrete marks of the Renaissance can be traced far back into the Middle Ages of the old schoolbooks. Yet if in the thirteenth century Dante already knows his Latin classics, if Giotto already paints in the round, if Frederick II, *Stupor Mundi*, is already as omnivorously curious about this world of the senses, as headstrong and as heartless as any Renaissance tyrant, it is still true that not until the late fifteenth century is humanism in the full tide of fashion. We must attempt shortly to define, at least in broad terms, what these new things mean as an attitude toward the world. But first we must sample the range of Renaissance humanism.

In many ways the simplest human activity that can be earmarked as "Renaissance" and set off from "medieval" is what we now call scholarship or, in an older term still useful, learning. The humanists proper, in the narrower historical sense of the word, were in fact scholars, though their position in society, at least that of the greater ones like Erasmus, carried a prestige among the ruling classes scholarship does not carry today. (The real analogy today is of course with natural science; Erasmus had in the sixteenth century the kind of prestige Einstein had today.) The humanists had what their medieval predecessors had not, a direct and widely spread knowledge of Greek; they had access to the originals of most Greek writing that has survived at all. Greek came slowly to the West, by means of hundreds of now forgotten scholars; it did not come suddenly after the fall of Constantinople in 1453 when Byzantine scholars fled from the Turk. Indeed, the medieval scholar after the thirteenth century was by no means as ignorant of Greek as we used to think, and by the late fourteenth century any ambitious, scholarly youth in much of the Western world could have access to Greek. The humanists also tried to write the kind of Latin Cicero and his fellows wrote. That is to say, they deliberately abandoned medieval Latin, which was a natural language developed over centuries, limited

it is true to an intellectual class, but written and spoken by them with
no more than customary respect for tradition. The humanist scholars
deliberately revived a dead tongue—which has in a sense been quite dead
ever since. They polished and refined the life out of Latin. They had
the use of the printing press, and were thus able to communicate more
readily with one another than had their medieval predecessors. The
humanists were, however, a small privileged group, not interested in a
wide audience; some of them damned the printing press as the vulgariza-
tion of learning. It is really only in religion that the printing press
in these early years touches a widespread audience of the people, most
of whom are illiterate or barely literate. How changed in spirit the
humanist scholars were from their medieval predecessors we shall try to
estimate in the next section. But for purposes of recognition their devotion to the Greeks, their Ciceronian Latin, their contempt for the
Schoolmen are ample signs.

In the fine arts, the men of the high Renaissance—the sixteenth century,
the *Cinquecento* of the Italians—produced work that looks very different
from medieval work. They produced it partly at least in a deliberate
imitation of the Romans, whose remains in architecture and sculpture
lay all about in the Italy which gave the lead to humanism in art and
in letters. But they did not produce it suddenly, and they owed a great
deal more than they liked to admit to their medieval predecessors.

In architecture the change is perhaps clearest, the break cleanest.
Actually Gothic, soaring Gothic, had never been really popular in Italy.
Builders readily took to the round arch, the dome, the classic orders,
and to lines that accepted the horizontal as something not to be transcended. They produced indeed a style, a compound of elements each
with a classical origin, but which when put together make something
new, something original. No Roman, no Greek, had ever built a building
quite like St. Peter's in Rome or the Renaissance palaces of Florence.
As it travels north, this style gets entangled with local medieval traditions
and produces some strange hybrids like the famous chateau at Chambord,
in France, all Renaissance in massive simplicity and horizontality in
the lower stories, all Gothic profusion and upward striving in roofs and
chimneys. In England, gentlemen's manor houses, though no longer
fortified, no longer medieval castles, show Gothic tracery right into the
seventeenth century.

In sculpture and painting again, work of the sixteenth century is
clearly distinguishable from work of the thirteenth. A painting of
Raphael's is not like one of Giotto's, nor is Michelangelo's David—even
apart from its heroic size—a statue that would fit into a Gothic cathedral.
Yet to the untrained layman trying to use his eyes, Renaissance painting
and sculpture look related to medieval painting and sculpture in a way
the cathedral of Chartres and St. Peter's at Rome do not look related.

If you take as a rough measuring rod what we shall crudely call naturalness, lifelikeness, what a stereoscopic camera sees, then from the thirteenth century on artists are working toward this kind of naturalness,
and away from certain conventions that may or may not be "primitive."
Those conventions are best identified with Byzantine art, which was stiff,
hieratic, flat-surfaced, and made no attempt to anticipate the camera and
Technicolor. (We are trying hard to report, and not to judge; but these
fields are in the heart of that kind of noncumulative knowledge known
as taste, where every word praises or blames; in general today to say that
a painting suggests anything photographic is to damn the painting.) As
early as the turn of the thirteenth to the fourteenth century the Floren-
tine Giotto was using highlights (*chiaroscuro*) to suggest in two-dimen-
sional painting the rounded figures we see in three-dimensional "natural"
perspective. That is to say that in painting and in sculpture the medieval
thirteenth and the Renaissance sixteenth century join together against
the Byzantine, and the Renaissance is clearly the daughter of the Middle
Ages, at least in one very central point of technique.

So too even more clearly in imaginative literature the obvious external
signs do not so much differentiate the Renaissance from the high Middle
Ages as mark a clear continuity of development. The use of the vernacular is certainly no criterion, for the vernaculars are used for poetry and
narrative, for literature in contrast to philosophy, even before great
medieval writers like Dante and Chaucer use them. No doubt certain
forms, especially in poetry, and certain kinds of polished style mark work
as that of the humanists. The sonnet, for instance, is a readily recognized
form that can at once be ticketed as Renaissance. But the continuity
from the thirteenth century on is none the less striking. For a concrete
example, take the note of bawdry or obscenity. If you will read in chrono-
logical order samples from the *fabliaux,* one of Chaucer's bawdier tales,
some Boccaccio, and some Rabelais, you will have gone from the Middle
Ages to the high Renaissance, and you will come out in the end with a
man always respectfully tagged as a humanist. And yet Rabelais has an
exuberance, a small-boyish obscenity, a freshness that has also been tagged
Gothic. His vast and miscellaneous erudition may at first sight seem
humanist, but it is an erudition piled on with little of the classical sense
of discipline.

Rabelais is describing, at great length and with a typical humanist
erudition in all fields, a marvelous (and fictitious) plant he calls panta-
gruelion, after his hero Pantagruel:

> I find that plants are named after several ways. Some have taken the name
> of him who first found them, knew them, showed them, sowed them, improved
> them by culture, and appropriated them: as the Mercurialis from Mercury;
> Panacea from Panace, daughter of Esculapius; Armois from Artemis, who is
> Diana; Eupatorium from King Eupator; Telephion from Telephus; Euphor-

bium from Euphorbus, King Juba's physician; Clymenos from Clymenus;
Alcibiadium from Alcibiades; Gentian from Gentius, King of Sclavonia. And,
formerly, so much was prized this prerogative of giving a name to newly discovered plants, that, just as a controversy arose betwixt Neptune and Pallas,
from which of the two the land discovered by both should receive its de-
nomination—though thereafter it was called and had the appellation of
Athens, from Athenæ, which is Minerva—just so would Lyncus, King of
Scythia, have treacherously slain the young Triptolemus, whom Ceres had
sent to show unto mankind the use of corn, previously unknown; to the end
that, after his murder, he might impose his own name, and be called, in immortal honour and glory, the inventor of a grain so profitable and necessary
to human life. For the wickedness of which treasonable attempt he was by
Ceres transformed into an ounce.

Other herbs and plants there are, which retain the names of the countries
from whence they were transported: as the Median apples from Media, where
they were first found; Punic apples—that is to say, pomegranates—from
Punicia; Ligusticum, which we call Lovage, from Liguria, the coast of Genoa;
Castanes, Persiques or peach-tree, Sabine, Stæchas from my Iles Hyères; Spica
Celtica, and others.

Rabelais' obscenity is often quite as learned, so learned that only a
humanist would find it very obscene. He makes long lists, like litanies,
of epithets in which only the original object is—or was—unprintable.

This comparative study of obscenity should at least bring home the
very great difficulty of pigeonholing works of art (in the widest sense
of art, which includes literature) to accord with big generalizations of
philosophy or sociology. The note of bawdry may well be peculiarly
timeless, and therefore an unfair test. Yet hardly any easily recognized,
single, external sign will clearly differentiate medieval art from Renaissance art.

The reader may indeed, if he has been thinking his way through this,
have come upon the idea that since the Middle Ages were primarily religious and since the Renaissance meant at least an attempted return to
the pagan, the unreligious if not the irreligious, medieval art should be
tied to the Church and Renaissance art should enjoy Bohemian freedom.
Now this is in part true. By the high Renaissance sculptors and painters are imitating the classical nude as they imitated everything else classic. The artist is beginning to lead something like the kind of life—wild,
indecent, improvident, but so interesting—he is still supposed to lead.
Benvenuto Cellini's autobiography, which is always appealed to by those
who want to simplify the sixteenth century as the Century of the Artist,
certainly sets up the myth of the artist as the genius above decency as
above dullness. Yet an autobiography of Villon's—did it exist—would
perhaps have outdone Cellini's. Of course, you can always maintain that
Villon (born in Paris in 1431, the year Joan of Arc was burned at the
stake) is not really medieval, that he anticipates the Renaissance.

But there is a grave difficulty in accepting the formula: Middle Ages equals religion and inhibition, Renaissance equals paganism and exhibition. All through the high Renaissance the artist is at work for the Church and on religious themes. If you will think of the universally known work of these men—Leonardo's Last Supper, Raphael's Madonnas, Michelangelo's frescoes in the Sistine Chapel, and the like—you will note that they are all religious in theme. Someone may tell you that these works are religious in a purely external way, and that their spirit is worldly, sensuous, pagan, humanistic, and quite the opposite of the medieval. Raphael's madonnas are, they may say, just Italian peasant women, no more spiritual than the winner of an American beauty contest. This contrast between a madonna of Raphael as all flesh and a Gothic sculptured Virgin as all soul is most misleading. Raphael's madonnas are descendants of medieval Virgins and by no means traduce their ancestor, who was very far from being an abstract principle. Indeed, it is chiefly because we exaggerate the asceticism and other-worldliness of the Middle Ages that we find Renaissance art so fresh, so pagan, so human. The Renaissance artists who gave most of their artistic lives to the task of making Christian beliefs tangible, visible, were carrying on a function they had inherited from the medieval forerunners. Only gradually, and only in comparatively modern times, is art so completely secular that religious art almost disappears or rather, becomes second-rate, derivative, conventional. Here again the modern has its firmest and most numerous roots not in the sixteenth, but in the eighteenth century. (We must note here a mid-twentieth century revival of willingness to experiment and create in religious art.)

The Nature of Humanism

The humanists were, however, conscious rebels, whether their main interest was in scholarship, philosophy, art, or letters. They are very modern in their awareness of being in revolt against their fathers, the men of the Middle Ages. Perhaps the scholars and philosophers, humanists in the narrower sense, were most articulate. Men like Erasmus expressed very freely their contempt for the Schoolmen, wretched slaves of a second-hand Aristotle, manglers of the noble tongue of Horace and Cicero, idle disputants over the number of angels who could occupy the point of a needle. We still echo their attacks today, though we should have a perspective they did not have. They were, it is true, rebelling against a decayed Scholasticism, not against the mature Scholasticism of the thirteenth century, which they made no real attempt to recover.

Even the artists were in rebellion, consciously striving to put off a tradition they felt to be a burden. Late Gothic was in as obvious a state of decay as was late Scholasticism, and especially north of the Alps those who welcomed the new Italian styles in all the arts did so as rebels against the complexities and fatuousness of late (flamboyant) Gothic. Early Renaissance (like early Gothic) is a simple style, relatively unornamented, consciously avoiding richness, consciously seeking in classical examples simplicity and discipline.

Perhaps at bottom humanists and Protestants were both rebelling because they felt the familiar, but to sensitive men and women never comfortable, gap between the ideal and the real had in late medieval times reached an excessive degree of obviousness. That gap, always pretty plain throughout the Middle Ages, was by the fifteenth century almost too wide for the most ingenious explanations to close. The ideal was still Christian, still an ideal of unity, peace, security, organization, status; the reality was endemic war, divided authority even at the top, even in that papacy which should reflect God's own serene unity, a great scramble for wealth and position, a time of troubles.

So, in a sense like Protestantism, this complex movement in the arts and in philosophy we call humanism is a very self-conscious rebel, a rebel against a way of life it finds corrupt, overelaborated, stale, unlovely, and untrue. The humanists seem to be opening a window, letting in the fresh air, and doing a lot of other pleasant things.

Yet the humanist figures of speech began to wear out for all save the very faithful. Renaissance art soon began to cultivate a lush ornamentation, a fondness for detail, a richness of color that would have satisfied the fifteenth century. Or more accurately, in most of the arts the victorious humanists divided into a lush or exuberant school and an ascetic or spare school. In architecture, for instance, one line of development went through Palladio, a sixteenth-century Italian who loved strict classic simplicity of the schoolmaster's tradition, into the kind of neoclassicism we are familiar with in the United States as "colonial"; another line led straight into the baroque and thence, in the eighteenth century, into the rococo styles of flowing curves and rich ornamentation. As for writing, the humanists were hardly at any time really simpler than their scholastic opponents, and very soon their scholarship got as pretentious, as heavy, as doctoral as scholarship ever got to be; Plato got rather confusedly substituted for Aristotle as The Philosopher; and even in imaginative writing men got so far away from the ideals of simplicity (which in fact the Renaissance never really did take seriously) that one finds in the sixteenth century two literary movements which cultivated a certain literary preciousness and obscurity more successfully than it has been cultivated until very recently—euphuism in England and gongorism in Spain. Recent popularity among the intellectuals has made us once more familiar with the metaphysical poets of seventeenth-century England, who were certainly not simple, clear, and reasonable. The Renaissance very rapidly created its own gap between the real and the ideal.

For the Renaissance, like the Protestant Reformation, was not really anarchical. It rebelled against one authority, one complex of ideals, habits, institutions, in the name of another, and by no means unrelated, complex. Again, as rebels the humanists had to work very hard to discredit an older authority, and in the process they often used libertarian language, at least to the extent of demanding freedom for the new education, freedom from the rules of Scholasticism, freedom for the individual to follow his own bent and not just parrot Aristotle. But even less than the Protestants, some of whom were antinomians, did the humanists really believe in the natural goodness and wisdom of man. Or if you prefer to put it that way, they never completely emancipated themselves from the long medieval intellectual tradition of looking for authority, looking for the answer, in the recorded works of famous predecessors. Only, for the Church Fathers, Aristotle, and the medieval doctors, the humanists substituted the body of surviving Greek and Roman writings, literary as well as philosophical, and, where they still were actively interested in religion, the text of the Bible, duly studied in the original Hebrew or Greek. As secondary authorities, they soon built up their own society of mutual admiration and began the modern process embedded in the scholarly footnote. But there is among them the same deference toward authority, the same habit of abstract and indeed deductive thought, the same unwillingness to make experiments, to grub around in an undignified way, that we find in the Schoolmen. They are not really forerunners of free modern scholarly research; they are vainer and more worldly Schoolmen.

The paragraph above is greatly exaggerated, but it is meant to drive home a point. The humanist scholars were not libertarians and democrats in the modern sense. They were a privileged group of learned men, very proud of their scholarly standards, with most of the traditional defects of scholars—vanity, possessiveness, quarrelsomeness, and a great fear of making mistakes. They had a large share of one of the traditional virtues of scholars, a lusty appetite for hard intellectual labor. Of critical acumen, of ability to set and solve problems they surely had no more than scholars must have. They were not the intellectual giants they now appear; they were rather pioneers moving slowly into rough country.

They set a pattern and standards for modern scholarship. In the study of ancient languages they introduced order, accuracy, and tools that we take for granted, like dictionaries arranged alphabetically. They developed analytical and historical standards of criticism. The stock example of the achievements of these scholars is still an excellent one to illustrate their methods at their best. The popes had in the early Middle Ages bolstered the prestige of the Holy See, already firmly based on the Petrine tradition, by the "Donation of Constantine." A document purported to come from the emperor Constantine as he left Rome to establish his capital in Constantinople made the pope his successor in Rome and gave to him the direct control of the land around Rome later known as the "States of the Church." This document was shown by one of the earliest of the humanists, Lorenzo Valla, who died in 1457, to be a forgery. Its language simply was not the language that could have been written in the early fourth century A.D. Valla made this evident by methods now familiar to us all; he showed that the document contained *anachronisms,* as if a letter purported to be Abraham Lincoln's should contain a reference to a Buick car.

The formal metaphysical thought of the humanists is not one of their strong points. In these early modern centuries most minds at once systematic and determined to answer the Big Questions were either theologians or rationalists of some sort. Italian humanists like Ficino and Pico della Mirandola were not merely Platonists; they were Neoplatonists, tender-minded believers in this most cerebral and scholarly mysticism. And in general it is true that through most of Europe the humanists welcomed Plato as a relief from Aristotle, as a philosopher closer to the purified but still sacramental Christianity they basically wanted. Erasmus, Thomas More, Colet, and other northerners came under the influence of Plato. The thesis that these men simply left one authority, Aristotle, to take refuge in another can no doubt be exaggerated. But they certainly added little to the Platonist tradition, and indeed they are not primarily philosophers.

It is, however, the imaginative writers, the artists, who are near the heart of the humanist attitude toward life. Petrarch, Rabelais, Shakespeare, Cervantes, the painters, sculptors, and musicians whose names we still know—these are the kind of men who sought some way between traditional Christianity as it was handed down by the Middle Ages and the new rationalism that seemed to take all the magic and mystery out of the universe. By the seventeenth century, some of them, like Milton, could invest with awe and mystery the world science was trying to make clear. But few artists could accept the world of Bacon and Descartes. It is from these centuries that the modern distrust of the artist for the scientist dates.

Now, as we have seen, these artists were in more or less conscious rebellion against the medieval Christian tradition. They repudiated one authority, but—and this is most important—they had to seek out, perhaps sometimes to set up, another authority. The scholar's simple acceptance of anything written by an old Greek or Roman was not enough for these men of imagination. Like everyone who touched at all things intellectual, these artists too went back to Greece and Rome. But like the architects they reworked their materials into something new. Indeed, we may take a lead from architecture, impersonal art though it may seem to be, in the difficult task of sorting these writers into some order.

One kind of Renaissance architecture—Palladio will do as a name to associate with it—found in its classic models simplicity, regularity, modera-

tion (nothing huge), quiet, graceful decoration (nothing stark). Now one
kind of Renaissance artistic and literary return to the ancients found
there essentially the same kind of authority; they found the classics were
"classical." They found, that is, substantially that ideal of the beautiful
and the good which has never yet quite been banished from formal Western education. They found that the Greeks and Romans—the ones that
count, the ones we have to read—were gentlemanly, disciplined, moderate
in all things, distrustful of the wild, the excited, the unbuttoned, the en-
thusiastic, free from superstition but by no means irreligious, controlled,
mature men of imagination, not narrow rationalists. One could go on
at great length, and indeed we shall return to some phases of these ideals.
Suffice it here to say that these Renaissance admirers of the classical culture of Greece and Rome found in that culture above all a *discipline*.
They did not see what Gilbert Murray thinks might have been seen there
had not generations of men like these humanists pretty well suppressed
it—exuberance, color, wildness, the desire of the moth for the star, high
adventure, and deep romance.

We shall call this the *spare,* in contrast with the *exuberant* interpretation of the classics. You can find traces of it even in the high Renaissance of the late fifteenth and early sixteenth century, and especially in
the more imaginative of the scholar-humanists like Erasmus. There is
much of it even in the essays of Montaigne, rambling, informal, allusive,
but never heaven- or earth-storming. And this spare classicism did become a movement, a fashion, a way of life. Its great flowering was in the
France of the sevententh century, and the Age of Louis XIV is in many
ways a good sampling of the ideal.

Here is a passage from Boileau, a ruling critic of that age, in which
both form and matter illustrate the classical ideal—clarity, sobriety, respect for authority, distrust of the unusual, the eccentric, the departure
from the norm:

> When authors have been admired for a great number of centuries and
> have been scorned only by a few people with eccentric taste (for there will
> always be found depraved tastes), then not only is there temerity, there is
> madness in casting doubt on the merit of these writers. From the fact that
> you do not see the beauties in their writings you must not conclude that
> those beauties are not there, but that you are blind and that you have no
> taste. The bulk of mankind in the long run makes no mistake about works
> of the spirit. There is no longer any question nowadays as to whether Homer,
> Plato, Cicero, Vergil are remarkable men. It is a matter closed to dispute,
> for twenty centuries are agreed on it; the question is to find out what it is
> that has made them admired by so many centuries; and you must find a way
> to understand this or give up letters, for which you must believe that you
> have neither taste nor aptitude since you do not feel what all men have felt.

The relation of this spare classicism to Christianity is by no means a

simple one. The great writers of the French classical period who are perhaps the best representatives of it are all good Catholics—or at least all
practicing Catholics. Indeed it would have been indecent self-assertion
for them not to have been Catholics; moreover, they could hardly hope
for preferment at the court of Louis XIV had they been heretics or skeptics. But the classicists were often separated by the thinnest of lines from
the rationalists, the men who were building up an attack on any form
of revealed religion. Obviously the Boileaus, the Bossuets, even the
Racines—and more important, the people who were the direct audience
of these writers—could not be enthusiasts, mystics, rebels, Protestants, and
still maintain the decorum that was part of their ideal. This decorum,
and much else prescribed for them, like the famous formal rules of French
drama, they would all maintaiń to be perfectly consonant with deep feeling, with a sense of mystery and the inadequacy of men to run their own
lives without the guiding hand of God. They felt they were good Christians.

And so they were, almost all of them. But they were enlightened and
conformist Christians, not evangelical ones. Some, like Racine, might
in their later years regret their worldly past and turn to a sincere but
still conventional piety. On the edge of this world there might be heresies
like Jansenism, which has been called the Calvinism of the Roman
Catholic Church, and which was indeed an austere and almost classical version of Christianity. Some of the gentler members, like Bishop
Fénelon, might go over to a much more modern heresy, the quietism that
seems in some ways an anticipation of the sentimental belief in natural
goodness of the eighteenth century. But the great bulk of these classical
humanists were surely marginal Christians, or at least Christians not
much moved toward the imitation of Christ, Christians for whom the
Church was above all a discipline for naturally unruly men who lacked
the sense of these classical humanists, their education, their feeling for
what was fit.

It is easy, and tempting, to consider the way of life and ways of thought
of the classical humanists as without influence on the formation of the
modern mind, especially in the English-speaking world, as something
that might move a schoolmaster or two—or a T. S. Eliot—but as not particularly germane to our own thinking and feeling. Yet one distinguished
French historian of ideas, Taine, maintained the thesis that what he
called the classic spirit (*esprit classique*) with its tendency to regard the
universal, the regular, the uniform as a kind of standard, its habit of
simplifying, its belief in rules and formulas, helped to produce the state
of mind we call the Enlightenment. Certainly rebels like Voltaire had
sat at the feet of the great masters of the seventeenth century. We shall
have to return later to this problem of the relation of *l'esprit classique* to
the Enlightenment. In their own time, the classical humanists believed

that they had found a principle of authority, a measure, decency and decorum, something that could stand with the medieval synthesis as a practical ordering of this messy world.

The exuberant humanists we Americans feel more at home with, and we commonly credit them as in very important senses makers of our own way of life. These are the heroes of the Renaissance proper, the men whose doings make good reading, even in textbooks—Cellini, murdering, whoring, sculpturing, posturing, talking with kings and popes; Leonardo da Vinci, painting, building, writing, inventing airplanes, submarines and armored battle-tanks (on paper), engineering. Then there are kings like Francis I of France and Henry VIII of England who not only looked kingly, who not only had the athletic and hunting skills essential to esteemed position in the upper class of Western society right down to the present-day United States, but who were also learned in the ancient tongues, witty, capable of turning out a poem or an essay, and, of course, great lovers. There are whole families like the Borgias, full of the most fascinating, immoral, and unconventional people.

Their flavor is unmistakable. There have been strivers, ardent pursuers of the ultimate, in all ages, and the whole spirit of some ages is sometimes as zestful, as pushing, as that of the Renaissance; late nineteenth-century America was a great age of push, and philosophers of history have labeled our whole Western culture, from the ancient Greeks on, or from the Dark Ages on, as "Faustian," "Nordic," "dynamic," restless, striving. But there is a curious childlike cruelty, abandon, and immediacy of aim in the striving of the high Renaissance. Cellini provides a mine of illustrations. Here is one:

Having discontinued my connection with that wretch Caterina, and the poor unfortunate young man who had conspired with her to wrong me being gone from Paris, I intended to have my ornament for Fontainebleau, which was of bronze, properly cleaned, and likewise to get the two figures of Victory, which extended from the side angles to the middle circles of the gate, furbished up. For this purpose I took into my house a poor girl about fifteen years of age. She was extremely well-shaped, lively, and of a complexion rather swarthy; and as she was somewhat rustic, spoke little, walked rapidly, and had a sort of wildness in her eyes, I gave her the name of Scozzona; but her name was Gianna. With her assistance, I finished my Fontainebleau and the two Victories intended for ornaments to the gate. By this Gianna I had a daughter, on the seventh of June, at three in the afternoon, in 1544. I gave this child the name of Constantia, and she was held upon the font by Signor Guido Guidi, one of my most intimate friends, physician to the King. He alone stood godfather; for the custom of France is, that there should be but one godfather and two godmothers. One of these was Signora Maddalena, wife to Signor Luigi Alamanni, a gentleman of Florence, and an admirable poet, the other godmother was a French lady of good family, wife of Signor

Riccardo del Bene, also a citizen of Florence and an eminent merchant. This
was the first child that I ever had, to the best of my remembrance. I assigned
the mother such a maintenance as satisfied an aunt of hers, into whose hands
I put her; and never had any acquaintance with her afterward.

It is not the sexual irregularity here that is striking, nor Cellini's obvious
lack of any sense of sin; it is his apparent self-centered unawareness of
others as persons, as objects of concern—it is his childlike innocence.

The exuberant humanists, it might seem, were in fact casting off *all*
authority, not merely that of the medieval Church; they were humanists
in the sense that they believed that man is the measure of all things, and
that each man is a measure for himself. The tag word is "individualism"—these men were great individualists as opposed to the timid conformists of the monkish Middle Ages; they were men who dared to be
themselves, because they trusted in their own natural powers, in something inside themselves. They were the kind of men we Americans like,
men with no stuffiness, men who might almost have come from Texas.

Rabelais again is a case in point. He loves to make fun of the monkish
Middle Ages, its superstitions, its pretenses to chastity, its Aristotelian
learning. He is going to free men and women from this nonsense. His
Abbaye de Thélème is a very lay abbey indeed, open to both sexes, and
inscribed on its gate is the pleasant command, *Fay ce que vouldras* (Do
what you like).

We must, be it repeated, avoid the excesses of debunking. These men
of the Renaissance in its more athletic phase were also makers of the
modern world. They helped greatly to destroy the medieval world, especially the political and moral phases of that world. They produced
many works of art that are an inescapable part of our inheritance. They
had taken on by the nineteenth century the stature of giants, and ful-
filled for almost all the great nations of Europe, except for Germany,
which had to wait for Goethe, the essential function of culture-heroes.
Do not think this unimportant; without Shakespeare, British self-esteem,
and even our own, would be not shaken, perhaps, but surely lessened.
No one else could take his place.

Yet these men of the Renaissance were by no means working for ends
like ours, and were we to encounter them in the flesh we should hardly
feel them kin. It is not merely, as we shall see in the next section, that
they had no sympathy with, hardly any idea of, democracy in our modern
sense. The difference is deeper, or rather, this fundamental difference
ramifies into all fields of life and can be expressed in many different ways.
Underlying our modern democratic beliefs there is an optimism, a notion of the possible orderliness and widespread prosperity for all, which
the men of the Renaissance did not have. There is today a doctrine of
formal progress, of better times that lie ahead in the nature of things.
There is a belief in the essential goodness and educability of ordinary

human beings. There is a very basic belief that man somehow fits into the universe, that, to put the matter with not wholly deceptive simplicity, men are made to be happy.

Now these are very big and very risky generalizations indeed. It may well be that in the mid-twentieth century the beliefs we have noted above are not really held by most men, that we are coming into a new age and a new faith. But these beliefs are clearly the beliefs of eighteenth- and nineteenth-century democratic optimism. On the Renaissance end of our generalizations, it must be admitted that since these early centuries of the modern era were a seedbed for our own ideas, since above all they were centuries of great intellectual fermentation and experimentation, since there was on the whole great freedom of thought in most of Europe, you can find examples of almost anything you search for in these times. A Jacksonian Democrat would find the English Levellers congenial enough. Science, invention, geographical discoveries gave a modern tone to intellectual life. Novelty and excitement were, if not commonplace, at least always available with a little effort. And it was a humanist of these centuries who gave us the word with which we sum up the notion that men might be happy and well adjusted in a perfect society on this earth—*Utopia*.

Yet this last should give us pause. We use the word *Utopia* usually with a slight twist of scorn. The word carries with it an unmistakable note of the dream, the myth, the unreal. And not unjustly, for Sir Thomas More's *Utopia* is no more modern than Plato's *Republic*. If you have a certain type of mind and training, you will add "and no less modern." Both are the work of metaphysical idealists, tender-minded men who hope that the spirit may somehow transcend the flesh. More's book reflects the early sixteenth-century interest in geographical discovery— Utopia itself is an island that the sailor Ralph Hythloday has visited— and it is much more preoccupied with economic questions than was Plato's *Republic*. But both are authoritarian in spirit, and neither seems aware of change in human relations as a process, let alone an evolution. Perhaps most writers who deliberately set out to invent a Utopia are by temperament authoritarian, even though, like Karl Marx, they put down on paper as an ultimate ideal the withering away of the state or some other distant, anarchical goal.

St. Thomas More (he was canonized in 1935) was one of the humanist-scholars, a Roman Catholic who suffered martyrdom at the hands of Henry VIII, and by no means one of the exuberant humanists we are now chiefly concerned with. And it is the exuberant humanists who have given the Renaissance the flavor that now seems so interesting to us— from afar. These active, adventurous, questing, excited men were at heart unsure of themselves and their place in the universe. They tried hard to believe in themselves, but not very successfully. They did not have the dogmatic security the spare classical humanists arrived at. They were always experimenting, always trying something new.

They had, however, certain ends, certain purposes, certain ways they sought to follow. They were contemptuous of their medieval forefathers, not so much because of what they thought was their empty logic-spinning, but because of what they thought was medieval fear of life—the life of the appetites. The Renaissance as a fashion among fashionable people—and the exuberant humanists were at the height of sixteenth-century fashion—set a great store on being frankly pagan about its enjoyments. These humanists and artists were not going to be like the late medieval decadents, worried and obsessed with sin while they tried to enjoy themselves. Theirs was to be no Dance of Death, but a Dance of Life.

But it was a public dance, and the performers were out to shine. Each dancer was determined to outdo the others in polish, in verve, in endurance. In the groups that set the tone of aristocratic life, competition was as frenzied, as intense, as it has ever been in human society. Within the elite that competition was perhaps even more deadly than the more widespread competition of late nineteenth-century life. The Renaissance was the age of the hero, the hero as artist, the hero as soldier of fortune, the hero as explorer, the hero as scholar, even the hero as poisoner. If you were less than a hero, you were a failure.

The great word—there is a big critical and historical literature upon it—which seems to point up this mad scramble of all the talents is the Italian *virtù*. The word, like our modern *virtue,* comes from the Latin *vir,* man. But Renaissance *virtu* emphasizes "man" in the way our manliness does, and adds a great deal more. Like the ideals of chivalry from which it in part descends, *virtù* is an upper-class ideal, to which a gifted person of lesser birth may indeed rise. Again like that of chivalry, this ideal can be made to emphasize a code of conduct not unchristian and can quite readily be turned into a rather overrefined, but decent, code for a gentleman, as in Baldassare Castiglione's *Libro del Cortegiano* (Book of the Courtier). Castiglione writes like a humanist, with abundant references to classical literature. But he is almost medieval in his tender-minded belief in the validity of the ideal; his prince is far nearer the prince of the medieval John of Salisbury than the prince of his own contemporary, Machiavelli:

> "Since it costs us nothing but words, tell us on your faith everything that it would occur to your mind to teach your prince."
> My lord Ottaviano replied:
> "Many other things, my Lady, would I teach him, provided I knew them; and among others, that he should choose from his subjects a number of the noblest and wisest gentlemen, with whom he should consult on everything, and that he should give them authority and free leave to speak their mind to him about all things without ceremony; and that he should preserve such

demeanour towards them, that they all might perceive that he wished to know the truth about everything and held all manner of falsehood in hatred. Besides this council of nobles, I should advise that there be chosen from the people other men of lower rank, of whom a popular council should be made, to communicate with the council of nobles concerning the affairs of the city, both public and private. And in this way there would be made of the prince (as of the head) and of the nobles and commonalty (as of the members) a single united body, the government of which would spring chiefly from the prince and yet include the others also; and this state would thus have the form of the three good kinds of government, which are Monarchy, Optimates, and People.

"Next I should show him that of the cares which belong to the prince, the most important is that of justice; for the maintenance of which wise and well-tried men ought to be chosen to office, whose foresight is true foresight accompanied by goodness, for else it is not foresight, but cunning; and when this goodness is lacking, the pleaders' skill and subtlety always work nothing but ruin and destruction to law and justice, and the guilt of all their errors must be laid on him who put them in office.

"I should tell how justice also fosters that piety towards God which is the duty of all men, and especially of princes, who ought to love Him above every other thing and direct all their actions to Him as to the true end; and as Xenophon said, to honour and love Him always, but much more when they are in prosperity, so that afterwards they may the more reasonably have confidence to ask Him for mercy when they are in some adversity. . . ."

The mixture of Xenophon and the Christian God is by no means uncharacteristic. The whole tone is that of Platonism, now watered down to the uses of an upper class—and its imitators, anxious to learn gentility from the new humanists.

In practice *virtù* can almost mean doing something, doing *anything*, better than anyone else. The skills it honors are the skills of the champion, the record breaker. Perhaps man is by some sort of instinct a record breaker; but a lot depends on what sort of records he tries to break. The Renaissance was as promiscuous in this as in other respects. It is true the Renaissance did not favor attempts to break records for asceticism; fasts, hair shirts, and hermits were not its style. But almost anything else would do. Don Juan, with his famous 1003 female conquests in Spain alone, is more in the Renaissance tradition of record breakers.

Don Juan clearly did not have a very good time setting up his record. Even in the earlier Spanish form of the legend, Don Juan is an unhappy man driven to his innumerable love affairs by some demonic push which is not quite what Hollywood and most of us mean by sex. Don Juan is indeed a brother of another figure of legend who by the Renaissance has become a literary figure—Doctor Faustus. Both Faust and Don Juan want something excessive—their very wanting is excessive. Yet they cannot satisfy their unending wants in a way the Christian tradition had long provided in its many variants of mystic other-worldliness. They have to get what they want in the flesh, here and now, like other men. But their

wants are not the wants of other men; they would blush to think they
had so little distinction of body and spirit as to have their wants re-
quited. They have the restless striving after something infinite that men
like Spengler find in northerners, in the Faustian man. But as good children of humanism, they want all this without God, without *theoria,
nirvana,* or any other mystic self-annihilation.

In real life, they get this sense of transcending limitations only by trying for the record, only by this conscious pushing to excess the quality
we have called exuberance. In the fine arts this striving for the excessive
is curbed by the degree of reverence all shared for Greek and Roman
work. The Renaissance artist is still so full of problems in working out
the natural, realistic representation of things on this earth that he feels
no need to be wild, or abstract, or unintelligible. He can do *big* things,
as Michelangelo was fond of doing; and admire Michelangelo as you
may, you will have to admit that there is in his work—in the David, in
God and Adam and Eve of the Sistine Chapel—a sense of strain, an heroic
strife to attain the heroic, the overpowering. Indeed, just putting God,
a majestic and powerful God, but a God not altogether without *virtù,*
on the ceiling of the chapel was the kind of thing that suited the exuberant humanists—and more than one humanistically inclined pope. It
is not that the high Middle Ages had had scruples about bringing God
too close to men by painting or sculpturing him. In the Last Judgments,
which were a favorite subject for the sculptor of the early Middle Ages
in particular, God has to appear. But he never looks like the perfect
knight. And in the later Middle Ages there is a tendency to confine concrete representation to Jesus, the Virgin, and the saints, as if God were
not in fact of our kind.

In writing of all sorts, even in the work of the scholars, this Renaissance quality of striving for the unique, the extreme, the grand, comes
out clearly; we have already noted euphuism and gongorism. But in fact
there is hardly a writer who does not at some phase in his career work
so hard at being himself that he becomes precious, difficult, full of alle-
gory and conceits. Sometimes there is an incredible piling up of details
of erudition, of odd lore, of odds and ends of experience of all sorts, as
in Rabelais. Later French writers of the spare classical school, shocked
by this Rabelaisian fertility and formlessness, called him "Gothic," which
he of course is not; he is merely an exuberant humanist, most emancipated, who would have been very uncomfortable *as an intellectual* in the
thirteenth century. (He would, of course, not have written in the thirteenth century, but followed his profession of medicine heartily and
creditably, with no undue worries about his ignorance.) Sometimes this
quality comes out in a prose style that in almost any other period would
be found intolerably artificial, like that of Sir Thomas Browne's *Urn*

Burial. You may say that this is the dead hand of Latin at its most Ciceronian, periodic, and spiritually periwigged. But it is what these writers thought a suitable style, something they quite deliberately sought for. Sometimes the Renaissance writer just doesn't know how to stop, a failing that again may well be timeless among the literary, but which in those days seems especially common. This is by no means true only of the early exuberant writers, like Rabelais. One finds it in later writers, among them the English poet Spenser, whose unfinished *Faerie Queene* runs on for eighty cantos.

Finally, this quality of excess may well be brought out in the work of a man who lived long after the last of the Renaissance worthies was dead. All the American critics at some time or other dragged out the epithet "Renaissance" for Thomas Wolfe, the North Carolinian novelist who died in 1938. The critics were well justified; the epithet had to be used. Wolfe's desires were all appetites, and his appetites were all Gargantuan. He tells in *Of Time and the River* how, as a young graduate student at Harvard, he got stack access to the library, even then of some two to three million volumes, and started to read them all, going up and down the rows of stacks, pulling down book after book. In a magnificent moment of concentration, he would register each book somewhere in his mind, and add it to his record. He came far short even of the first million, but this means no more than that the Renaissance can hardly come again. Certainly a dip into Wolfe should make clearer the note we have been attempting to describe.

It must not be thought that these exuberant humanists were all wild men, that none of them ever enjoyed a quiet moment. Some of them tired, if they lived long enough. Some of them won their way through storm and stress to what their world had agreed to call wisdom. Some of them seem always to have had a certain kind of wisdom about human beings. Yet the serenity, the wisdom, the recognizable state of balance that does come out of this Renaissance way of life is very different from that of the medieval Scholastic, very different from that of a spare classicist like Boileau. Shakespeare by his whole career and environment belongs to what we have called the exuberant humanists. He has most of the Renaissance mannerisms, followed most of the Renaissance fashions. He was a wise man, but to judge him from his works—and fortunately, perhaps, that is all we have to judge him from—there is a bitterness in him not found in orthodox Christianity, and seldom found in the Enlightenment of the eighteenth century. There is the full Renaissance contempt for the many, for the vulgar; Shakespeare is not in the least a democrat. There is no good evidence that Shakespeare was a Christian. He certainly has no Christian warmth, no Christian feeling for the will of God. Fate, the universe, the scheme of things seem to him not quite meant for man, not even meant to test man. He does not seem to believe in any way of changing this; he is clearly no man for good causes. He ends up extraordinarily close to Montaigne, who never went through as much turbulence and exuberance as did Shakespeare. The world is an interesting place, while you are young a rather exciting place, but not really a very nice place, and certainly not a sensible place.

The humanism of the early modern centuries is not an attitude that can be summed up clearly. As we have noted before, the systematist, the taxonomist, in the natural sciences does not expect his classifications to be like watertight compartments; he knows that in real life his species vary and shade into one another, and he knows that his own work is not perfect. Men who shared some of the humanist ways and beliefs were also in part theists, men in the direct Christian tradition, St. Thomas More, for instance; other humanists, perhaps even the Lorenzo Valla who exposed the spuriousness of the "Donation of Constantine," come pretty close to the rationalists we shall discuss later. Nevertheless, the humanist attitude is one that can be in part isolated and described. It differs from the historical Western Christianity of its own time in its distrust of Scholasticism and the whole medieval complex and in its dislike for the more evangelical, Old Testament aspects of Protestantism; it differs from rationalism in that, persuaded though it is of the superiority of the natural to medieval formalism, sacerdotism, and convention, it clings, or seeks to cling, to the notion that man is not wholly a part of nature, that he is not just the cleverest of animals, *but actually not wholly an animal.*

The human being, the full, complex human being, is for the humanist a standard. To oversimplify, his slogan might be: Neither superhuman (theism) nor subhuman (mechanism). Humanism as a system of values, however, we have already noted, has the range, the spectrum, of concrete behavior that any of the other great Western systems of value have had. Man may be the measure of all things, but he is not a neat standard meter or yardstick. He can, for instance, get bestially drunk, or sparkle wittily and benignly on a few glasses of wine, or take a little wine for his stomach's sake, or abstain severely, and try to make others abstain, from all forms of alcoholic drinks. In the last four or five hundred years, the cultivated minority that has liked to call itself humanist has tended quite definitely toward the second of these practices; it has sought a pleasant temperance. But in the lustier days of the Renaissance humanism was not quite so confined. It could be rowdy with Rabelais, gentle with More, academic with Erasmus, frantically active with Cellini, skeptical and tolerant with Montaigne, even, at the court of Lorenzo the Magnificent in Florence, Neoplatonist with some very charming ladies and gentlemen.

The Political Attitudes of Humanism

The two centuries, roughly 1450-1650, with which we are here concerned are commonly tagged in political history the "period of absolutism." It is a fact that in these centuries the modern territorial state
emerged from the medieval state all over the Western world, even where,
as in the Germanies, the territorial unit was not our nation-state, but the
lands of a prince or a free city, perhaps no greater in area than its predecessor of the Middle Ages. The simplest practical manifestation of this
change was the existence in the new territorial unit of a single chain of
authority backed by a graded system of law courts and an armed force,
police and military, paid, controlled, and administered by those at the
top of the chain. Feudal remnants persisted almost everywhere, and this
new state had by no means the tidy table of organization and chain of
command a modern army is supposed to work with. But the difference
from the complex medieval nexus of rights and duties, of counterbalanc-
ing authorities and limiting custom, was very great. The new state—
even if you take Soviet Russia as its ultimate embodiment—has never
quite been the ruthlessly efficient, antlike, regimented society its many
critics have made it out to be. But historically it originated at least in
part from a demand for standardization and efficiency, for some curbing
of the human tendency to stray, to be lazy, to be eccentric.

We may once more make use of a simple dualism. If you set up a polar
contrast between authority (compulsion) and liberty (spontaneity), then
in the balance the new state *in all its forms,* even when those forms are
democratic, belongs on the side of authority. There are, of course, great
historical and geographical variations, and some states can be put nearer
the absolute pole of authoritarianism than others. But all of them have
more political control over most individuals than was common in the
Middle Ages.

Certainly the theory of the absolute state was put in these years about
as nakedly as it has ever been put. (Modern totalitarian theory seems
rather reluctant to come out flat-footedly against such nice words as
liberty and *democracy.*) The English seventeenth-century philosopher
Hobbes invented for the new state the term *Leviathan,* which has ever
since been a reproach among libertarian writers. Hobbes made use of
an old concept of political theory, with a long tradition of respectability
from Rome through the Middle Ages, that of the contract. But he
twisted this concept, which on the whole had been used on the libertarian side, so that it fits neatly into authoritarian theory. The contract
had been supposed to put *limitations* on all parties to it, rulers and ruled
alike, but above all to provide a kind of fence within which the individual

could be on his own. With Hobbes, the contract is entered into by all individuals in order to avoid the horrible war of each against all that would prevail were man to remain in a "state of nature." (We shall have to return to this notion of a state of nature; for the present we may note that for Hobbes this was a most unpleasant state, so unpleasant that it had perhaps never existed.) These individuals contract among one another to create the sovereign, the authority that prescribes the laws all must obey and that substitutes order for the disorder of the state of nature. *But there is no contract between the individual or any group of individuals and the sovereign.* The sovereign is absolute, and the individual must obey the sovereign absolutely. Hobbes does make one reservation: The sovereign is there to preserve order, to make the individual secure, and if he should fail in this purpose and the state become disorderly and life insecure, then the individual has the right to protect his own life and security as he can. But Hobbes's heart was not in this hypothetical reservation; it was very much in setting up a sovereign above the contract that created him.

The contract theory, as we shall see, was not altogether safe ground for the partisans of absolutism in its characteristic Renaissance form of monarchical absolutism, and indeed became one of the most useful of wedges for the introduction of democratic ideas. But there were whole arsenals of argument and theory available to the monarchical absolutists in the new historical erudition that was available to all educated men. The Bible—especially the Old Testament—Greek and Roman history, patristic literature (at least for the Catholics), and even the first and very uncritical beginnings of fields of knowledge like prehistory and ethnology were all drawn upon for arguments. That these same fields were increasingly drawn upon by opponents of monarchical absolutism in the seventeenth and eighteenth centuries need not surprise us. Common sense has long admitted what only the very tender-minded will deny, that the devil also can quote scripture.

It would be tedious and unprofitable to review a great number of these defenses of absolutism. A fair example is the patriarchal theory, which among English writers reached its perfection in the book Locke spent so much time tearing apart, Sir Robert Filmer's *Patriarcha.* The patriarchal theory is well worth study as an example of the complex and devious ways of what it is now fashionable to call "rationalization" or something even more scornful. We are obviously not here dealing with scientific theories, with cumulative knowledge. But we are dealing with an essential part of intellectual history, with an essential part of human relations.

The monarchist writer is seeking, in simplest terms, to put into words reasons why individuals should obey the government of the new centralized state, a government at least symbolically headed by a monarch. In the patriarchal theory he makes use of an analogy between the relation of father and son and that of monarch and subject. He is free with metaphors that call the subjects "children," "the flock," and the monarch "father," "shepherd," and the like. Now even today and in the United States, where it has been remarked by epigrammatic European travelers that the children often bring up their parents, the feeling that the normal child-parent relationship is one of obedience by the child is still very strong. Its strength has varied in different times and places, but the weight of Western cultural inheritance in its favor is great. It seems to many just one of the facts of life. The Hebrew society in the midst of which the Old Testament was put together was a strongly patriarchal society in which the son was very firmly indeed under the control of the father. You can find suitable texts to emphasize the wickedness, the unnaturalness, of filial disobedience almost anywhere you look in the Old Testament. In Roman society too the *patria potestas,* the power of the father, was in republican days quite absolute, even extending to power over the son's life. Roman law as it filtered down into medieval society continued to carry this firm paternal authority. Christianity had made much use of the paternal power and the sentiments that had grown up around it. The metaphor of the shepherd and his flock was of long standing; the priests of the Church are called "father."

It was easy to extend the metaphor from the Church to the State, the more since the new model modern state in Catholic as well as in Protestant countries took over where it could the spiritual prestige, the nexus of human sentiments, which in the Middle Ages had centered in the Church as an institution. How deliberate this taking over was no one can be sure. Certainly men like Filmer were not of the mental disposition to say to themselves, "The Pope managed to make the idea of his being Holy Father very useful toward strengthening his power. Why can't we strengthen the power of the state if we keep hammering at the idea that our king is the Father of his people?" On the contrary, Filmer was surely as persuaded of the truth of his theories as was Tom Paine of the truth of his opposite ones.

But the patriarchal theory is a set of arguments that depend for their persuasive force largely on the sentiments, not on the logical capacity and training, of those who accept them. It is a metaphor and not a theory, and can be made invalid, untrue, for anyone who simply says that he feels that a king is to him in no way a father. Especially if one stays within the terms of humanism or rationalism, one can say that there is only one kind of father-son relation, the kind that we call biological and that they in those days called natural. The patriarchal theory, as a justification of unquestioning obedience from subject to monarch (citizen to government), can be still more readily refuted, granted your sentiments flow the right way, by substituting another and contrary metaphor with its own claim to be the right theory. This the Lockeans did when they maintained that the true relation between subject and king was that of agency. The king is not the father of his subjects—he is their agent. He exists to give them good government, and if he fails to do so, they are fully justified in dismissing him as one would dismiss an agent who proved unsatisfactory. To most Americans, this agency theory of government seems very sensible. But over the long course of Western history, there is no doubt that the patriarchal theory is much more representative of common opinion.

Indeed, the patriarchal theory in one form or another seems immortal in writing on social relations. We all know that, following the lead of Freud, modern psychologists have emphasized the importance of the parent-child relation. The psychologists, too, write on political theory, and once more they have recourse to the patriarchal theory. It is true they emphasize the son's ambivalent feeling of dependence on, and desire to revolt from, the father. It is true that they consider themselves scientists, and maintain that they are adding to the sum of cumulative knowledge. But read Geoffrey Gorer's *The American People*. Mr. Gorer explains our politics and our culture largely in terms of the father complex and the Oedipus complex, and comes up with a wonderfully Freudian explanation of the young American male's fondness for milk. He is oblivious to what is nowadays an even greater fondness for carbonated soft drinks, which are harder to fit into Freudian schemes. It is highly likely that in the twenty-third century Mr. Gorer's adaptation of the age-old father analogy will seem at least as silly as Sir Robert Filmer's does now.

There were other arguments in favor of absolute monarchy. One went back to Roman precedent, not of the Republic, but of the later Empire, when the Roman state was itself well streamlined with a bureaucracy and an absolute prince at its head. A favorite tag was *quod principi placuit, legis habet vigorem*—"what has pleased the prince has the force of law." This put the matter with excessive baldness, and was perhaps the most irritating of arguments from the point of view of the republicans.

The consecrated phrase, however, the one that has gone down into history, is the "divine right of kings." The king is, in no blasphemous sense, God on earth; in the language of the theory, he is God's deputy on earth, and to oppose his will is to oppose God's will, which is indeed blasphemy. He is God's anointed—and in fact by medieval precedents European kings received at their coronation ceremony a special anointment with a consecrated oil. Most of the rest of the arsenal of arguments for royal absolutism could, of course, be subsumed under this one.

It is significant that in all these defenses of the new absolutism the basic arguments are all traditional. The notion of contract is merely given a slight twist, and you have Hobbes's Leviathan instead of the Christian feudal state of John of Salisbury. The notion of the spiritual shepherd, the Christian father, is given another twist and you have the father-king who cannot be disobeyed.

Admirers of the Middle Ages are particularly shocked by what they regard as the Renaissance perversion of the medieval doctrine of the divine right of kings. In the medieval doctrine, they maintain—and quite rightly as far as the words go—that the ruler rules by divine right as long as he rules as God wants him to; he rules by divine right not just in the sense of right as possession, an incontrovertible claim, but in the sense of right as morally just. When he rules wickedly and not in accordance with divine right, then he has no right to rule, and his subjects are released from their duty of obedience and justified in revolting. At this point we should inevitably inquire, who judges whether a king is ruling in accordance with God's intentions? Suppose one group in the state say the king does so rule, and another says he doesn't. How do we know which is right? The medieval and indeed the Renaissance mind could answer these questions much more serenely than we can, for they were not as yet disturbed by the idea that God's intentions are by no means as clear as scientific truth, which of course could never be found in such problems. The medieval *and the humanist* mind were both firmly in the habit of believing that God's will was as clear as anything on earth.

The argument we nowadays, at least in English-speaking countries, regard as a clincher is never used clearly. This is the argument that the new-style monarchic state is more efficient than the old, that the monarch has to have absolute power in order to sweep up the debris of feudal autonomous areas, in order to rationalize, standardize, so that the new middle-class businessmen can sell in a wider market and with greater security and greater convenience. The justification of an institution by its *utility,* an argument familiar enough to us, does crop up in defense of monarchy, even as far back as Pierre Dubois in the early fourteenth century. But in most of the writers here considered it is mixed with many other arguments. The French *politiques,* writers who in the religious wars of the late sixteenth century put the nation as represented by the Crown ahead of both Catholic and Protestant parties, seem to have some such modern notions as might be labeled nationalistic in the back of their minds. But they do not speak our language.

One of the best of them is Jean Bodin, who is often regarded as rather more than a *politique.* Bodin was a scholar-humanist of wide learning, and with many interests. He has an important place in the history of historical writing as one of the first writers to concern himself with systematic historical methods in research and composition in his *Method for the Ready Knowledge of History* (1566). In political theory, he is perhaps the most balanced writer on the vexed subject of sovereignty. He is by inclination a moderate and a sensible man. He wrote in the late sixteenth century, after the prestige of Aristotle had rebounded from the first humanist disparagement, and he had the benefit of the abundant common sense evident in Aristotle's politics. Bodin comes out in the end as a defender of the absolutism of the sovereign prince. As the maker of laws, according to Bodin, the sovereign was—because he had to be—above laws. But Bodin hastens to qualify this as a legal principle only; morally, of course, the prince is bound by the law of God and the law of nature, and by the decencies. If he does not so abide he is a tyrant, though apparently still a sovereign. Bodin too brings in the patriarchal argument, reinforced by the Roman *patria potestas,* and the usual arsenal of Biblical quotations.

It would not be fair to say that all the political thought of the humanists and the classicists of the early modern centuries was on the side of absolutism. From the start of the revival of Greek and Roman classics in the Renaissance sense, there is discernible an attitude that can be followed as a clear thread in the Western political tradition right down into the French Revolution, which made Brutus one of its heroes. This is the tradition of *classical republicanism,* with its heroes from Livy, its Roman hatred of kings—and, often, its Roman distrust of *mobile vulgus,* the inconstant common people.

We have again come up against a word that has had a history and therefore can be ambiguous. We Americans are likely to think that "republican" is really just another way of saying "democrat"—and this entirely apart from our liberals' fondness for saying that our two parties, Republican and Democrat with capital letters, are as alike as Tweedledum and Tweedledee. But the *res publica Romana* was no more than the Roman political organization, which was—and remained right through to the founding of the Empire—politically and socially aristocratic. This tradition of aristocratic republicanism, which had little ground to work on in the Middle Ages, began to thrive in the Renaissance. From its very nature it could hardly be a mass belief. It has been a creed above all among artists and intellectuals, especially artists and intellectuals of good birth, an assumption of aristocrats. It is a creed that, with such holders, naturally enough conforms to no simple, common, stereotyped pattern. Classical republicanism is almost always libertarian rather than collectivist, or socialistic; or at any rate, where it emphasizes that the necessary order and discipline of a society involves care for the lower classes, it is the collectivism of *noblesse oblige,* of what nineteenth-century Englishmen called "Tory democracy." Where you do find men working toward some basic and radical reform of society to get rid of poverty through the efforts of the poor, you will find that these men are in these early modern centuries inspired rather by religion than by humanism, and by a violently sectarian kind of religion.

One kind of humanist republicanism is really at heart directed against a specific monarchy. In the late sixteenth century political thought in France was sharpened by the great civil wars of religion, and a body of theory resulted that has on the surface a pretty democratic look. Huguenots like Etienne de la Boétie and François Hotman came out firmly against all theories of monarchical absolutism, and urged instead that ultimate authority lies in the hands of the people. The author of the pamphlet *Vindiciae contra Tyrannos*—he was probably du Plessis-Mornay —brought in the contract theory and much scriptural and medieval history to justify actual revolt and even tyrannicide. You can extract from this literature something very close to what came to be the conventional eighteenth-century doctrine of the rights of man, the need for constitutional government in the hands of a representative parliamentary body, the supremacy of the law, and so on. Yet the temper of these works is definitely not eighteenth-century. They *sound* medieval, if only because of their usual reliance on arguments from precedent, historical or Biblical, and their rather heavy scholarship. These men are by no means rabble rousers. They have not the popular touch, moved though they are by the justice of their cause. One feels that they are inevitably antimonarchical because the French monarchy was against them, but republican also by necessity, since they have no other choice. Some of them set up a principle of "natural leadership." They are a long, long way from Thomas Paine, or even Benjamin Franklin; they are republicans, not democrats.

Yet another pattern is nearer the center of this aristocratic republicanism, nearer in the sense of setting a pattern that survived into the nineteenth century in men like Lord Byron and even into the twentieth in a Wilfred Scawen Blunt or that curious American representative of the type, the late John Jay Chapman. Algernon Sydney, an Englishman of noble family who died on the scaffold in 1683, a martyr to republicanism, is an admirable example. His *Discourses Concerning Government* was not published until 1698, and was much read in the next century. It is full of Roman history, seen in the glow of gentlemanliness that has long accompanied British classicism. It attacks divine right and defends popular sovereignty. It has no radical social doctrines—indeed it talks the language of moderate constitutionalism, and had Sydney lived into the next century he might well have been a good moderate whig with no "republican nonsense." Sydney is against the upstart Stuarts with their doctrines of divine right, and in favor of an English ruling class that will have all the Roman virtues and none of the Roman vices.

Milton himself belongs in this group of aristocratic republicans, as far as his politics goes. He is a humanist by taste and training, and rather on the spare than on the exuberant side. His most famous prose writing is doubtless the *Areopagitica,* one of the classic defenses of liberty of speech and its train of attendant liberties. There is no doubt a timelessness about any eloquent defense of freedom of speech in Western culture, which has hardly ever been absolutist enough not to nourish some spark of this freedom. But it is very doubtful if Milton even in this pamphlet was anticipating laissez-faire notions of the usefulness of individual freedom. At any rate, it is an interesting if very delicate exercise in intellectual history to read together and compare the *Areopagitica* and John Mill's *On Liberty* of 1859. Milton's rolling classic eloquence may get in the way of an understanding of what he is about; but even when this allowance is made, he seems to be arguing for freedom for the elect, for the humanist, for men like himself, and not, like Mill, for freedom even for the crank, the mistaken, the ignorant—in short, the people.

The aristocratic quality in Milton's political and moral ideas is quite clear in his lesser writings, in the *Eikonoklastes* or the *Ready and Easy Way to Establish a Free Commonwealth*—the latter an unsuccessful attempt to prevent the recall of King Charles II. Of course, Milton hated the sectaries and their uncouth hopes for heaven on earth, and he was disillusioned by the failure of moderate Puritanism to establish a comfortable halfway house between the Anglicans and the millenarian sects. Like many another refined and cultivated defender of individual liberty, Milton in the end proved that it was refinement and cultivation he really meant to defend, and not the liberty of men who were coarse and unthinking. He came in the end so much to distrust common men voting by head, or by pressure groups, that in his plan for a commonwealth he made the legislature a self-perpetuating body with lifetime tenure of office, a kind of House of Lords without peerage.

But the most fully rounded work of this school of humanists with leanings, not precisely toward the Left, but at any rate toward a more popular form of constitutional government, is that of another seventeenth-century Englishman, the *Oceana* of James Harrington. In form this is an imaginary commonwealth, a Utopia, a form perhaps dictated by the need to evade the censorship of the new dictator Cromwell in the year of its publication, 1656. It is a treatise on government, a very thoughtful one in which the importance of the distribution of wealth and the class structure is recognized very specifically. It recommends a constitutional state with proper balance of interests, and including a senate of natural aristocrats and a popular representative body to approve or reject the proposals of the senate. Harrington has many modern ideas, among them the secret ballot and universal compulsory education. Indeed, the *Oceana* might well be classified as the work of a rationalist, and its influence on the next century was great. But Harrington has the classical style, the classical set of mind, and seems in this book rather to sum up the best thought of the politically moderate humanists than to break any new paths.

Of necessity, the category of humanists cannot be as neat as that of the other two strains in the early modern centuries, the Protestants and the rationalists. In the search for standards, for an authority, which at all times in Western history has been one of the main activities of the intellectual classes (even when they thought they were just casting off *all* authorities), the humanist appeal to something peculiarly *human*— not divine, not animal—has tended in practice to have as its first consequences a bewildering variety of possible standards and authorities. For, in simple language, *human* is a blanket word that can stretch to cover almost anything—including the divine and the animal.

Simply for convenience, and knowing well that our systematic work of classification must be most imperfect, we may separate these humanists of the sixteenth and seventeenth centuries roughly into the groups we christened "exuberant" and "spare." Most of the earliest are in some senses exuberant, even when they are sober scholars; and by the seventeenth century most of the men who are predominantly interested in humanism are of the spare or disciplined sort. Crudely, but at least simply, it may be said that predominantly the earlier men who went back to Greece and Rome found there freedom for the individual to be himself, to follow his own bent even if that bent were a series of contortions; and that the later men, for whom the first had made the way to Greece and Rome easy, indeed a part of ordinary schoolwork, found there discipline, quiet, order, simplicity. The first group tended to believe that the many would let the few be free to cultivate their uniqueness—or they were just not interested in the many; the second, who had known the horrors of the wars of religion, tended to worry a great deal about the masses, and the ways of keeping them in a decent place—they were, in short, monarchists and authoritarians. But neither group was passionately and actively interested in what we should now call the democratic cause. Even that sub-branch of the classical humanists, the aristocratic republicans like Algernon Sydney, were not democrats.

The humanists have left imperishable works of art. They had their part in the destruction of medieval attitudes, and, in a positive way, in the establishment of the modern territorial state with its standardization and its drive toward efficiency. Still, on the whole, we have less of the humanists in us than the textbooks usually tell us. The humanists were by no means the major architects of the modern world, nor the makers of the modern mind. Insofar as these two centuries went to make us what we are, by far the most important makers were the Protestants, the rationalists, and the scientists.

CHAPTER TWO

MAKING THE MODERN WORLD

II. PROTESTANTISM

Sources of Protestantism

Martin Luther was an Augustinian monk. There is some appropriateness—though, of course, no causal connection—in this faint link between the two men. For though it is true that St. Augustine's life work made him one of the pillars of the Catholic Church, there is in his personality that mystical straining for perfection which has always presented problems to the less saintly persons who have to run things on this earth. The Protestant movement is, in one very important sense, simply another manifestation of the persistent Christian tension between this world and the next, the real and the ideal. We moderns hardly need reminding that Luther, Calvin, and Zwingli headed movements that differed greatly in aims and organization from medieval attempts to reform existing religious practices. For one thing, they succeeded in establishing churches, where Wycliffe and Hus failed. Or, from another point of view, they were not, like the mendicant friars, tamed and absorbed into the Catholic Church.

We hardly need reminding of the part played by economic institutions, by nationalism, by the personalities of the leaders in differentiating the Protestant Revolt from medieval reform movements. We rather need reminding that, no matter how deep its economic and political causes, Protestantism won men's hearts and minds by appeals to Christian tradition. Even formally—and form is by no means unimportant—this is true. The Protestant reformers all insisted that they were not innovating, but were going back to Jesus and the early Church, the *real* Christian Church. It was Rome, they maintained, that had changed, by corrupting it, the *true* Christian tradition. The Protestant reformers believed quite sincerely that theirs was an *imitatio Christi,* an imitation of Christ. They did not think they were changing but restoring, and they would have been astonished and puzzled to be told they were agents of progress. Theirs was, as a performance visible to a neutral observer, an extremely different imitation from that of St. Francis. If Protestantism is simply one manifestation of the Christian effort to best the old Adam in men, we must remind ourselves that there are many ways in which the old Adam comes out, and many ways of trying to best him. We must ask ourselves what was new in the Protestantism of the early sixteenth century—new even though its makers thought it was old. These elements of novelty will go a long way toward explaining why the Protestant groups became schismatic churches instead of mere heretical groups leading a more or less underground existence, like the Lollards and the Hussites.

But we must first record the fact that the Roman Catholic Church itself was subject in the fourteenth and above all in the fifteenth century to pressures from the time of troubles that then marked a decline of medieval culture. Just as the church buildings took on the flamboyancy of the overripe Gothic, so the life of the Church grew more worldly, more decadent, lost that careful balance of the age of Aquinas. The Schoolmen grew emptily disputatious, the monastic orders grew richer, unpriestly priests grew more numerous, or at least more conspicuous. As a general rule, we may say that no institution is as bad as those who attack it—especially if they attack it successfully—make out. The old regime in France was not nearly so bad as the French Revolutionists made out; George III was by no means the tyrant American Revolutionists painted him. The Church of Pope Alexander VI (Rodrigo Borgia) was by no means as immoral as that scandalous pope, by no means the sink of iniquity it appears in Protestant propaganda. Like our newspapers, history loves the headlines; but the routine and not newsworthy still goes on. Many a quiet fifteenth-century priest or monk led quite as Christian a life as his thirteenth-century predecessors.

Still, there was a real decline in the level, and certainly in the peaks, of Christian life and institutions in the last years of the Middle Ages. Efforts were made to stem this decline. There were the open revolts anticipating that of Luther, notably that of Wycliffe in England and Hus in Bohemia; there were humanist reforming groups well short of revolt, such as that around the French scholar, Lefèvre d'Étaples, or Erasmus himself. Many of the ideas, many of the organizing methods used by later Protestants are to be found in these movements, and there is undoubtedly here what the historian rather loosely calls "influence." Did not Luther himself, perhaps reluctantly, acknowledge his debt to Hus?

Second, there was the movement to reform the Church from within by methods we should today call constitutional, the Conciliar Movement of the fifteenth century, which produced many writings held in high esteem by the historian of political thought. These clerical intellectuals of the late Middle Ages, of whom Jean Gerson may stand as a type, were still clearly working within a frame of medieval ideas. You can extract from Gerson something like the standard recipe of a mixed constitution, mingling elements of monarchy, aristocracy, and a polite democracy. This recipe has been attractive to moderate, sensible men from Aristotle to Montesquieu and Victorian Englishmen. Gerson and his fellows have the full academic faith in the quiet "ought," the full medieval belief that God has really ordained the right running of the universe so clearly that no reasonable person can fail to understand it. Since in fact they did meet in councils that came into active conflict with popes, the men of the Conciliar Movement did their bit toward preparing the way for the Reformation. They did not succeed in making the pope subject to a parliament-like group of the clergy, but they did challenge the growing power of the Roman bureaucracy. Their words, their attitudes, however, lacked the bite, the fierceness, the frank appeal to popular passions of Luther's; they lacked the revolutionary intensity of Calvin's; they lacked the touch—so familiar to us today—of the hard-boiled realist Machiavelli. All this is perhaps to say not that Gerson and his colleagues were medieval rather than modern, but merely that they were examples of that constant Western phenomenon, the moderate idealist and reformer, the man of words, nice words.

Words, however, do things in this world of human relations. They do not do things all by themselves, any more than the gas in an internal combustion engine explodes by itself. We need not ask whether Protestant ideas made economic changes or economic changes made Protestant ideas. The reader should be warned, however, that the Protestant Reformation is one of the great battlegrounds of the contemporary debate over economic determinism. From the point of view taken in this book, economic changes, changes in the way men of Western society did their daily work, are an important element in the whole social situation in which the Protestant Reformation proved a success. They are, in medical terms worth the reader's trip to the dictionary, part of a *syndrome* of which we do not fully understand the *etiology*. Grave changes like those involved in turning a self-sufficing manorial economy into a money economy based on extensive trade we should expect to be accompanied by, and followed by, grave changes in all human life. We should not expect them necessarily to be accompanied by, or followed by, a Protestant Reformation, as in fact they were. Similar changes in simple non-European economies in recent times—in Japan, for instance—have not been accompanied by a Protestant Reformation but by quite other changes.

The simplest economic explanation of the Protestant Revolution well antedates Marx, and is perhaps most vigorously stated by the English radical William Cobbett, who lived at the turn of the eighteenth into the nineteenth century. The Catholic Church everywhere, so runs this explanation, had over the pious medieval centuries grown enormously

wealthy from bequests of rich donors anxious to ensure a place for themselves in heaven. Kings, princes, and their followers, the ruling classes
in short, always in need of money, looked enviously at this wealth. They
seized upon the abstract ideas of Luther and his co-workers as a means
of making the spoliation of the clergy seem respectable in the eyes of
their subjects. They were also heavily indebted to the new merchant and
banking class, and were able to pay them off in part with lands and other
property seized from the Church. Thus was created a new, money-hungry
ruling class, out of which came our modern capitalists.

This whole explanation is too neatly tailored to English experience.
In Germany, the territorial princes were the chief gainers from the ex-
propriation of the Roman Catholic Church. In France, where the Reformation, though not triumphant, played a very important part, the
economic stakes were not nearly so clear. Furthermore, there is no evidence that in most parts of Europe that remained Catholic the ruling
classes were less needy or less greedy than in those parts that turned
Protestant. The Italian princes needed money as badly as did the German; even the Spanish Crown saw the wealth of the New World sift
away and was in chronic financial trouble. Obviously we need a subtler
explanation. This the Marxists have provided.

According to the Marxist interpretation, there is first a whole series
of material economic changes, adding up to a new trading economy. (Let
us, for the moment, not ask what caused these elemental changes.) The
people who make this new economy run, or at least who benefit by it,
are the money men, the traders, the first of a class destined to fame and
power, the *bourgeoisie*. These men cannot get on with the older feudal
ruling class, whose habits of mind and body are fixed by their position as
landed gentlemen. The older feudal class taxes the trader, scorns him,
cheats him, and helps the Church try to enforce those class notions of
fair price, those prohibitions of interest in the name of usury, the whole
medieval attitude toward business. The new trader wants simply to buy
in the cheapest and sell in the dearest markets. He does not want to be
father and protector of his workmen; he just wants to be their employer.
He is already by 1500 the modern businessman in embryo—a good, big
embryo. Naturally he makes use of Protestantism against a Church
that tries to enforce economic ways contrary to his interests. Naturally
Protestantism is successful in parts of Europe where the new businessmen are most prosperous, a failure where they are least so. Progressive
England and Holland go Protestant, for example; backward Spain and
Naples stay Catholic.

Another fillip is added to the economic interpretation by the distinguished German sociologist Max Weber. Weber accepts part of the
Marxist explanation, in particular its emphasis on the class struggle, and

on the adoption of Protestantism by the rising middle classes. But he maintains that the Protestant attitude toward life, Protestant ethical ideals, were not just seized upon by greedy moneymakers as an excuse for despoiling the Catholic Church (the Cobbett thesis). He maintains that these Protestant ideas molded the people who adopted them, made them more fit to make money, made them into the middle class we all know. Luther's idea that each man had a vocation from God, that work in that vocation was God's will, helped form this businessman's ethics. But Calvin was the real source of these ethics, and it was in Calvinist countries that the capital which financed the later Industrial Revolution was saved in these early centuries. Calvinism not only preached the dignity of labor: it insisted on labor, since the devil lies in wait for idle hands, and since work is a part of man's debt to an overpowering God. Success in business was a sign of God's favor—interest, of course, was quite legitimate—so your Calvinist works hard and produces income. But on the side of outgo, Calvinism discouraged luxury, ostentation, sport, decoration of churches—in short, it discouraged spending, except for the necessities of virtuous but solid living. Income is greater than outgo, so your Calvinist saves. This saving is capital, plowed back into the business. So the Calvinist becomes a capitalist, a rich man—and he will go to heaven, too. More than that, he has the pleasing assurance that the heavily indebted nobleman who lorded it over him so unpleasantly the other day will not only die poor, but, since he is not a Calvinist, will go to hell.

We have in the last few sentences somewhat vulgarized Weber's thesis, but in the main lines we have reproduced it clearly enough. Altogether, the arguments for *some* economic interpretation of Protestant origins and growth are pretty convincing. Nevertheless, something else is necessary. Economic symptoms, even with subtly sociological and psychological additions thereto, do not wholly exhaust the syndrome. Moreover, were Protestantism and Capitalism rigorously linked together, they would at all times coincide, so that a map of Europe showing the newer, richer banking and trading centers would coincide with a map showing the growth of Protestantism. There has never been such complete coincidence, even after 1800, when Protestantism and Industrialism *tended* to coincide geographically. In the early modern period, before the Lutheran outburst, the great centers of the new economy, Milan, Florence, Augsburg, the Low Countries, were in regions little affected by pre-Protestant movements. And after Luther, all through the sixteenth century, northern and central Italy, the Catholic Netherlands, the Rhineland, and Catholic northern France continued to be leaders of the new economy. Calvinism certainly helped maintain and strengthen the spirit of capitalism; but the capitalist ethics of Calvinism by no means explains the success of the Protestant movement. It is but one of the sources of Protestant success.

Another source is the complex of habits, interests, and sentiments we call nationalism, one of the most powerful forces in the modern world. Nationalism is a subject to which we shall return. Here it will be enough to suggest that the place of nationalism in the Protestant Reformation may be regarded under two heads—the nationalism of the ruling groups, and the nationalism of the great masses.

One can readily be cynical about the motives of makers of Protestantism like Henry VIII of England. This Renaissance monarch, after the fashion of his newly intellectual times, aspired to be an all-around man, scholar as well as athlete and statesman. He accordingly composed (or had a ghost writer compose) a defense of Catholicism against Luther's recent pamphlet on *The Babylonish Captivity of the Church,* and was rewarded by the pope with the official title of *Defensor Fidei,* "Defender of the Faith." He then proceeded to break with the Roman Catholic Church and set up what became the Church of England (Protestant Episcopal). In the process of change, as we have indicated, much of the corporate wealth of the Roman Church in England went to endow the new Tudor nobility and gentry, supporters of the Tudor monarchy. Henry himself became the head of the English Church, a pope of sorts in his own right. Similar histories would hold for dozens of German princelets.

Yet we must beware of the narrow economic motivation. These rulers and their followers were not merely lining their pockets; they were also clearing the way for the new bureaucratic state, eliminating clerical privileges, canon law, that whole claim of the Catholic Church to be at a certain point wholly free from lay control. These new Protestant rulers sought to build up churches that would be, so to speak, the moral police force of the state. But if power and wealth were both at stake for these rulers, why not also their conscience? Men like Henry VIII, or the German Philip of Hesse who stood by Luther, were good patriots, who really believed that corrupt Italians were exploiting the souls as well as the bodies of their countrymen. Their patriotism seems so clearly in accord with their worldly interests that we incline to discount it; whereas John Hodge and his German fellow man-in-the-street could satisfy little more than their emotion by railing at the papists, and we therefore somehow feel they were sincere. But surely one can believe, even when one profits?

The common people clearly did satisfy their emotions. Notably in England, Scotland, Holland, and Germany, Protestantism came to identify itself thoroughly with the "in-group" of the territory. From Luther's own pamphlets—especially those written in German—from most of the literature of the conflict, indeed, there sounds the love and praise for Germany, the hatred and contempt for "foreigners"—in this case Italians —that we have heard now for so many generations:

> For Rome is the greatest thief and robber that has ever appeared on earth, or ever will. . . . Poor Germans that we are—we have been deceived! *We were born to be masters,* and we have been compelled to bow the head beneath the yoke of our tyrants. . . . It is time the glorious Teutonic people should cease to be the puppet of the Roman pontiff.

The same note is sounded, perhaps a bit less blatantly, in other Protestant lands. Later, and defensively, certain lands begin to identify patriotism and Catholicism. This is notably true of subject nationalities, like the Irish and the Poles. But the Roman Catholic Church has always maintained an international organization, an organization with many of the attributes of state-power. Protestantism has never achieved such an organization; its international meetings are groups, conferences, leagues, with no shred of what is called "sovereignty" or even authority. Thus Protestantism has been identified with certain given territorial entities, and with no true international entity.

Protestantism, then, found in the sixteenth century many sources of strength that were lacking in earlier movements of reform. Above all, Protestantism in the sixteenth century took on many forms, adapted itself to many different concrete situations in different parts of the West, so that no one formula can explain its success. Some of its doctrines, some of the ways of life it encouraged, were doctrines and ways that made the life of the businessman, the new *bourgeois,* easier. Protestantism owes something to capitalism. Other doctrines made it easier for rulers and their followers to grow in wealth and power. Protestantism owes something to simpler and older economic and political drives. Protestantism came to reinforce the common language, common culture, common *behavior* of the in-groups we call nations, in-groups already clearly marked as such even in the thirteenth century. Protestantism came to an open and successful break with a Roman Catholic Church, which for several centuries had had its own time of troubles, its own conciliar movement, its Babylonian captivity, its discontented intellectuals, its crude careerists, its conspicuously worldly leaders. Luther may have been no stronger than Wycliffe or Hus; his opponents were almost certainly weaker than theirs.

What has become, if we accept this interpretation, of the rightness, the progressiveness, the modernity and democracy of the Protestant movement? Isn't the Protestant Reformation one of the great landmarks in Western history? Above all, did not the Protestants side with individual freedom and democratic self-rule, the Catholics with authority and privilege, and weren't the Protestants therefore modern, the Catholics retarded and medieval?

Now these questions do suggest an element lacking in our previous analysis of the sources of Protestantism. One of the livest and most abundant of those sources was the perennial human capacity for being moved by high ethical ideals. Most Protestant movements did enlist this most human force on their side, along with other forces the realist and the cynic like to focus on. For a period disastrous to the cause of the religious unity of the West, the Roman Catholic Church made no successful, concerted effort to enlist this moral force on its own side; and when, with St. Ignatius Loyola and the Catholic Reformation, the Church finally made such an effort, it was too late to preserve Western religious unity.

Since Protestantism was an attack on established institutions, part of its vocabulary was the vocabulary of resistance to authority, part of its appeal was an appeal to the individual, to his rights and his liberty, and against authority. Luther appealed from good works, which are prescribed by authority, to faith, which is locked in the bosom of the individual. There is a certain congruence between the Protestant appeal to the individual (men did not then talk of "individualism") and the nineteenth-century appeal to individualism. Furthermore, as we have noted, Protestantism in its actual working out helped the individual initiative of the capitalist businessman; it helped break down the medieval feudal nexus in politics, and made the way easier for the more streamlined and efficient royal bureaucratic state.

To attempt to understand in concrete territorial cases the reasons for the success or failure of Protestantism (of any and all kinds) against Catholicism is a fascinating exercise in the still immature social sciences. All the variables we have discussed are at work in any one case, and many more. There is clearly no simple litmus-paper test. Blonds did not all turn Protestants, nor brunets all stay Catholic; Northerners did not all accept Protestantism, nor did Southerners all reject it; "Germanic" peoples were not wholly Protestants, nor were "Latin" peoples wholly Catholic; enterprisers, businessmen, did not all turn Protestant, farmers and peasants did not all stay Catholic.

Yet some variables are more important than others. To this writer, the concrete instances of England, Ireland, France, the Low Countries, and the Germanies indicate that where Protestantism became identified with the dominant in-group feeling (or nationalism) it prevailed, and where it did not, it failed. In France, for instance, Protestantism had great strength in the sixteenth century. Calvin himself was a Frenchman and, despite common American notions about the French national character, Frenchmen make as good Puritans as any others. But the French Crown, the focus of French patriotism, had nothing of importance to gain from a split with Rome; it already possessed great independence. Most Frenchmen never identified Frenchness with Protestantism, as most north Germans identified Protestantism with Germanness. Indeed, toward the end of the civil wars in sixteenth-century France, most middle-of-the-road Frenchmen identified Protestantism with treason to France. Again, Calvinism meant patriotism to the Dutch, and resistance to Calvinism, or loyalty to the Catholic faith, meant patriotism to those unassimilated, indeed rival, southern provinces of the Low Countries which were to become independent modern Belgium. Incidentally, this contrast between Protestant Holland and Catholic Belgium is an interesting one for the simple economic determinist to grapple with, since these small contiguous areas have both been trading and industrial centers for centuries, have both had, in short, very similar economies.

There is a great gap between sixteenth-century Protestantism and the nineteenth-century individualism of the Americans who wrote textbooks equating the two. The men who made Protestantism, especially Luther and Calvin, were not really modern in spirit (the term *modern* is not used in this book in praise or blame, but merely to indicate attributes of Western culture since roughly 1700), and they certainly did not believe in freedom. Protestantism, historically considered, can look quite medieval. Rightly held to be one of the forces that made the modern world, Protestantism turned modern almost in spite of itself and its leaders. Protestantism was in nature and purpose a last medieval, a last great purely Christian, effort to justify in action God's way to man.

The Nature of Protestantism

There are, in fact, many Protestantisms. The ways of the High-Church Episcopalian have little in common with those of the convinced Unitarian or those of a primitive fundamentalist. We shall shortly attempt some classification of the varieties of Protestantism as they appear in the sixteenth and seventeenth century. Yet some things can be predicated of Protestantism as a whole. Most of these things are negative things, but one very important one is positive.

The Protestant movement displays a special form of the tension, the contradiction we have noted in Western culture. Protestantism was a revolt against an established authority possessing the external attributes (organization, laws, ritual, tradition) of authority. It asked men to *disbelieve and disobey*. It did indeed, and most earnestly, ask them to believe in better things and obey better men, better laws; its most successful advocates, Luther and Calvin, insisted that what they called on men to believe and obey was the true Christianity of Jesus, and no new thing. But no Protestant of the early years could wholly disavow the fact of his rebellion, a rebellion each individual had to decide to make. Luther, who had the man of action's indifference toward philosophical consistency, an indifference that seems to the logical person almost a kind of stupidity, frankly put the case for revolt in its most risky terms.

Since the papist priest has come as an obstacle between man and God, runs Luther's appeal, let us get rid of anything that might again prove such an obstacle; let every man be his own priest. It is presumptuous to suppose that God the all-powerful and all-knowing would let any such petty human device as the Church interfere with his relations with his own creatures. Moreover, God had made his intentions clear in the Bible, which each man could read for himself without priestly intermediary. With some of the theological implications of this famous Lutheran appeal to the conscience of the individual we shall come in a moment. Politically and morally, the Luther who preached thus was preaching anarchy, was telling each man to listen to something inside himself and disregard all outside himself—law, custom, tradition, the Christian inheritance of the Middle Ages. But really—and some things in this world are disconcertingly simple—Luther was telling the man to listen to what his conscience, heart, Germanness, whole soul prompted, in the firm, naive, and most human belief that this prompting would be wholly consonant with what conscience, heart, Germanness, and whole soul kept hammering into Luther himself. Luther appealed to free men because he believed free men were all Luthers—quieter little Luthers, not indeed so gifted, but still Luthers. When during the Peasants' Revolt he began to discover that free men wanted very different things, wanted social and economic equality, wanted heaven on earth as soon as possible, wanted something more done about the problems of sex than just letting priests marry, wanted a lot he did not want them to want, then Luther willingly supplied some intermediary between God and these benighted men. He provided the Lutheran Church, which has its own laws, dogmas, bishops, priests—and its own practical doctrine of good works. Justification by faith could never, to Luther, justify Anabaptism or antinomianism. The rebel against authority ended by building up his own authority.

Many, perhaps most Protestants of the earlier years would have been outraged or baffled by our last paragraphs. They did not think of their movement as an attempt to free men so that they could somehow spin anew their fate from their own inner resources; they thought of their movement as getting men back under the right authority, the right master, God. The Roman Catholic Church had perverted God's word, but fortunately that word was available, ready for translation into the living languages of Europe. With the Bible available in the vernacular, the priest no longer had the monopoly he had enjoyed when only a Latin version existed. The great reformers, Wycliffe, Hus, Luther, Calvin, all made possible the wide circulation of the Bible in their native tongues. The printing press by the sixteenth century had begun to make something like mass production of Bibles possible. Any reader could now lay his hands on a Bible. The Bible was thus to be the real, the incontrovertible authority, God's words, not man's.

Those who still believe that reading the Bible is a solution for the problem of liberty and authority are a minority we rather patronizingly call fundamentalists. From the point of view we have deliberately assumed in this book, it is clear that the Bible is not what most people mean by an authority. If you get into a dispute about the population of New York City at the last census, you can find an authority in any one of a dozen reference books. If you get into a dispute about the real meaning of the Last Supper, you can nourish your argument from the Bible, but you certainly won't settle it. In oversimple terms, men seem to have found in the Bible what they were looking for. The Protestant appeal to the Bible pushed the search for authority back just one more step; *somebody* had to say what the Bible meant on given points, *somebody* had to do the kind of thing the Fathers, Canon Law, the Roman Church had done long ago. Not the Bible, but the interpreters of the Bible, provided authority. Once more, the nonconformist had to have his own conformity.

Such conformity is the common fate of all revolutionists of this world, if they survive their revolution. In practice it has usually been easy for political revolutionists, even economic revolutionists, to rebuild an authority to take the place of the one they rebelled against; Jacobin France and Bolshevik Russia soon made obedience respectable. But for some reason, perhaps in truth because of the high level of aspiration to eternal truth with which the theologian and philosopher work, and because Protestants, like Catholics, are held in Christian tension between this world and the next, between real and ideal, the Protestant Revolution has never quite so successfully lived down its revolutionary origins. It has preserved alive, at least in its borders, in its depths, the impossible tension of its birth. It would have men justified only in their faith, it would see none but free men; but it would also have an orderly, a disciplined world. From the Catholic point of view, as Bossuet for instance put it, this means that Protestantism is always spawning new sects, protesting against the original protesters, world without end, that Protestantism can have no unity because it has no principle of authority. Put more sympathetically, perhaps, Protestantism is the true heir of the striving for an unearthly perfection on earth, the striving that in medieval Christianity was expressed in mystic flight, in crusades, and in monastic reform, the eternal heresy. Or *was* the true heir, until the Enlightenment brought another, more worldly, promise.

For—and this is a first negative generalization—the major Protestant faiths accepted the old Christian dogma of original sin. Calvin, we know, intensified the gloomier side of the Catholic view of animal man. Extreme Calvinism is most pessimistic about man's ability to lead the good life in this world. Luther's doctrine of justification by faith was by no means an affirmation that men are born good, that they can by following their natural desires find the best guide to life. Even at his most anarchical moments, early in his struggle with Rome, Luther held to the doctrine of man's natural weakness. It is God who gives man faith, who *makes* him and *keeps* him good. On the periphery of Protestantism, among some of the wilder sects, you will find anticipations of the later doctrine of the natural goodness of man. Among the so-called anti-nomians you will find an open anarchism, the doctrine that no law, no prescription, no ritual should bind the free human spirit in the individual, since all such laws, prescriptions, rituals, are simply fixed formulations that strait-jacket the infinitely various human soul. Now antinomianism and later ideas of the natural goodness of man may well be affiliated; but even the antinomians talk the language of Christian theology. This human spirit that cannot rightfully be caged is also the divine spirit, is a personal God at work in this world.

A second negative follows clearly. Protestantism is not, in these cen-turies, in any far-reaching sense a rationalistic movement. Later ration-alists of the eighteenth and nineteenth centuries claimed Protestantism as a parent—or, in a less exacting metaphor, claimed that Protestantism was the thin edge of the wedge that began prying humanity loose from Catholic "superstition." There are difficulties of definition here. If you believe that paring off worship of saints and of the Virgin Mary, reducing ritual, emphasizing the sermon, altering greatly or even abolish-ing the role of music and the decorative arts, and making corresponding reductions in theology—if this process seems rationalistic, then Protestant-ism as compared with Catholicism is rationalistic. But many of these changes took place only in the eighteenth and nineteenth centuries, when it was most evident that rationalism had greater influence in Protestant churches than in the Catholic. If you will go to the sixteenth century itself, and read the polemical religious literature of the time, you will hardly feel yourself in a rationalistic environment.

Millions of tourists have seen the dark spot on the walls of the castle of the Wartburg where Luther threw his inkpot at the devil. There is nothing in spirit apocryphal here. Luther believed in the supernatural as firmly as any more loyal Augustinian. Calvin's terrible God was as real as old Jehovah, whom he often recalls. Early Protestantism resisted the new scientific theory about the relations of the earth and sun as did the Catholic Church, and for much the same reasons. Modern American Protestant fundamentalist distrust of geology and biology has sound roots in the sixteenth century. If Protestants (with some exceptions, such as the Anglicans) ceased to believe in saints, they continued to believe in the devil, in witches, and in the whole court of darkness. Indeed, to just the extent that Protestantism meant for the individual a renewing of deep religious emotion, a getting away from the perhaps too comfortable formalism of the Catholic Church of the late Middle Ages, it revived the sense of the miraculous, the irrational.

Thirdly, early Protestantism was not tolerant. The first Protestants neither preached nor practiced religious toleration. Historically, it is true that the practice of religious toleration first developed in Protestant countries, notably in England. The extreme hard-boiled formula, that religious toleration came solely because the many sects were weary of trying to kill—or at least to argue—one another off, that practical and unbelieving politicians achieved adjustments among exhausted sects no longer afire with zeal, that theories and ideals about religious toleration played no part at all in the process—this formula will not do. It is unfair to such genuinely religious groups as the Quakers, for whom toleration was a positive good, as it is to hundreds of writers and workers of all faiths and no faith who came in these strife-ridden centuries to defend religious toleration as in itself a desirable goal. But religious toleration was not the goal of Luther, nor of Calvin, nor of the other more conspicuous and successful fighters for a cause they felt to be above experimentation and above doubt, and hence, of course, above the cowardice or laziness men called toleration. Defenses of religious toleration as in itself morally good did indeed occur even in the early years of the Reformation, but they came from the lesser figures. Among some of the early humanists there was a disposition toward toleration—Chateillon or Castalion, a French theologian, made a positive defense of toleration as early as 1551—toward rationalism, and even toward skepticism. Yet many of the humanists preserved more than a touch of the desire for perfection that underlay Protestantism. Many of them, like Erasmus himself, had not the courage and drive to work for real toleration.

After these negatives, it is hardly necessary to add that early Protestantism was not, in the conventional modern American sense, democratic. A great deal has been written about the relation between the Protestant movement and the growth of modern Western democracy. Much, of course, depends on the definition of democracy. If you stress the importance of individual freedom in democracy, then clearly neither Luther nor Calvin was a democrat, for neither believed a man should in practice be left free to sin (see below). If you find that in democracy equality rather than individual freedom is the crucial point, then even more clearly the great Protestant groups were not democratic. The tiny group of the Calvinist elect, the saints, the saved, are among the most exclusive of aristocratic groups. Few attitudes are less democratic than that of the English Puritan who, in answer to the suggestion that men who were going to hell anyway might as well enjoy a few pleasures on earth, replied that their behavior stank in the nostrils of the faithful. As for Lutheranism, after the Peasants' Revolt its authoritarian and aristocratic flavor is very clear. It is early the suitable Church for the Prussian Junker. Out of early Protestantism, let us repeat, much that helps make modern democracy was to come, but not intentionally.

There are exceptions to the above statement, as to most big historical generalizations. The seventeenth-century English Revolution—not the "Glorious Revolution" of 1689, but the great Revolution of the 1640's—

was one of the main sources of modern democracy. The left-wing movements of that Revolution are bewildering combinations of religious, political, and economic ideas and aspirations. There are chiliastic sects, there are antinomian sects, and there are sects that are more Calvinist than Calvin. There are groups, like the Levellers, that aim at political democracy in very close to our modern sense. Even major groups like the Presbyterians and the Independents (Congregationalists) in their attacks on king and bishops set up parliamentary supremacy, a bill of rights, a constitution, much of the institutional side of democracy. More, there are to be found among many of these groups democratic notions of social equality, democratic distrust of an authority whose decisions are beyond the control of the whole people. The spirit of the leaders who set up the Puritan Commonwealth in Massachusetts Bay, we know well enough today, was *not* democratic. The government founded by Winthrop and his associates was the government of the elect, of the saints. Yet even in Massachusetts, resistance to this oligarchy soon developed. And in Roger Williams you find in full seventeeth century a Protesant leader who is also—indeed, above all—a democrat.

Yet it must be repeated, in the general view the negation holds: the Protestants of the Reformation are not democratic in spirit, if only because they believed so firmly in Hell and Satan, concepts hardly consonant with democratic equality.

Put all this together—a vivid and extensive supernaturalism, the more vivid perhaps for being focused on the divine trinity and its satanic opponents, or rather, agents; a heightened sense of sin; a renewed drive toward the ideal; a hatred for other religious groups that banished toleration from theory as from practice—and you have a whole that does not much resemble the staid and established American Protestantism of the twentieth century, the Protestantism of Ladies' Aid, Boy Scouts, church suppers, African missions, and all sorts of good causes, from temperance to world government. Early Protestantism is a much more untamed thing, a ferocious, and to the calm rationalist or the innocent idealist, a rather unpleasant thing. For the early Protestant still has the medieval man's sense of the violence and uncertainties of a universe ruled by a terrible, inscrutable God, a God not confined by statistics, science, or common sense. Indeed, to the extent that the Protestant God is a darker and more inscrutable God than the God of the Schoolmen, the Protestant of the sixteenth century lived in a world more violent and more uncertain than the world of the Catholic thirteenth century. Early Protestantism came to bring not peace, but a sword.

The Protestant Spectrum

We have hitherto sought in the main to make generalizations about Protestantism as a whole. And yet, as even the most kindly Catholic

writers enjoy pointing out, the most obvious generalization you can make
about Protestantism is that it is *not* a whole. Protestant unity, if it exists,
must be sought among the abstractions and the generalities of the spirit.
In mundane matters of organization, administration, finance, in the outward signs of group existence, there is only the bewildering variety of the
sects. That familiar American reference book, the *World Almanac*, notes
that "there were in the continental United States in 1962 259 Religious
Bodies." Look under "Churches of God," for example, and you will find

> Church of God (Anderson, Ind.)
> Church of God (Cleveland, Tenn.)
> Church of God of Prophecy
> Church of God, Seventh Day
> Church of God, Seventh Day (Denver, Colo.)
> Churches of God in North America
> The Church of God
> The (Original) Church of God
> The Church of God by Faith

The systematist who undertakes to classify the Protestant churches
finds no single test at his hand; and indeed the title we have used for
this section, "The Protestant Spectrum," if taken literally suggests a regularity of disposition that does not conform to reality. You might classify
Protestant groups, at least for a given country, by their social prestige,
the wealth of their members, their theological distance from the Roman
Catholic Church, their degree of evangelical warmth, their Biblical fund-
amentalism. We shall here take the two great national—and in their
critics' eye, Erastian—churches, the Anglican and the Lutheran, as the
Right Wing of Protestantism, the Calvinist sects as the great Center, and
the more "radical" sects as the Left Wing. Note that Methodism is an
eighteenth-century development that cannot come into our reckoning
here.

Erastian was once a fighting word, as certain to warm our forefathers
to argument as *socialist* is to stir us. Briefly, it is the doctrine, fathered
on the German-born Swiss theologian Erastus (not to be confused with
the great humanist Erasmus of Rotterdam), that makes the Church no
more than a department of state, the clergy the moral police of the
state, the laymen patriots who equate God's word with that of their
rulers.

Now a national church, by the very fact that it is limited in its
temporal organization to a given nation-state, is inevitably somewhat
Erastian. In England, the national church has never had anything like
a monopoly in the religious life of the country. It was very early opposed
by strong separatist movements, and was split within by groups so "high"
as to be nearly Roman Catholic and so "low" as to be nearly Unitarian,

with a broad or latitudinarian group in the middle. The Church of England, in short, has been a paradox of churches, a single Church with both aspirations toward catholicity (universality) and a singular variety of minds and dispositions. Even so, the Church of England has seemed Erastian to its enemies, and there is no doubt that over the early centuries it was the reflection of the way of life of the new gentry and the conservative classes generally. The Church of England had for the first few decades of its existence a most stormy history of ups and downs, from which it emerged under Elizabeth as a classic example of English ability to compromise—or, if you prefer, to pretend that certain difficulties do not exist. Even in the first two centuries after Luther, then, the Church of England is no simple thing, but a sort of microcosm of the Protestant world. Basically a conservative Protestant Church, respectful of civil authority if not slavishly Erastian, theologically and liturgically close to the Roman Catholic Church, lacking the Protestant zeal to clean up this world, the Church of England nevertheless kept under its elastic control— the metaphor here is fairly exact, for the Anglican mind can *stretch*—a whole host of potential rebels who might go over to Rome, or to Geneva, or direct to heaven itself. At various times, these potential rebels have become real rebels, but the Church has stayed on, a puzzle to the logically minded, an offense to the moral perfectionist, a delight to the admirer of the irrational English.

The doctrinal history of the Church of England from the Supremacy Act of 1534, when Henry broke away from Rome, to Elizabeth's Act of Uniformity in 1559 is an extraordinary example of masses of human beings carried through a series of mutually conflicting orthodoxies. The phenomenon is not new or unique in Western history, where in periods of social and intellectual change men have often had to adjust their minds, if not precisely to keep them open. The changes in the official party line of the Communists since 1938 are a classic example familiar to us all. A good party member had in 1940 to believe in Hitler's goodness and in 1941 to believe in his wickedness; he had in 1952 to believe Stalin a national hero, and in 1962 to remember him as a villain, and at the same time, forget him. But the party is already an elite, a relatively small group even in Russia. These changes in sixteenth-century England were undergone by a whole churchgoing people. The same quiet, ordinary subject of the king had first to accept Henry VIII in place of the pope, the use of English instead of Latin in church services, and a few other changes, of which the most conspicuous must have been the priest's taking a wife. Archbishop Cranmer, the king's right-hand man in these momentous affairs, a priest who had studied abroad and knew his German Reformation firsthand, had set the example by marrying. Next, our faithful subject was to learn that Henry thought Cranmer had gone too far. The enemy of Luther, the defender of the faith, was not going to see that faith destroyed. He wanted to have his people Catholics under Henry, not under the pope. So in 1539 Henry in person pushed through Parliament the Six Articles, the "bloody whip with six strings." By the third article "priests, after the order of priesthood received, as afore, may not marry, by the law of God." Auricular confession was restored, and the Roman doctrine of the Eucharist reaffirmed.

But this was only a beginning. On Henry's death his young son Edward VI succeeded. The boy had been brought up in Protestant ways, and under his brief rule our good subject went to a church where the services were very Protestant, and in 1551 subscribed to forty-two articles drawn up by this same Cranmer, compromising with the extremes, but still repudiating much Catholic doctrine. Once more his priest might marry. But Edward died childless in 1553, and was succeeded by his elder sister Mary, who had been brought up a Catholic. Under Mary, the "Bloody Mary" of later English history books, the whole English nation returned, in form at least, to the Roman Catholic fold. Cranmer was burned at the stake, a martyr to something a little less clear than martyrdom usually warrants. Our good subject went back to his Paternoster and his Ave Maria. But Mary herself died in 1558 after only five years on the throne, and was succeeded by her younger sister Elizabeth, destined to the long life denied her brother and sister, and to an ultimate place in English Protestant hearts.

Elizabeth was a Protestant, and under her the national Church was once more thoroughly reorganized, a new Supremacy Act setting the Crown in place of the pope was passed, an Act of Uniformity prescribing a uniform worship all over the kingdom put through, and another set of articles of faith and doctrine drawn up, the famous thirty-nine articles that are still the charter of the Church of England. Our faithful subject went back to services in English, to a theology that banished the old sacraments and preserved only the apostolic or more English of the saints, became, in fact, an Anglican. His son might live to see Cromwell stable his horses in the church; but at any rate, the crisis with Rome was over.

Now unless our faithful subject was irresponsible to the point of feeble-mindedness, he cannot possibly have believed the quite contradictory things he professed, if he duly conformed, in those twenty-five years of ups and downs. Here is a classical case of a difficulty that will confront us to the end, when we attempt to estimate the importance of ideas in social relations. If our faithful subject took with full seriousness all the ideas he had to accept, he must have gone mad. Perhaps he by temperament preferred one shade or another, but lacked the energy or courage to do anything about it, and so took what came along. If many people behaved this way, it is most important for us to understand this behavior. Perhaps he really didn't care about any of these ideas; perhaps he went to church as some people are said to go to movies, just for the sake of something to do. Naturally he wouldn't care whether Edward, Mary, or Elizabeth were directing. If there are many such people, it is important that we know it. Probably most people took no such simple position, but adjusted their behavior in subtle and complicated ways we cannot yet understand. But one thing is clear from these twenty-five years of English history alone: Masses of men can and do accommodate themselves to changes in abstract ideas, philosophies, theologies, to conflicts among these ideas, in a way that the sincere and single-minded idealist cannot possibly explain except by ceasing to be an idealist about his fellow men.

The Lutheran Church has been the established national church in most of northern Germany and Scandinavia. Especially in Prussia, it has seemed to outsiders to be a stock example of extreme Erastianism, governed through submissive ministers by the rulers of the state, and inculcating that very strong German sense of the propriety of obedience which is not at all a myth of Allied propaganda in two world wars. No more than the Anglican has the Lutheran Church taken to Calvinist austerity. It has always encouraged music, has preserved a dignified ritual and enough of Catholic theology so that the Eucharist remains a miracle, and no mere rationally sentimental recollection of the Last Supper. Luther himself was adamant—he loved being adamant—on this matter. Christ had said "this is my body," and a body is no mere symbol. The Catholic doctrine of transubstantiation he had to repudiate, since it was so central a Catholic belief; he produced his own doctrine of *consubstantiation,* and defended it with what we shall have to call late scholastic argumentation. Luther's doctrine uses the Latin *con,* "together with," instead of *trans,* "across, through." His thinking is hard to follow: The untrained layman has to understand that the elements are bread and wine *together with* the body and blood of Christ, are *both* natural and miraculous, *really* both, not just apparently. It is in some ways a typical compromiser's doctrine, a rather empty effort to have a cake and eat it. And yet men died for *con* against *trans,* as they had died for *homousion* against *homoiousion* and as they were to die for democracy against totalitarianism.

Calvinism is the center of Protestantism. The way of life that grew out of Calvin's work on earth is still a very great element in Western culture. Unfortunately, there is no royal and easy road to an understanding of Calvinism. It has a founder and a great book, the *Institutes of the Christian Religion,* which Calvin published in 1535, but a mere reading of this book will give you less insight into Calvinism than a mere reading of *Capital* would into Marxism. Calvinism grew from a book and a little theocratic community at Geneva into a world-wide religion through the efforts of thousands of men and women in hundreds of communities. The intellectual historian, try though he will, finds that he cannot encompass a movement that is in some senses identified with all Western history since the sixteenth century.

There is an obvious contrast between the excitable, inconsistent, undisciplined Luther and the cold, logical, systematic Calvin. You can expand this contrast into a book, as you could the contrast between the Parthenon at Athens and the cathedral of Chartres. But you must not lose sight of the fact that Calvin too was a rebel, a man who *wanted things different.* For Calvin too the Roman Catholic Church was handling men in the wrong way, was not living up to what God intended when he sent Jesus to earth. For Calvin too a way had to be found back to true Christianity.

He found it, as so many have, in the works of that pillar of orthodoxy, St. Augustine. There is not much use attempting to apply a system of psychological analysis to Calvin, nor to begin, at least, with sociology. It is probably true that Calvinism as it worked out was a most fitting system of beliefs, cosmological, theological, ethical, for a commercial and industrial capitalist middle class. But Calvin did not sit down to work up such a system for a middle class, as in a way Marx sat down to work up such a system for what he called a proletariat. Calvin sat down to put once more before men the true word of God.

Calvin's God had the conventional monotheist's attributes—he was all-powerful, all-knowing, all-good. But he was all these so completely, so inhumanly, that he could not conceivably allow what men vainly call free will. God is not precisely outside space and time, but he is the creator of space and time, and of all that goes on inside them. He has absolute and complete foreknowledge of all he has created. No man has any choice in anything he does. God has determined everything. He planned—or willed, if we can use these limited human words to try to describe the action of a Being so far above us poor worms—Adam's fall and its consequences. Planning the fall of Adam may seem not to accord with the attribute of perfect goodness but again it is highly presumptuous of us to use our wormlike vocabulary to judge the works of God. God can do nothing but good in his own eyes, so the sin of Adam must have been good—for God.

Ever since Adam's sin men have been damned to hell. Damnation is no doubt a sort of punishment for the human presumption in Adam's first disobedience; you will remember that he disobeyed God's clear personal command not to eat the fruit of the tree of knowledge. True, Adam could not help himself, since God had willed Adam's presumption and had moved Adam's teeth as Adam bit the apple, and it might seem that God was being a trifle unfair. . . . Again, from the Calvinist point of view we are obtruding most unfairly into our analysis our petty human rationalist views of justice. God is *above* logic; indeed, God made logic just as he made the apple.

God next sent Jesus to earth to bring to a happy few salvation through election. Once more, it would be too human and wormlike to say that God relented and decided to give some of Adam's descendants a chance to redeem themselves. Out of the fullness of his Godliness, God through Jesus has given grace and consequent salvation to a few, a very few. Who these few are in fact is known only to God. But it is not unlikely that most, perhaps all, of them are Calvinists—the Calvinists who are the *elect.*

Calvin's is a far more rigid and radical determinism than St. Augustine's. The Bishop of Hippo tried hard to give men free will and keep determinism for God. Calvin seemed to feel no need for any such concessions. Yet the logic seems inexorable: If I have no thoughts, no desires of my own, but only those God has arranged for me, I am surely justified in taking my thoughts and desires as they come. That state of moral tension which I speak of as "resisting temptation" is surely unreal? To resist what I want to do is to resist God. If I want to commit fornication, God wants me to do so. If I am to be saved, that salvation is wholly through God's grace, and nothing that delusion I call my conscience may say has anything to do with the process. Therefore, I might just as well sin to my heart's content.

The reader need hardly be reminded that such is not the Calvinist position. At some point the Calvinist slips from under his logic, and sets up the Christian moral conscience at its most tense. In fairness to Calvin it should be said that this point is basically the same one at which all the great Christian thinkers escape from the moral nihilism that seems to flow from a complete determinism: To say "I know that, whatever I may do, I do because God wills it" is in fact to claim that I understand what God wants, that I am God's equal and not just his helpless agent. To be sure of one's salvation—this is the great sin of pride, the antipodean opposite of the humility so central to Christianity. Though they are not humble in the folksense that equates humility with weakness, as a disposition to yield, though indeed they are often decided and commanding men, the great Christians have had this humility. Even Calvin has it.

I cannot then be *certain* that what I want to do is what a man chosen by God as one of the elect would want to do; what I want to do *may* be what a man chosen by God as one of the damned would want to do. Note that we are being very careful of our language. Later and more careless Calvinists might say I cannot be sure that what I want to do is what God wants me to do—but that would imply that I can resist God's will, which would destroy determinism. The point should be clear: I cannot *resist* God's will, but I can never, even if I am of the elect, *fully know* God's will. Indeed, if I think I know God's will it is a sign I am damned. But only very humble Calvinists could be quite consistent here, and *on a general level,* among its ordinary adherents, Calvinism did not precisely breed humility.

The Scottish poet Robert Burns, in his *Holy Willie's Prayer,* has his Calvinist elder begin

> Oh Thou, wha in the heavens dost dwell,
> Wha, as it pleases best thysel,
> Sends ane to heaven, and ten to hell,
>   A' for thy glory,
> And no for ony guid or ill
>   They've done afore thee!

Burns puts the doctrine with satirist's scorn, but it is quite good Calvinist doctrine. A few stanzas later, however, Holy Willie breaks into the spiritual pride outsiders—and not only outsiders—have for three centuries so readily detected in Calvinists:

> Yet I am here, a chosen sample,
> To shew thy grace is great and ample;
> I'm here a pillar in thy temple,
>   Strong as a rock.
> A guide, a buckler, an example,
>   To a' thy flock.

The way is now clear for the ethics of Calvinism, for what the last few generations of intellectuals in America, under the illusion that they were free from it, call Puritanism. I cannot know God's will, according to the Puritan, but he has given me some indications of the way a member of the elect would behave. These indications are chiefly in his own words as recorded in the Bible. The Calvinist, however, though he repudiated the historic Catholic Church, did not wholly repudiate a more general Christian tradition of authority; moreover, the elders, the men in authority in the Calvinist communities, were held to possess rather more reliable premonitions of God's intent than the laymen.

Now the Bible and Christian tradition, reinforced by the minister and elders of the church, made it overwhelmingly clear to a Puritan that if he really wanted to commit fornication this desire was put there by God working through Satan and not (this language is not Calvinistic, but should be clear) by God working directly, on his own. It is the kind of desire that would come to one of those destined for damnation; it is the kind of desire that should give our Puritan grave concern over his future life—perhaps he is not to be saved; it is the kind of desire he had better suppress completely and wholly if he really wants to be saved. If he really is to be saved, he will have the strength to suppress it. God, who for all his inexorable determination apparently listens to prayer, at least to Calvinist prayer, will help the man who asks him for help in avoiding this sin.

We are back in the full tide of Christian piety and Christian morals. Calvinism as a way of life is one of the forms of idealistic or other-worldly Christianity. It has often been reproached for un-Christian exclusiveness, for holding that the elect are no more than a tiny minority. Yet in fact it represents an attempt to extend to life in this world something of the ideals the historic Catholic Church had long given up trying to extend beyond the monastic and the secular clergy. Spiritual pride there certainly was in many a Calvinist, but they were not better Calvinists for that. The Calvinist would not let sinners sin freely, if he could help it, even though in strict logic it might be maintained that God obviously intended the sinner to sin. Where they were in power, the Calvinists censored, forbade, banished, and punished behavior they thought sinful. In this they were clearly in their own minds God's agents, doing God's work. In practice, these firm believers in the inability of human effort to *change* anything were among the most ardent of workers toward getting men to change their behavior. To an amazing extent they succeeded. They helped make the Industrial Revolution and the modern world.

The note of Christianity the Calvinists most clearly emphasized is that of asceticism. But it is easy to misunderstand and caricature Calvinist asceticism. The Calvinist is not the mystic who seeks to annihilate sense awareness, not the mystic who seeks passiveness, the quieting of the will, seclusion from this world. He seeks rather to select among his worldly desires those which will further his salvation, and to curb or suppress those which will not. The Calvinist thought the world a very serious place indeed, in which laughter was somewhat out of order. This world is for most of us, the Calvinist believed, an antechamber to hell and eternal suffering, and if you really feel this you are not likely to be much amused. The Calvinist thought that many pleasures to which the human race is addicted—light music, dancing, gambling, fine clothes, drinking, and playgoing, among others—were the kind of thing Satan liked, the kind of thing, not that God disliked, for he did nothing so human as like or dislike, but that somehow, somehow, derogates from that awful Majesty.

The Calvinist did not hold, as some Christians have held, that sexual intercourse is sinful. He did hold firmly to the notion that it was sinful if indulged in outside a monogamous marriage duly entered into with the sanction of the Church. You will find in Calvinist literature the notion that the purpose God had in mind in providing sexual intercourse was the continuation of the race, and not the sensuous pleasures of the

participants. Those pleasures are all the more dangerous since they may
lead to extramarital indulgence, which is a very great sin. But there
seems to be no reason to believe that the Puritans who produced such
large families, notably in New England, did so out of a painful sense
of duty. The Puritan was not often addicted to mortifying the flesh in
one great form of the ascetic tradition. He liked to eat well, sleep well,
live in a comfortable house. Indeed, one of the reproaches certain modern liberal intellectuals have made to our Puritan forefathers is that
they neglected the fine arts and the nobler ways of the flesh in favor of
stuffy commercial success, earthly comforts of a vulgar sort—in short, that
they were ancestors of George Babbitt. Paradox is perhaps more fair:
Calvinism is this-worldly other-worldiness. It is Christian Stoicism, a
bit worried, often very worried.

Calvinism also sounds very loudly another Christian note, that of ethical meliorism. The Calvinist had a high moral code, pushed to extremes
in certain directions precisely by his serious-mindedness, but still essentially a code in the tradition of all the higher religions. In spite of, or
because of, his belief in determinism, he was always trying to live up to
his code, and see that other people did so too. Both inward and outward
directions of this effort are important.

The Calvinist certainly felt the "civil war in the breast," the struggle
between what has become famous as the Puritan conscience and the
temptations of this world. This notion of a higher part of human consciousness that can and should censor and suppress the promptings of
a lower part has left a firm imprint on the West, an imprint especially
strong where Calvinism has set the dominant tone. Neither Rousseau
nor Freud seems to have seriously shaken this conception of the role of
conscience—not even in themselves.

In its outgoing direction, this ethical meliorism has taken many forms
other than that of the outright, police-enforced prohibition the critics
of Puritanism single out for condemnation. The method of outright
prohibition of dancing, theater, and the like is certainly there, and was
resorted to by the early Calvinists the more naturally because, as we shall
see, they had no democratic worries about the freedom of the individual.
But the Calvinist also believed in persuasion; he made the sermon a central part of his worship. He did not force the note of anti-intellectualism
we have found in Christianity—indeed in the long run the influence of
Calvinism was to further what we can call rationalism—but in these early
years the Calvinist is certainly no rationalist. He believes in hell-fire
and in the moral uses of fear of hell-fire; he believes in emotional conversion, and is a good missionary, though not at his best among primitive
peoples.

Puritanism, which we Americans commonly use, to the despair of the
semanticist, in a very loose way as shorthand for the Calvinist way of

life, is one of those great clusters of ideas which cannot in fact be analyzed with chemical exactness. In the scientist's sense of "define" you cannot define Puritanism. We have attempted very cursorily to indicate some of the elements of the Puritan way of life in its first two centuries, but we have barely skimmed the surface. Even so, there remains one major and very difficult problem we cannot neglect, that of the political aspects and results of Calvinism.

One of the tensions in Christianity, of course, is that between its sense of the importance of the individual as an immortal soul, and its need to overcome the individual's ego (selfishness, self-importance) either by submission to God or by melting in with a community, or by both. Something of this same tension exists in modern democracy as a way of life, or ideal, a tension usually expressed as that between liberty and equality. The more individual liberty, the more competition, the more big winners and just plain losers; the more equality, the more security, the more limits on competition, the less individual liberty.

In Calvinism this tension exists in a particularly complex form. Calvin, like Luther, was forced to a certain degree of individualism just because he broke with an established church. He had to sweep away the authority of the Catholic Church in the minds of his followers, and to do that he had to urge them to think for themselves. He and his followers, as Weber, Troeltsch, Tawney, and others have pointed out, did much to encourage the competitive individualism of the businessman. The Puritan's struggle with his conscience was the struggle of an individual keenly aware of his self-sufficiency—or insufficiency. Even the Calvinist's sense of the littleness of man in the face of the awfulness of God was in no very paradoxical sense a heightening of the individual's importance here on earth, for only as an individual, not as one of a mass, could he grow to an awareness of God. Finally, Calvinism had throughout its early years to struggle against constituted authority for the mere right to survive as an active religion. The power it early attained in Geneva and in Boston, the security it attained in later centuries everywhere it survived, it did not have in France, England, and Germany in the first years. It had to defy authority—Calvin himself, so authoritarian in Geneva, could at moments be a libertarian in his advice to followers elsewhere.

Put all this together and you can almost think Calvin anticipated what the social Darwinists of the nineteenth century were to picture as the right state of man, a fine free-for-all of competition in all walks of life, with the devil appropriately taking the hindmost. Such a view would be wrong, and you have only to dip into the practicing Calvinism of sixteenth-century Geneva or of seventeenth-century Boston to see a community in some ways almost Spartan in its discipline and its collectivism. These communities were ruled from above by a minority of the virtuous; they were not in our sense of the word *democracies*. They were not societies

in which collectivism was extended to economic goods, though in both
societies the poor were a public charge—if only because the morals of the
poor usually needed tending to. They were even in a sense societies of
status, as anyone who has studied early New England social history knows.
For instance, early class lists of Harvard students are arranged in a complex order of status—social standing—difficult for us to understand. We
do see that they are not simply arranged alphabetically, nor according
to excellence in studies, nor even according to the income of their parents.

In the balance, however, Calvinism has swung toward democracy. The
decisive influence here has probably been the form of its church government, congregational or presbyterian, in any case one in which all church
members in good standing take part in meetings that handle the affairs
of the parish, and that are free from authority of bishops or other constituted authority, lay or priestly. In the sixteenth century and in seventeenth-century New England the practice of this government is more
clearly an oligarchy of the "saints" than an egalitarian democracy. The
fact remains, however, that Calvinist experience, hammered out in years
of resistance to established churches, gave training of a sort that perhaps
was transferred to democratic government, and in New England, at least,
provided some of the machinery of that government. It may even be
that the Calvinist habit of appealing to the Bible as the written word of
God prepared men to appeal to a written constitution; but this is the
kind of generalization one can hardly test.

The Left Wing of the Protestant movement is made up of a great number of struggling sects. Perhaps they are to be classed as on the Left
merely because none of them ever became powerful and established
groups identified with a great country. Even the Quakers, in many ways
the most successful of these sects, and certainly one of the most interesting, have always remained small in numbers. They have for the systematist relatively little in common beyond their scattering, their general
opposition to established churches, their small membership, and their
great variety. Seventeenth-century England is one of the best places for
a modern American to study them, for there is no language difficulty—
that is, no such difficulty as with Latin or German, for the innumerable
tracts of English seventeenth-century religious dispute are not written
in our present language.

A full list of the sects would be a very long one. There are the Diggers,
simple Biblical communists who took to digging up certain commons—
the rough equivalent of our public parks—on the ground that God had
given the land to all. There are the Fifth Monarchy men, or Millenar-
ians, who held that the fourth monarchy of Biblical revelation was draw-
ing to a close, and that they were destined to usher in the fifth or final
monarchy. They were divided into a passive group who believed that
God would take care of the work of making his prophecy come true, in

good time, and an active group who proposed to get out and help bring the prophecy true by violence if necessary. There were the Levellers, whose name is self-explanatory, but who were rather a political than a religious sect. There were the Muggletonians, followers of Lodowicke Muggleton, the inspired tailor, who survived as a sect until the 1860's. There were the Behmenists, the Bidellians, the Coppinists, the Salmonists, the Dippers, the Traskites, the Tyronists, the Philadelphians, the Christadelphians, the many variants of Adventists and Baptists. The prevalence of proper names—the names of the leaders or prophets of the sects—suggests that they represent the ultimate splintering down of Protestantism in search of *some* final authority.

Many of the sects belong clearly on or beyond what has been called the "lunatic fringe." Their study should be of great interest to the sociologist and the psychologist, who will find three hundred years ago symptoms he may otherwise think uniquely modern, and thus not really understand. Their very existence is one of the signs of grave social changes in the making. These extremists confront the historian who attempts to treat human affairs objectively, without wrath or zeal, with a serious problem, for they themselves are full of wrath and zeal. They are immoderates, heaven-stormers, men to whom the qualities the objective historian tries to cultivate in himself are abhorrent. He fancies that he can see clearly how much more satisfactory, how much more decent, more humane, the course of history would have been without these troublemakers, these impossibilists. He can see their unpleasant side— their readiness to persecute (if they attain a position in which they can persecute), their authoritarianism (if they attain a position of authority), their delusions of grandeur, their egocentricity, their inability to appreciate the rich variety of the good lives men may lead.

In his too easy condemnation of these extremists, the man of moderation misses their greatness and fails to understand their usefulness in society. The obvious metaphors are weak; these heavenstormers are not quite the leaven, not quite the gadflies, not quite the vanguard of society. Sometimes they are, and often they are not, what these metaphors would have them. They are reminders to us all, though we do not often heed them, that men cannot decently do without the prick of the ideal, cannot lapse safely into comfort—not even the comfort of scientific objectivity. Montaigne, who liked extremists as little as any man, could say of the excesses of revolutionaries:

> I see not one action, or three, or a hundred, but a commonly accepted state of mortality so unnatural, especially as regards inhumanity and treachery, which are to me the worst of all sins, that I have not the heart to think of them without horror; and they excite my wonder almost as much as my detestation. *The practice of these egregious villainies has as much the mark of strength and vigor of soul as of error and disorder.*

Some of the wildest of the sects seem almost abstractly chiliastic—that is to say, they promise heaven on earth, but with no concrete touches, or in the misplaced concreteness of a revelationary symbolism taken mostly from the Old Testament and the last book of the New. But many of them, and many of the less crazy ones, are what we call loosely socialistic; they are the kind that appear in histories of socialist thought. Their main emphasis is the solution of the problem of poverty—no more rich, no more poor, just good men sharing as nature and God meant them to share the riches of this world. Many insist they are but going back to the primitive Church, which they found to be communist. They all use the vocabulary of religion, even when they are concerned with economic matters. They are not really very different from their late medieval predecessors. They are hostile to conventional Calvinism—though they may well share some Calvinist theological and ethical ideas—because it is clear already that conventional Calvinism does not believe in sharing the wealth.

We should not be surprised to find that some of the most collectivists of these groups should also be radically individualist, indeed anarchical. We have already noted that human beings can apparently live happily in the midst of various logical contradictions. The socialists of modern times have always had their anarchist wing. At any rate, one of the few valid generalizations that link these early Protestant extremists is the tendency to what was then call antinomianism. The antinomian carried the fundamental Protestant position—justification by faith as opposed to justification by works—to the utmost extreme. To him a law, a custom, any command was in fact a "work," and should therefore be disregarded unless his inner voice told him that what was so prescribed was right—and usually in those excited early days it did not. The inner voice is all that counts. Some of the antinomians actually followed out in practice the logic we have earlier traced as flowing from an absolute determinism; they argued that if their inner voice told them they were saved, then clearly whatever they did was ordained of God, and would not interfere with their salvation. The radicals who in Westphalia in the 1530's enjoyed brief periods of power were accused by their enemies of all sorts of debauches; and though conservatives have always accused radicals of shocking personal, and especially sexual, morals, there seems to be no doubt that some of the antinomians did follow their logic into behavior usually thought well beyond logical justification.

But, as has often been suggested of the proliferation of heresies in the second and third centuries of Christianity, the proliferation of the sects is in some ways a sign of youthful strength in Protestantism, a sign that men take in fecund seriousness the hope of a much better life here, if only in due and necessary preparation for a perfect life in the hereafter. These sects—and they are really Protestant heresies, offensive though the term may be to conventional Protestants today—have in them a wild energy, even when their goal seems an absurd heaven.

By 1700, Protestantism had settled down. Its rebelliousness had been tamed by success, and even the Calvinists were now established or tolerated almost everywhere. Protestantism had not necessarily become stuffy and self-satisfied; it still had much missionary fervor, especially in work overseas, and it still numbered many zealous Christians. But it had come to a stalemate with its old Catholic enemy. The Catholic Church itself had from the mid-sixteenth century on summoned great sources of spiritual strength, had reformed many abuses of worldliness, indifference, and corruption that had crept into the late medieval Church, and without in any basic way altering its theology and liturgy, had in the Council of Trent knit the fabric of Catholicism firmly together. The revived Church had reconquered spiritually rather than by force much of Germany and of eastern Europe, and after the Thirty Years' War it was clear that Protestantism was not likely to make further large territorial gains in Europe. Protestantism was in the main and in its historic forms no longer a fighting faith. The very sects that split off after 1700—Pietists in Germany and Methodists in England and America—were at bottom what may be not unfairly called *consoling* sects, groups aiming at making the individual happy (in a Christian way, of course) rather than at the conquest of this world and the next. There was much emotion in Pietism and Methodism, much courage and devotion among their leaders, but one misses the stormy idealism, the channeled violence, of earlier Protestantism. The search for perfection on earth was moving elsewhere, into what became the Enlightenment.

CHAPTER THREE

MAKING THE MODERN WORLD

III. RATIONALISM

Rationalism—A Broad Definition

Once more we confront a big word—*rationalism*. Like most such words, this one can be defined in a variety of ways. We shall here define it very broadly as a cluster of ideas that add up to the belief that the universe works the way a man's mind works when he thinks logically and objectively; that therefore man can ultimately understand everything in his experience as he understands, for instance, a simple arithmetical or mechanical problem. The same wits that showed him how to make, use, and keep in repair any household contrivance will ultimately, the rationalist hopes, show him all about everything.

The foregoing is a rather informal illustration of rationalism, but it should bring home the extent to which the complete rationalist departs from Christian belief, even from such forms of Christian belief as Scholasticism with its emphasis on the ability of the human mind to understand at least in part God's plan for the universe. There are, of course, all sorts of compromises between rationalism and Christianity, some of which we shall encounter in the Age of the Enlightenment. But the push of rationalist belief is away from Christianity. The rationalist tends to the position that the reasonable is the natural and that *there is no supernatural*. At most there is for him the unknown, which should someday be the known; and if, to use the term of the nineteenth-century English philosopher, Herbert Spencer, there is an "Unknowable" (i.e., God) it's rather silly of us to try to know him, or even know about him. There is no place in his scheme for a personal God, no room in his mind for the mystic surrender to faith. Violent antithetical dislikes are often useful as bench marks; what the rationalist most dislikes is the mood of Tertullian's "it's certain because it's impossible."

Rationalism tends then to banish God and the supernatural from the universe. It has left only the natural, which the rationalist holds to be ultimately understandable, almost always by what most of us know as the methods of scientific investigation. Historically, the growth of scientific knowledge, the ever more skillful use of scientific methods, is closely tied with the growth of the rationalist attitude toward the universe, with the rationalist cosmology. For most rationalists have indeed a complete world-view, a way of life tied up with their belief in reason. Many practicing scientists have been rationalists; any scientist who holds that we have no other true knowledge except knowledge arrived at by the use of the scientific method is logically either a ratonalist or a skeptic. But— and this is a very important point—science and rationalism, though historically intertwined, are not by any means the same thing.

Science, both in the sense of a body of accumulated scientific knowledge and in the sense of a way of going to work on problems (that is, scientific method), is not concerned with metaphysics. *As science* it provides neither a cosmology nor an ontology, nor a full teleology. Science *as science* makes no attempt to answer—does not even ask—the Big Questions of human destiny, of God's ways to man, of Right and Wrong and Good and Bad. Some scientists as individuals come near not asking any of the Big Questions, come near guiding themselves in daily life by custom and authority, as do most of us most of the time. Some scientists, that is, may be without metaphysical curiosity, or metaphysical anxiety— as may be many of the human race. (This is a point about which even professional psychologists seem to know little—the writer's guess is that very few human beings indeed are altogether free of metaphysical anxiety, or at any rate, metaphysical concern.) As soon as the scientist asks and tries to answer any of the Big Questions, however, he is ceasing to behave as a scientist. He is at the very least doing something *additional;* he is probably doing something *different.*

The point of view that science is in no sense directly normative is, as we noted in the Introduction, rejected by some modern thinkers, and does challenge the long Western tradition that man must use his mind to make sense of his whole experience, his universe. Yet the orthodox tradition within science is that the scientist *as scientist* does not make any value-judgments. The philosophic depths of this question are very great indeed. Here we can but record the orthodox position, and note that there are heretics, heretics who are by no means agreed, save in their opposition to the orthodox. If anything is common to those who oppose the orthodox doctrine of science as non-normative, it is the doctrine that human intelligence can solve problems in morals, aesthetics, even theology, as successfully, *and by the same methods,* as it solves problems in natural science. The evidence seems to be against them today, but the case is still open, and the court has not decided. Perhaps there is no court.

The rationalist, on the other hand, has usually a full set of answers for the Big Questions, or at any rate is confident that time and diligence on the part of right-thinking men will produce answers, *correct* answers, not just widely accepted answers. Rationalism as it grew up in the sixteenth and seventeenth centuries in the West is in fact a complete metaphysical system; more than that, it served for a minority, and continues so to serve, as a substitute for religion. If it is a semireligious system, rationalism is perhaps better given specific labels, such as materialism, positivism, and the like, which indicate more exactly the whole complex of beliefs, habits, and organization involved. Thus, to take a rough parallel, rationalism is the broad general term, like Protestantism; materialism, positivism, atheism, yes, even unitarianism, even deism, are the sect names, like Anabaptist or Quaker.

Natural Science

By 1700 most of what we call the natural sciences—then, with the exception of mathematics, known as "natural philosophy"—had reached a stage that made the great synthesis of Newton possible. In the two previous centuries most of the separate disciplines of science, and in particular physics, astronomy, and physiology, had become mature—although not, of course, finished—sciences. There was once more on earth what there had been in Hellenistic Alexandria two thousand years before, a body of researchers and teachers, laboratories, collections, means of exchange of information and ideas—in short, a social and intellectual environment suitable to the advancement of science. The earlier generation of humanists had been no more favorable to natural science than had their medieval scholastic predecessors, but as the sixteenth century wore on scientists like Galileo flourished in the midst of the artists of the Renaissance; and the seventeenth century is not only the century of genius, of men like Newton, Harvey, Descartes, Pascal, it is also the century of the founding of the great scientific societies, such as the British Royal Society (1660), and the French *Académie des Sciences* (1666), the century when, with hundreds of active workers tied together by societies, their publications, and an extraordinary system of private correspondence, science as a social activity came of age.

Science was not yet, in 1700, the most respectable of intellectual occupations. It had by no means acquired the position of wealth and prestige it has achieved in the twentieth century. Classical or liberal education still gave to natural science only the kind of attention the Middle Ages had given to the *quadrivium;* that is, to mathematics and the better-known applications of mathematics in music and mechanics; experimental science, laboratory science, was not yet quite respectable in ordinary education. But the scientific knowledge of these early modern times did seep down into the minds of the literate public; science was one of the vehicles that helped carry rationalistic notions throughout the Western world.

We cannot answer simply and finally the question, Why did the study of natural science flourish at this particular point in space and time? As in the somewhat analogous question of why the Protestant Reformation of the sixteenth century broke out from the Catholic Church in the West in a way no other heretical movement did, there are certainly many variables involved. One of the major variables, and one our own generation understands so well that it is not here emphasized, is the economic one, the growth of a complex money economy run by capitalist businessmen (entrepreneurs). We see readily enough that these businessmen were eager to innovate, willing to endow research, undeterred by the undignified, ungentlemanly nature of much scientific work, untied to the prejudices of a classical education. We see all this too readily, perhaps, because most of these factors operate far more clearly from the late eighteenth century onward than they do in these early years. As we have pointed out, the scientists learned from the craftsmen and technologists, rather than as today, the technologists from the scientists; the most distinguished scientists were gentlemen, sometimes noblemen, and very rarely indeed businessmen. From the start, science was genuinely international and knew no religious bounds. If Spain produced few scientists, and England and France many, again there is no simple answer why. Still, we must note that wealth and increasingly modern economic organization are related to the flourishing of science. This relation is not the whole story, but it is clearly part of it.

There is no wholly satisfactory formula for relating the rise of natural science to the social environment in which it rose. But with somewhat deceptive simplicity it may be said that almost every cultural change in these centuries had its influence on the growth of science. For science, though it can go on to most abstract concepts, rests on things, on facts, on great numbers of different material objects. Thus any multiplication of its data is in itself of great importance to any natural science. The geographical discoveries of the early modern period, themselves furthered by scientific investigations in astronomy, navigation, and geography, brought before Europeans thousands of new facts, thousands of challenges to the inquiring mind. The medieval discovery of gunpowder began with these centuries to be used for practical purposes of warfare, and its use stimulated efforts to defend against it. Then in turn efforts were made to produce more powerful explosives. This is technology and invention, not science; but this multiplication of "things," this preoccupation with things, this attempt to get more and more complex things, is in itself and in its influence on men's minds one of the indispensable conditions for the growth of science.

Warfare is a good instance. There have been theories—the best known is associated with the German economist Werner Sombart—that the growth of large-scale nationalistic warfare in these centuries was the root cause of everything else we call modern, since the need of the state for money to pay a professional army stimulated efforts to make the state structure more efficient, since the demand for material things to fight with stimulated economic change, and since the demand for more effective weapons of offense and defense stimulated technology and invention. Naturally this thesis of organized warfare as the mother of modern civilization proved extremely offensive to good liberals and democrats, and they proceeded to write books showing that warfare had nothing to do with the rise of modern culture. Actually both extremes are nonsense of the chicken-or-egg-first kind. Warfare, geographical discoveries, inventions, business techniques, fashionable luxuries, discoveries, and many other factors worked together, each influencing the other, and all together providing the material setting for modern science.

The psychological setting is quite as complex as the material, and of course greatly influenced by this multiplication of "things." Some men have always been curious, and a great many have been willing to hunt for new experiences. Some men have been patient and systematic in sorting out details, and a great many have had some share of the collector's instincts in amassing material. In fact, the scholar of the Middle Ages already had most of these traits to a very high degree. What was needed to provide a state of mind suitable for the cultivation of natural science was first, a willingness to turn these gifts for patient, meticulous investigation and collection of facts from the dignified world of philosophical and literary scholarship to the undignified world of smells, weights, measures, chills and fevers, and all the rest so familiar to us now; and second, a willingness to give up a good deal of the very strong medieval respect for the authority of previous writers, especially Aristotle, and adopt the habit of checking up on, subjecting to the test of experimentation or verification even the very nicest explanations of natural phenomena.

It was necessary, then, to make the study of natural science respectable by providing it with a philosophy, not necessarily a metaphysics, but at least a method and an aim. That was achieved in the course of these centuries, and notably by Francis Bacon, to whom we shall come in a moment. But do not be misled by the scientist's often naive notion of his newness and uniqueness. The transition from the scholar, indeed from the Scholastic, to the scientist was no miraculous revolution creating something out of nothing. The modern scientist took over from those scholarly predecessors he now so often looks down on almost all those slowly learned habits of mind and work so necessary to natural science—patience, accuracy, the hard-won accumulation of mathematics and logic, the great community of men and women devoted to the cultivation of the mind.

But before we come to Bacon's attempt to make science philosophically respectable, we must consider another possible factor in the rise of science, one that has perhaps already occurred to the reader. Isn't *freedom* one of the essentials for the cultivation of the sciences? Didn't the scientist have to win his freedom from all sorts of medieval restraints and taboos, just as did the Protestant and the humanist? How about Galileo?

Once more let it be noted that the relation between a flourishing natural science and the degree of individual or group freedom from legal or moral restraints in a given society is by no means clear and simple. It would be pleasant to hold that there is a direct correlation, the more freedom (as we Americans understand freedom) the greater scientific advancement. Now it is clear, of course, that in a society where all novelty is forbidden there can be no science, since science depends on someone's producing something new. But such despotic societies exist only in imagination, at least in the Western world. The actual record shows that science grew up in a Europe for the most part ruled by absolute monarchs, and that it owed much to the patronage of these monarchs and their ministers. Indeed, as science slowly proved itself useful in adding to man's command of his material environment, the possessing classes were persuaded of its value to themselves, and were delighted to endow and protect scientists. After all, the discovery of the law of gravitation did not endanger in any obvious way their interests. Freedom for scientific investigation is by no means the same thing as freedom for artistic, philosophical, political, or moral experimentation. No doubt scientists need some kinds of freedom, but most of all they need freedom from the dead weight of custom and authority *in their own fields*.

When a scientist announces a discovery that upsets widely and deeply held beliefs, it is not surprising that he meets resistance and has to struggle to be heard. The interesting part about the record in Western society is that he does get heard, that the censorship that would shut him up is an ineffective and sloppy censorship, that somehow or other such censorship seems rather a stimulus than a hindrance. Even in the most famous case of scientific martyrdom, that of Galileo, censorship did ultimately no more than dramatize Galileo's work. This Italian scientist himself built on the work of still earlier scientists, going back indeed to the late Middle Ages, but especially on that of the Polish astronomer Copernicus. The issue is familiar to all. Galileo's newly invented telescope enabled him to register additional facts, such as the existence of satellites of Jupiter, suggesting a model for the solar system, and the existence of dark spots on the surface of the sun which by their apparent foreshortening seemed to indicate that the sun was revolving. These and many other observations bolstered up the Copernican (and Aristarchian) theory that the earth revolves in an orbit around a sun that is also revolving. Christian belief had thoroughly committed itself to the other theory, that the earth is stationary and that the sun revolves around it. Sentiments of great strength held many intelligent men to the belief that our planet, the place of Christ's sacrifice, *must* be the center of all things. The interests against Galileo were in fact a coalition, and by no means a united Catholic Church that simply refused to cultivate astronomy. One of the strongest interests against him was a group of Jesuits whom he had offended by seeming to neglect prior Jesuit investigations. In fact, the coalition against Galileo is a fascinating mixture of old and new, of academic rivalry (no new thing, surely), of vested interests, of plain neophobia, perhaps even of a kind of metaphysical anxiety, for the prospect of an infinity, or at least a plurality, of worlds opened up by the telescope horrified many. Ultimately Galileo was brought to trial before the Inquisition and chose to recant rather than be judged guilty. But nothing could undo and unprint Galileo's writings, and no power in seventeenth-century Europe was strong enough to suppress such ideas as Galileo had set circulating. The triumph of the heliocentric theory was assured.

The man who came closest to systematizing in general terms what this new "natural philosophy" was about was the Englishman Francis Bacon, later Lord Verulam. Bacon has had a bad press. He was not a good man, not a kindly man. He was ambitious for power and wealth; his political career, which culminated in the Lord Chancellorship, was marked by time-serving and lack of scruple; he was finally impeached. Later scientists have rarely been able to pardon him for being such a bad scientist, such a poor practitioner of what he preached. Yet he was a good, if almost posthumous, child of the humanist Renaissance, immensely learned, versatile, energetic, eager to push forward in all directions. His admirers in later generations have even advanced one of the most remarkable ideas in all intellectual history, the notion that Bacon wrote the works commonly attributed to Shakespeare.

Bacon planned, and in part carried out, a great work called the *Instauratio Magna* or *Novum Organum* (1620), written in Latin. Many of his ideas, however, come out as well in the English *Advancement of Learning* of 1605. It would be misleading to say that this great opus was planned as a sort of *counter-summa* against Aristotle and the Schoolmen. It was rather an ambitious classification of and program for the new scientific studies by which Bacon hoped that men would secure new mastery over their environment. It is full of attacks on Aristotle and his medieval disciples, on deductive reasoning, full of appeals to go to the evidences of sense perception, to employ induction. Here are some of the key passages from the *Instauratio Magna*:

> The subtlety of nature is greater many times over than the subtlety of the senses and understanding; so that all those specious meditations, speculations, and glosses in which men indulge are quite from the purpose, only there is no one by to observe it.
> The syllogism is not applied to the first principles of sciences, and is applied in vain to intermediate axioms; being no match for the subtlety of

nature. It commands assent therefore to the proposition, but does not take hold of the thing.

The syllogism consists of propositions, propositions consist of words, words are symbols of notions. Therefore if the notions themselves (which is the root of the matter) are confused and over-hastily abstracted from the facts, there can be no firmness in the superstructure. Our only hope therefore lies in a true induction.

There is no soundness in our notions whether logical or physical. Substance, Quality, Action, Passion, Essence itself, are not sound notions: much less are Heavy, Light, Dense, Rare, Moist, Dry, Generation, Corruption, Attraction, Repulsion, Element, Matter, Form, and the like; but all are fantastical and ill defined.

There are and can be only two ways of searching into and discovering truth. The one flies from the senses and particulars to the most general axioms, and from these principles, the truth of which it takes for settled and immovable, proceeds to judgment and to the discovery of middle axioms. And this way is now in fashion. The other derives axioms from the senses and particulars, rising by a gradual and unbroken ascent, so that it arrives at the most general axioms last of all. This is the true way, but as yet untried.

Historians of philosophy and of science have written a great deal about Bacon's idea of induction. Perhaps he has, from our point of view, a naive notion of induction, a belief that if the scientist will only observe enough facts he will somehow find these facts arranging themselves in an order that will be true knowledge. Certainly in polemic against the Schoolmen he often seems to imply that the process we call thinking has no part in the work of the scientist; but this is surely because he identifies the syllogism, which he scorns, with mental activity pure and simple. A close reading of Bacon should convince a fair critic that, although he by no means understood even as well as we do (and that isn't very well) what goes on in the mind of the great creative scientist, he did not really hold that the scientist merely hunts out and records facts.

Far from it. What has misled critics of Bacon is at bottom what ties him to the Schoolmen he so bitterly fought, and to the generation of Renaissance humanists to which he belongs. Bacon was out after answers to the Big Questions; he thought he had found a way to *certainty,* and therefore to agreement, in those matters men had so long been debating without achieving agreement. As we shall see, the modern scientist does not aim at theories that will be absolutely, unchangingly true. Bacon does so aim. He is by temperament a nominalist in almost the medieval sense; he starts with the reality of the "objects" he apprehends with his senses. But he is hunting for a way to get at the kind of permanent form amid the flux of sense knowledge the medieval realist declares he knows offhand, just by thinking or believing. Bacon, to oversimplify greatly, wants to start with nominalist notions and end up with realist ones.

He will achieve that by a long patient series of observations and recordings in which gradually—to use scholastic terms that would have infuriated Bacon himself—the *substance* emerges out of the *accidents,* the permanent out of the fleeting. Bacon himself, in spite of his dislike for the old terms of philosophy, finds himself forced to use the word *form.* Here is a passage of major importance:

> For since the Form of a thing is the very thing itself, and the thing differs from the form no otherwise than as the apparent differs from the real, or the external from the internal, or the thing in reference to man from the thing in reference to the universe; it necessarily follows that no nature can be taken as the true form, unless it always decrease when the nature in question decreases, and in like manner always increase when the nature in question increases.

To attempt to go much further would be to trespass on the fields of the professional philosopher. It may be that Bacon was no more than foreshadowing in terms like *apparent* and *real* what Locke was to call *secondary* and *primary* qualities—that is, for example, color, a secondary quality about which our sense impressions differ, and mass, a primary quality objectively measurable by scientific methods. Bacon's *forms* are perhaps no more than what later scientists meant by *laws* or *uniformities;* but for Bacon these forms are ultimately knowable, are in fact absolutes.

The role of the separate sciences now begins to be so crowded with names and discoveries that the historian of science needs at least as much space as the conventional historian of politics and war used to take up. We can here but summarize briefly. Mathematics continued the progress it had made since the high Middle Ages and reached a point at which it was able to cope with the new problems the astronomers and physicists were presenting. Decimals, no more than a device, but like zero an indispensable device, were invented by the Fleming Simon Stevin in the late sixteenth century. The Scottish mathematician John Napier invented logarithms at about the same time, and in the next century Descartes, about whom we shall hear more, developed the useful device now known as the Cartesian coordinates from which stemmed those graphs which even the man in the street now understands. Pascal, chiefly known to us as a man of letters, made important advances in geometry and in the theory of probability.

In astronomy there is a famous sequence—Copernicus, Tycho Brahe, Kepler, Galileo—out of which the heliocentric conception of our own solar system emerged clearly, together with the beginnings of knowledge of the great universe outside our planetary system. We have already noted how Galileo's summing up and confirmation of all this brought about his trial—and good publicity for his ideas. Taken together with the work of Kepler, that of Galileo set up the conception of a universe that ran in accordance with mathematical laws, but that definitely *moved,* unlike the fixed and unchanging heavens of the Aristotelian tradition.

Kepler's first law, for instance, noted that the planets do not move around the sun in perfect circles (if they had moved in Aristotelian tradition, they would, of course, have moved in perfect circles, and no one would have made the fine observations and complicated calculations necessary to prove that they did not so move) but that they do move in ellipses of which the sun is one of the foci. The Greeks knew the ellipse from the study of conic sections, but they had never applied it to an attempt to ascertain any "law of nature."

Kepler was a German Protestant, full of visions and enthusiasms. He seems to have taken astrology seriously, as did all but the most skeptical, or the most Christian, of his time. In his younger days he worked out an elaborate scheme, the *Mysterium Cosmographicum,* which attempts to discern mathematical relations among the planets and the sun such that they confirm a long-standing and purely abstract sequence of relations worked out long long ago by the Pythagoreans of early Greece—the five perfect or "Platonic" bodies, pyramid, cube, octahedron, dodecahedron, icosahedron. But when Kepler found he had made a mistake in his data—he had wrongly estimated the distance of some of the planets from the sun—he gave up his theory. Perhaps we can get no better capsule summary of the significance of scientic method than this. Kepler was looking for a cosmology, a set of truths about the real nature of the universe, just as Plato or Aquinas had looked; but, since he had been trained as a scientist, a corrected observation—a measurement—made it necessary for him to scrap his system and start all over again. Factual data do not so obviously get in the way of the philosopher.

Physics, and especially two of its branches, mechanics and optics, came fully into its own in these centuries. Here too Galileo is of great importance. His experiment with falling objects is one of the most familiar in the history of science. Aristotle had said that bodies fall with velocities proportional to their weights, a heavy body falling faster than a lighter one. Galileo let two such weights fall—though modern research has shown, almost certainly not from the picturesque Leaning Tower of Pisa—and noted that they did not behave as Aristotle said they should. From these observations by much more elaborate experiments and mathematics he developed our modern notions of acceleration and of compounded motion. Again, the Aristotelian notion is that of something "perfect"—circles instead of ellipses, straightforward motion determined by the nature of what is moving; the modern scientific notion is much more complex, takes more complicated mathematics to express, and must be constantly checked against observation to see if the motions it postulates (or predicts) really do take place.

Another Italian, Torricelli, invented the barometer, a German, Von Guericke, the air pump, and many obscure workers helped in the steady improvement of lenses and other instruments that made more refined measurement and observation possible. Boyle and his helper Hooke studied the air and other gases, and began the century-long process that ended in the discovery of oxygen and the founding of modern chemistry.

All these investigations pointed toward some great underlying mechanical principle in nature, a set of very elaborate rules that could be put only in terms of higher mathematics, but still rules suggesting that all nature was a machine. Inevitably this notion inspired researchers in the field we now call biology, and the great seventeenth-century discovery in physiology is an attempt to follow some of the leads given by physicists. Harvey in 1628 published his demonstration that the human heart is in fact a pump, and that the human blood is driven by the heart along a system of circulation. Borelli showed that the human arm is a lever, and that the muscles do mechanical "work." Finally, the microscope as well as the telescope came into use, and scored its first triumphs in the discovery of microorganisms. The Dutchman Van Leeuwenhoek is perhaps best known among these early microscopists, but as has constantly been true in the growth of science, many lesser and now forgotten workers helped in the patient accumulation of data and in limited interpretations of their meaning.

Someone, finally, comes to bring together all this work into a major scientific generalization, a law or uniformity that—still within the limits of natural science—simplifies and explains, coordinates many separate laws or uniformities into one general law that sums up millions of man-hours of investigation. The new law is not (still within the limits of science) a final, unalterable, perfect law. It will almost certainly be modified or even, conceivably, shown to be in some sense wrong, given time and long further investigation. But still it is *relatively* permanent, a plateau, a temporary resting place. Galileo almost made this achievement, and a dozen other major figures such as Kepler made essential contributions to the big generalization. It was Newton, however, who drew everything together into that grand mechanical conception which has been called the "Newtonian world-machine." To Newton we shall return in our chapter on the century that revered him, the eighteenth.

Now any such big generalization as that achieved by Newton seems inevitably to influence human thought in many ways, to have its repercussions in fields outside science, in philosophy, in theology, in morals, even in art and literature. Science, we must repeat, does not *as science* provide a cosmology, does not answer, does not indeed *ask*, what in this book we have called the Big Questions. But scientific achievements, at least in the modern world, have been translated into metaphysics. The scientists of these two centuries were a most varied lot, with varied religions and varied *Weltanschauungen*. Some could not resist the temptation—indeed they could hardly have thought a temptation was involved —to see God as the master mechanic, or to hold that their mathematics were a clue to all life and death, or to hunt in the laboratory for some kind of absolute truth. Some, indeed, like the pious Robert Boyle, kept their science and their religion pretty well in separate compartments, an achievement many scientists can bring off happily even today.

The increasing body of scientific knowledge was chiefly, however, translated into the attitude toward the universe we have here called rationalism. The scientists of the early modern world had shown how great a degree of orderliness underlay many different physical phenomena, how notions natural enough to common sense, like that of the rising and the setting of the sun, were not accurate descriptions of what really went on. Appearance and reality were in their work sharply contrasted. Indeed, their work suggested that the great order of the universe was not altogether what Aristotle and the Christian Fathers had said it was, that this order could not be apprehended by faith, or by reasoning according to a received word, but could be apprehended by rigorous re-examination of everything in the human cultural tradition—a re-examination to be conducted by that deceptive and well-known faculty, reason.

Philosophy

Francis Bacon might well lead off this section, for he was rather a philosopher than a scientist, and we have already noted that he was searching for absolute truth and an infallible way to arrive at it. But Bacon's position in intellectual history, and perhaps his major influence on Western thought, has been as the enemy of deduction and the champion of induction, and though many of his aphorisms have been of great use to the kind of people we call rationalists, his work has on the whole been that of a prophet of natural science. So too was in his own time at least the work of the man who represents with unusual completeness the full philosophic development of seventeenth-century rationalism, the Frenchman René Descartes, whose name we have noted briefly as a mathematician. Descartes is, like so many of the figures we have glanced at in these years of the Renaissance, a polymath, a man of very wide scholarly and scientific interests.

Though Descartes broke with both medieval Scholasticism and with the vague, watered-down Platonism that was about all the high Renaissance produced in formal philosophy, he talked the language of philosophy, cast his thought, revolutionary though in a sense it undoubtedly was, in what anyone would recognize as a philosophic mold. Like all great philosophers, he was by no means a simple thinker; commentators can still find something in him no one else has quite found—at any rate, doctoral theses can still be written about him. For our purposes, however, he can be simplified. Here, as throughout, we are interested in what ordinary educated men made of the work of a great thinker. Descartes, it must be admitted, can hardly be said to have filtered down to the uneducated, save in the most general and vaguest way as one of the men who prepared for the Enlightenment. He presents to the layman unused to the rigors of formal philosophy the kind of difficulties that most of the great philosophers present. Yet he wrote a clear if dry French, and even in translation his work is quite readable. The background of his most important philosophic ideas is in the *Discourse of Method* (1637).

Descartes grew up in a learned world full of conflicting groups and ideas, a learned world clearly in transition from persisting Scholasticism to some new synthesis. He early decided that his contemporaries and teachers were in a muddled state of mind about the universe, and that he was born to set it right. He has himself described the steps he went through in his progress from repudiation of all authority to his discovery of what he thought was a solid, absolutely certain, rock-bottom truth on which he could build:

> I thought . . . that I ought to reject as absolutely false all opinions in regard to which I could suppose the least ground for doubt, in order to ascertain whether after that there remained aught in my belief that was wholly indubitable. Accordingly, seeing that our senses sometimes deceive us, I was willing to suppose that there existed nothing really such as they presented to us; and because some men err in reasoning, and fall into paralogisms, even on the simplest matters of Geometry, I, convinced that I was as open to error as any other, rejected as false all the reasonings I had hitherto taken for demonstrations; and finally, when I considered that the very same thoughts (presentations) which we experience when awake may also be experienced when we are asleep, while there is at that time not one of them true, I supposed that all the objects (presentations) that had ever entered into my mind when awake, had in them no more truth than the illusions of my dreams. But immediately upon this I observed that, whilst I thus wished to think that all was false, it was absolutely necessary that I, who thus thought, should be somewhat; and as I observed that this truth, *I think, therefore I am,* was so certain and of such evidence, that no ground of doubt, however extravagant, could be alleged by the Sceptics capable of shaking it, I concluded that I might, without scruple, accept it as the first principle of the Philosophy of which I was in search.

It should be clear that however brazen Descartes' defiance of tradition, this is the language of high philosophy. A true skeptic might ask unpleasantly, Why not "I sweat, therefore I am"? But from this famous "I think, therefore I am" Descartes went ahead to build a system of philosophy that went right on up to God. It was a somewhat remote and impersonal God—Descartes in his sixth Meditation writes, "I now mean by nature . . . nothing but God himself or the order of created things established by God." We need hardly be surprised that the Catholic Church did not feel that the philosopher had redeemed himself from his early doubt, and that the Church has ever since regarded him as belonging to the ranks of its enemies.

Descartes much more clearly than Bacon put the central position of the rationalist. The world is not the confused and rather messy place it seems to be in our first crude, common-sense reflections. On the other hand, the world is not the world of Christian tradition, with its immanent, interfering God and his unpredictable miracles, with its absurd other-worldliness, with all its irrational clutter of medieval ways. Nor is it the Neoplatonic world of the innocent and youthful Renaissance lovers of life and their disillusioned successors. The world is really a vast number of material particles spinning, combining, forming fascinating patterns of such complexity that we are fooled into all sorts of false common-sense and pre-Cartesian philosophic notions. Yet the particles do in fact obey one set of rules, perform their complicated rondo to one tune, and work harmoniously as worked the geometer's mind of René Descartes. The clue to unraveling the obscurities and confusions of our experience is then mathematics. We should think out all our problems as we think out mathematical problems, being careful of our definitions, taking each step carefully and reasonably, seeking above all for clarity and consistency, but never embroiling ourselves in scholastic complexities, never arguing for the sake of arguing. Descartes is not the worshiper of induction Bacon was, and he has the full rationalist contempt for the raw facts our sense impressions pick up.

As a polymath, he interested himself in many fields, and has for instance a small place in the history of physiology, for he did some study in the working of the nervous system. But here as usual he is the philosopher, not the patient laboratory investigator. He was really looking for the seat of the soul (which he thought was uniquely human, not possessed by other vertebrates). He thought he found the seat of the soul in the pineal body, now considered to be a remnant of a sense organ once important in ancestral forms.

Descartes thought it important to find a place for the soul in the body because his system had involved him in a technical problem of great importance in the future history of formal philosophy. We shall not here do more than call the reader's attention to this problem. He can follow it down through Locke, Berkeley, and Kant right into the nineteenth, and even the twentieth, century. It is not, however, a problem that moved the world, however much it moved philosophers, and is, indeed, a good example of how the historian of philosophy and the historian of ideas at work in the crowd must employ different methods and focus on different topics.

Very briefly, then, Descartes was driven from his initial *cogito ergo sum*—I think, therefore I am—to a psychology and a theory of knowledge in which clear thought is contrasted with a muddy sense world somehow outside thought and yet, if we're not all quite mad, in some relation to thought. The soul guides our thinking—perhaps Descartes meant *does* our thinking—and in some way, probably through the nervous system, tells the body what to do. Other animals Descartes definitely thought were mere machines, responding through something close to what we call conditioned reflexes, to environmental stimuli; but men were not quite machines in this sense. Men ran themselves through their souls, souls that shared the rationality of universal laws, mathematics, and God.

From Descartes on, many philosophers tried to remedy this dualism of soul and body, spirit and matter, thinking and perceiving. The matter came closest to popular levels in the next century, as may be seen from Boswell's *Life of Johnson*. An English philosopher, George Berkeley, had solved the problem by deciding that "matter" does not exist, that, in a Latin aphorism much like Descartes' own, *esse est percipi*—to be is to be perceived—and that all reality is an idea in the mind of God. Sam Johnson's common sense was outraged by Berkeley's proposition that matter does not exist, and according to Boswell he kicked a hitching post on the street-side and announced firmly, "I refute it *thus.*"

But the more absurd reaches of the dilemma come out in the problem of solipsism, which is a problem that could hardly arise except in the Cartesian sequence. My thought processes tell me all I know; these processes depend for information on the sense impressions recorded on the nerve-ends and transmitted to my brain; but I never *really* touch what lies beyond those nerve-ends, those telegraph wires that come into my brain; perhaps all these messages are fakes—perhaps there is nothing there; perhaps I am the only person in the universe, and all the rest is an illusion; I *think*, therefore *I* am—but nothing else need be. This is, of course, a position on the lunatic fringe of philosophy, but the whole problem raised by Cartesian dualism is really insoluble, and there exist philosophers today who would class it almost with Zeno's famous paradox as no more than an intellectual puzzle.

It must not be thought that Descartes is the sole philosophical rationalist of these centuries, though he is probably the best example of one. Hobbes, whom we have met as the philosopher of the Leviathan state, was in many ways as complete a rationalist as Descartes. Many historians and philosophers have thought it profitable to contrast with rationalism what they call empiricism. Such a classification actually *accepts* the terminology and point of view of the Cartesian dualism. The rationalists are those who emphasize the mental, rational, or "ideal" side of the polarity of soul and body; the empiricists are those who emphasize the material, bodily, sensation side of the polarity. Both sides, however, both empirical and rationalist philosophers, from Bacon through Descartes and Hobbes to Locke himself, held that the universe made sense because it was reasonable, because it had the kind of underlying pattern we see best in the great mathematical and scientific advances of these two centuries. In other words, one philosopher's spirit did the same kind of work another philosopher's matter did. Of course, there are many and great differences in the world-views of such men as Hobbes and Locke, and many philosophical problems on which they do not agree. Still, rationalism and empiricism in the early modern centuries do have one significant thing in common: They hold that the world makes sense—mathematical sense, at bottom.

In fact rationalism with the seventeenth-century philosopher Spinoza reached quite as far into the intense inane as ever Plato did. Baruch Spinoza, of a Portuguese Jewish family settled in Holland, lives up completely to popular notions of the disinterested philosopher. He refused to succeed in a world which to sensitive souls measures success so crudely and vulgarly. In a century that rewarded men like Descartes with very great public attention, Spinoza turned away and earned his living grinding lenses in The Hague—a job at which he was very expert. He was banished from the synagogue for his unorthodox ideas. He lived the simplest of lives and wrote, in the fashion of his times, most subtly devised metaphysics. We cannot here attempt a real analysis of this philosopher's philosopher. His best known work, perhaps, is an ethics, *mathematically demonstrated,* in which he uses the outward forms of mathematical demonstration to arrive at God and perfect goodness. Spinoza is sometimes given the label of "pantheist," but the label is a cold and unfeeling one for so ardent a seeker after a God at once perfect and remote, and yet not quite beyond our imperfect human understanding. Reason leads him to mystic surrender, to the "intellectual love of God":

> And this intellectual love of the mind toward God is the very love of God with which God loves himself, not in so far as he is infinite, but in so far as he can be expressed by the essence of the human mind, considered under the form of eternity; that is, the intellectual love of the mind toward God is a part of the infinite love with which God loves himself. From this we clearly comprehend in what our salvation, or blessedness, or freedom, consists; to wit, in an unchangeable and eternal love toward God, that is, in the love of God toward men. This love or blessedness is in the sacred Scriptures called glory.

It is a shame to dismiss Spinoza thus curtly; he is worth the attention of anyone who wants to penetrate into a temperament intellectuals have always admired, the sweet, unworldly rebel capable of amazing firmness in matters of the mind. For us, however, it must be enough to note that Spinoza in the great century of scientific advance, and working with the concepts of mathematics, arrived at as "other-worldly" a philosophy as ever any medieval thinker did. Many, many roads lead to the no-place of the mystic.

Political Ideas

The political ideas of the early rationalists are for the most part of the kind we discussed in the last chapter. Hobbes, notably, rejected theories like that of the divine right of kings, for the rationalist has to deny the divine in the traditional Christian sense. But he still believed that there was a system of *right* political relations that could be discovered by thinking about certain given propositions concerning human behavior—such as the proposition that all men want security first and the proposition that in a state of nature they do not have security. From this, according to Hobbes, it follows "rationally" that men will get together and make a contract to create a sovereign quite as absolute as any divine one, but the creation of men in nature. Thinkers like Hobbes, Harrington, and Bodin were humanists influenced by the rationalist current of their times, all working in a traditional frame of reference. They prepared the way for the politics of the Enlightenment, the political attitudes we Americans inherit firsthand, but they did not quite reach the full optimism of the eighteenth-century philosophers.

What is new and original in the political thought of these centuries is the work of Machiavelli. Now Machiavelli shares with all those we have called rationalist a complete dismissal of the idea that there is anything supernatural, that there is any kind of God who intervenes in the day-to-day affairs of men. Machiavelli simply pays no attention to the medieval notion that God is behind the moral order. He sets out with Renaissance curiosity to find out how men actually behave. We shall see that he also has really pretty firm notions of how men ought to behave. But there is certainly a basis for Francis Bacon's praise of him: We owe a lot to Machiavelli, said Bacon, for telling us what men do instead of what they ought to do. In other words, some part at least of Machiavelli's work seems to be of the kind the natural scientist does; it is based on observation, on the collection of the facts, as the starting point of all thinking on the subject. Some of his thinking is based on patriotism, on an Italian's hatred for the foreign powers who dominated Italy. He is by no means a modern anti-intellectual. Like Bacon, he carries with him much of the Middle Ages. But, again as with Bacon, notably in some pages of *The Prince,* he is trying to analyze his data and put them together without concern for morals or metaphysics.

Machiavelli's famous—and to many still infamous—little book *The Prince* was published in 1531, four years after its author's death. With the *Commentary on Livy,* it gives a fair cross-section of Machiavelli's mind and method. In *The Prince* Machiavelli sets out to describe the ways in which an individual ruler (prince) can most readily retain and strengthen his position as ruler. He does not attempt to ascertain what the good or the best prince will do, nor what is the justification for obedience, nor indeed what are the rights and wrongs of politics. He sets himself a technical problem: given certain conditions, what other conditions will maintain, strengthen, or weaken the original conditions. But let him say it:

> We now have left to consider what should be the manners and attitudes of a prince toward his subjects and his friends. As I know that many have written on this subject I feel that I may be held presumptuous in what I have to say, if in my comments I do not follow the lines laid down by others. Since, however, it has been my intention to write something which may be of use to the understanding reader, it has seemed wiser to me to follow the real truth of the matter rather than what we imagine it to be. For imagination has created many principalities and republics that have never been seen or known to have any real existence, for how we live is so different from how we ought to live that he who studies what ought to be done rather than what is done will learn the way to his downfall rather than to his preservation. A man striving in every way to be good will meet his ruin among the great number who are not good. Hence it is necessary for a prince, if he wishes to remain in power, to learn how not to be good and to use his knowledge or refrain from using it as he may need. . . . Further, he should have no concern about incurring the infamy of such vices without which the preservation of his state would be difficult. For, if the matter be well considered, it will be seen that some habits which appear virtuous, if adopted would signify ruin, and others that seem vices lead to security and the well-being of the prince.

Machiavelli then goes on to test in concrete problems the validity of this general thesis. Should a prince be generous or mean? Should he be *thought* to be generous or mean? Is cruelty or clemency the wiser course? Machiavelli answers, as a physician or indeed in low ordinary matters anyone of common sense would answer, that it all depends on the other elements in the situation, on the other *variables* in a human situation too involved to be put into any mathematical equation. But again let us sample Machiavelli:

> Here the question arises; whether it is better to be loved than feared or feared than loved. The answer is that it would be desirable to be both but, since that is difficult, it is much safer to be feared than to be loved, if one must choose. For on men in general this observation may be made: they are ungrateful, fickle, and deceitful, eager to avoid dangers, and avid for gain, and while you are useful to them they are all with you, offering you their blood, their property, their lives, and their sons so long as danger is remote, as we noted above, but when it approaches they turn on you. Any prince, trusting only in their words and having no other preparations made, will fall to his ruin, for friendships that are bought at a price and not by greatness and nobility of soul are paid for indeed, but they are not owned and cannot be called upon in time of need. Men have less hesitation in offending a man who is loved than one who is feared, for love is held by a bond of obligation which, as men are wicked, is broken whenever personal advantage

suggests it, but fear is accompanied by the dread of punishment which never relaxes.

Yet a prince should make himself feared in such a way that, if he does not thereby merit love, at least he may escape odium, for being feared and not hated may well go together. And indeed the prince may attain this end if he but respect the property and the women of his subjects and citizens. And if it should become necessary to seek the death of someone, he should find a proper justification and a public cause, and above all he should keep his hands off another's property, for men forget more readily the death of their father than the loss of their patrimony. Besides, pretexts for seizing property are never lacking, and when a prince begins to live by means of rapine he will always find some excuse for plundering others, and conversely pretexts for execution are rarer and are more quickly exhausted.

These passages may seem true or false, or a mixture of both, to a reader of the mid-twentieth century; but they will not seem new. The psychologists have got us used to the notion that men's bad actions should be studied as well as condemned, or even studied rather than condemned. But all this was very new when Machiavelli committed it to print. Though men in the Middle Ages conducted themselves no better than in Machiavelli's description of the constants of human nature, the people who wrote books did not do much more than note the existence of such behavior. Chiefly, they preached against it, they were indignant at its immorality, and, most important of all, they held it to be unnatural behavior for human beings, even though they could hardly help admitting that it existed.

Machiavelli is then original, at least in the context of Western Christian culture, in his realistic political analysis. He is in some senses trying to do what the natural scientists were just beginning to do—observe phenomena carefully and arrange these observations into laws (uniformities, generalizations) that would enable successful prediction of the future phenomena in the given context. But he did not succeed in his field as well as the scientists did in theirs. We may here note three ways in which Machiavelli fails to apply the scientific method to the study of politics (it has not yet been wholly successfully applied, and there are those who do not think it can be at all profitably applied, to the study of politics).

First, even in the brief quotations given, you will have noted an excessively low or pessimistic view of human nature. Men in general, he says, are ungrateful, fickle, and deceitful. Scientifically speaking, it is probably impossible to make any sensible generalization of this sort about human beings; on one view of science, a problem of this sort is meaningless. Most of us do, however, make some sort of judgment, in the balance, about our fellow creatures seen as a whole. But all the way from a trusting love of one's fellows to a passionate contempt for them there are variant attitudes which, though often wise and useful to individuals who take these attitudes, are most certainly not to be classified as scientific judgments. Machiavelli's attitude is far out toward extreme cynicism. It was probably inspired partly as a reaction against the pious commonplaces of Christianity, which, if it accepts the doctrine of original sin, is not in fact cynical about human beings, is indeed much concerned with their possible salvation. Machiavelli seems to want to shock, to seem to be a wise and wicked fellow.

He may, of course, be an inverted idealist, a man who is cynical just because he wants so much perfection. There are grave psychological problems here, difficult to solve in the study of living men, almost impossible with figures of the past. Machiavelli does indeed seem the balked intellectual; he is clearly taking a position not that of the vulgar, the average, the conventional intellectual of his day. It is possible to go even further, and maintain, as did the distinguished American historian, Garrett Mattingly, that *The Prince* is in fact satire, and Machiavelli an ironist meaning the opposite of what he says, meaning to condemn "immoral realism" and defend the eternal verities. The writer cannot agree, but he confesses that in these matters no "scientific" cumulative knowledge seems possible.

Second, and less disputably, Machiavelli's detachment is greatly limited by his warm Italian patriotism. *The Prince* is not in intent an academic or scientific treatise on the art of governing. It is a treatise on the art of governing in Italy in the Cinquecento; and it is a treatise in which the duty—quite as much as the benefits—of uniting Italy and expelling the foreigner are urged upon the prince. Machiavelli's last chapter in *The Prince* is an ardent paean to Italy, and helped redeem Machiavelli's reputation with later generations who found Italian nationalism a noble cause. We need here no more than note that this too is a distortion in Machiavelli's effort to see things as they really were. He wants things so different, he wants Italians so different, that he cannot quite attain detachment.

Finally, though Machiavelli had had a certain experience of international relations and of other government business on an appointive or bureaucratic level, he wrote these most famous works of his in something like academic retirement. Just as he leaned over backward in an effort not to write piously about unreal human beings (as, say, John of Salisbury must have seemed to him to write) so he leaned over backward in his effort to be no academic intellectual but a man of the world. This last is a disastrous pose, a distortion of the worst sort. Machiavelli tries too hard to be worldly; he has shocked quite unscrupulous but conventional people for several centuries. His very reputation for wickedness—or for counseling wickedness—in itself is proof of his failure. Scientific knowledge does not contain the corrosive acids of Machiavelli's wit.

Yet Machiavelli is rightly, in our opinion, regarded as one of the pioneers of the effort to study the behavior of men in society as the scientist studies the behavior of gases or of insects. This effort may be doomed in advance to failure; in another few centuries the "social science" of today may seem one of the blind alleys men have followed. But at present, committed as we are to their pursuit, we must be grateful to Machiavelli. Much of what he said had indeed been said before, much of it in Greek political thought; Aristotle, for example, had observed some of the ways men behaved in political life and had noted them down. There is a whole literature of aphorisms and short essays on human nature, on the quirks and foibles and little and big follies of men. But most of this adds up to common sense or to a sort of equivalent folk-wisdom. It is like the weather-wisdom of the old inhabitant. Science must always attempt to systematize and measure and put into somewhat formidable terms—in the long run most useful—what folk-wisdom puts in hunches. The first meteorologists may be less reliable than the weather-wise old salt. They may seem rather crude and brash and impractical. But in the long run the systematic science wins out.

Machiavelli is the scientist in his initial and very self-conscious stage. He is going to get at what really lies behind all these fine words men write about politics and ethics. He is not going to be content with a few random reflections on these matters. He will study systematically certain problems, not to find what is right, but just to find what is. He does not wholly succeed in keeping an even temper, in being as detached as he should be. Above all, he fails in general—though there are signs that he sees the factor concerned—to realize that men's ethical ideas and ideals, even though they do not stand in a simple causal relation to men's deeds, stand in *some* relation to men's deeds. In other words, Machiavelli makes the mistake still repeated by some of our deliberately hard-boiled writers on politics and morals; he writes off men's professions of good just because they do not wholly live up to them.

Francis Bacon, too, belongs in his own right to the list of those who have attempted to study human behavior as the scientist studies anatomy or physiology. Notably in the first book of his *Instauratio Magna* he outlines a subject that has much concerned social and political psychologists in our own time—the systematic study of the way in which the human mind is influenced in its workings by nonlogical, nonexperimental factors. Again, men have known since our culture began that the "human understanding is no dry light," as Bacon put it. We have long known that the wish is father to the thought, that men entertain prejudices, that our very language is full of ambiguities and double meanings, so that even if the will to be precise and objective is there the way is still hard. But Bacon's analysis of these difficulties under the name of "idols" is still suggestive, still one of the best systematic attempts to classify our rationalizations.

He finds four classes of idols which beset men's minds, the Idols of the Tribe, of the Cave, of the Market-place, and of the Theater. By Idols of the Tribe he means the errors that have their origin in human nature itself, in our sense apparatus and in our minds. The statement "man is the measure of all things" means in fact that even in science our standards tend to vary subjectively. By Idols of the Cave Bacon means something close to the ordinary meaning of prejudice, the errors molded and produced by our own personality, the little cave we have hollowed for ourselves in this harsh world. By the Idols of the Market-place he means what we should call the distortions of propaganda and advertising, the mutual excitation men work upon one another in crowds or in almost any kind of social intercourse, the errors of men gathered together. By Idols of the Theater Bacon means the errors men accumulate when they try to work out systematic interpretations of the universe—these are the errors of philosophers and intellectuals, the errors of system-building in which it is easy to hold that Bacon himself erred. But let him define this last Idol:

> Lastly, there are Idols which have immigrated into men's minds from the various dogmas of philosophies, and also from wrong laws of demonstration. These I call Idols of the Theater; because in my judgment all the received systems are but so many stage-plays, representing worlds of their own creation after an unreal and scenic fashion. Nor is it only of the systems now in vogue, or only of the ancient sects and philosophies, that I speak; for many more plays of the same kind may yet be composed and in like artificial manner set forth; seeing that errors the most widely different have nevertheless causes for the most part alike. Neither again do I mean this only of entire systems, but also of many principles and axioms in science, which by tradition, credulity, and negligence have come to be received.

It goes without saying that the attempt to apply to the study of human relations methods similar in some respects to those of the natural sciences bore no such fruits as did the application of these methods to the natural sciences. Even today, there is no unanimity about the social sciences— though it is definitely fashionable to contrast them unfavorably with the "real" sciences.

Just as Cartesian rationalism or Baconian empiricism did in fact aim at achieving a cosmology, a certainty about all possible relations in the universe, so most of those who broke with medieval notions of political thought were themselves working up a system of politics that seemed to them somehow outside the imperfections of politics as practiced. We shall see in the next chapter that the political and moral thinking of early modern times had by the eighteenth century turned definitely into rationalist channels. But the result was not so much a science of politics as another political ideology, or rather a group of ideologies. All this is not said in complaint. Unless men change their nature radically, political ideologies and metaphysical systems seem essential to human spiritual needs. We are still living in the system of ideas about the Big Questions that was prepared in the early modern centuries and came to fruition in the eighteenth century.

Making the Modern World—A Summary

Between the fifteenth and the eighteenth centuries the modern culture of Western society was formed. By the eighteenth century educated men and women, and we may believe many of the uneducated, had come to hold certain beliefs about themselves, about the universe, about what was worth doing on earth, about what could be done on earth, beliefs that their ancestors of the Middle Ages had not held. They lived in a world that seemed to them new, since their ideas about it were new. They were not, of course, totally new; most of Western society was Christian in 1700, as it had been in 1400. It is a central thesis of this book that much of what men and women of the eighteenth and later centuries believed was incompatible with some very important parts of traditional Christian belief; or less ponderously, that the Enlightenment *radically altered* Christian belief. Still it is clear that a very great deal of Christianity has remained—and not merely the formal organization of the churches.

Yet one very simple and unambiguous change is there for all to see. In the thirteenth century there was but one organized ecclesiastical body in the West, the Roman Catholic Church; in the eighteenth there were already several hundred sects in the whole of Western society. Even in such countries as France where on the surface the Catholic Church was still supreme, there were several hundred thousand Protestants and an unknown number of deists, atheists, and skeptics, all pretty open about their beliefs or lack of belief, and very few exposed to any serious danger of the medieval punishment of their kind. Voltaire's pamphlets against the executions of Calas and de la Barre by Catholics must not mislead us; theirs were the *rare* case, at least in the West. The working unity of Christianity had been broken, and already by 1700 there was a body of writings that defended the notion that religious differences *ought* to be tolerated, that Church and State are rightfully separable, that the individual should make up his own mind in matters of religious belief. Indeed, the way was clear for such eighteenth-century ideas as the notion that there is *some* truth in all religions—even in non-Christian religions.

To Americans today such notions are so common that it is difficult to realize how very new they are, how sharply contrasted with what men and women of only a few centuries ago assumed with equal confidence to be true. They are notions that imply a new criterion of truth—metaphysical and theological truth—rather than the abandonment of the search for this sort of truth. In the Middle Ages these truths were held to be revealed, and perfect in their revelation; men might lose sight of them, might even as heirs of Adam's sin go against them; but no one could be *right*, no one could know the truth, and be against them. In the light of these medieval notions, the burning of heretics was understandable. They were rotten fruit, and if left alone they might corrupt the sound fruit; moreover, they were damned, and to cut them off from actual living was doing them no real harm—they had done that to themselves already. In short, if you know you are right, anyone who differs from you must be wrong. People should be right, and not wrong. You cannot let wrong notions spread without doing very great harm.

Now although the rationalizations or justifications of religious toleration are only beginning to spread and develop in the early eighteenth century, the main lines of defense are clear. Though they vary in detail, they add up to one of three propositions: that there is a new truth, deeper than that of traditional Christianity, which will if tolerated ultimately supplant or thoroughly modify it; that truth is not revealed perfect and complete to men, but must be discovered progressively by trial and error, by investigation, by human effort; or to the proposition, *little held in these early days,* that there is no such thing as truth or certainty in such matters, that all truth is "relative," that neither revelation nor thinking and studying will arrive at absolutes. But all these propositions agree in rejecting at least something in the Christian heritage from the Middle Ages; they all claim to lead to something new and something better.

The change in fundamentals is neatly pointed up at the turn of the seventeenth into the eighteenth century by an apparently insignificant debate among men of letters in France and in England, a debate usually called by its French name *la quérelle des anciens et des modernes*—the quarrel between the ancients and the moderns. One of the memorials of its English phase is Swift's amusing *Battle of the Books*. Briefly, one side maintained that the Greeks and the Romans had achieved a culture in general and in detail unsurpassable; they were the giants who staked out the fields of human culture and set examples we can but imitate from afar. Classical culture was to these people a kind of lay or humanist Eden; it was blasphemy to suppose that the like could ever again appear on earth. The other side maintained that, although the achievements of the Greeks and Romans were very great indeed, they were, so to speak, records that modern Europeans had the chance to break; modern culture could be as good, or better, in every field; there was no use in holding the men of old to be inevitably our superiors, for we could benefit by their works, we could stand on their shoulders and reach all the higher.

The position of the moderns in this quarrel is one of the first forms of the very important doctrines of progress so familiar to all Americans today, the idea that novelty is neither a delusion nor a falling off, but the natural working out of some kind of universal plan. We do not know how this basic, revolutionary change in outlook came about. We do know that it was a very complex and relatively slow process, in which we can discern three main intellectual constituents.

First came a great series of changes in the practices and ideals of Christianity under the name of Protestantism. The Protestant movement had its full share of human heroism and human weakness, of struggle and accident and strange ends. Its narrative history, over which in a book of this sort we have to pass wholly, is a fascinating record. But for the intellectual historian it is probable that the chief importance of Protestantism is as a *dissolvent*—the strongest at work in these years—of medieval authority. The Protestant movement broke through the formal unity Western Christendom had preserved for a millennium and a half, and set up a dozen major and hundreds of minor groups or sects in the position of claiming full religious authority in their fields. Protestantism, by the fact that it split into sects and subsects, prepared the way for religious skepticism. For to a mind at all inclined to doubt, or addicted to logic, the spectacle of a great number of contradictory and antithetical beliefs—each claiming monopoly of truth—could be taken as evidence that there existed no truth to be monopolized. More positively, Protestantism, especially in its Anglican and Lutheran forms, worked as a buttress to strengthen the patriotic sentiments of members of the new territorial national states. God was still—to put it otherwise would have been to leave Christianity wholly behind—a God of all the human race; but in a sense he played favorites, treated the English or the Prussians or the Danes as his preferred children. In the practice and administration of day-to-day religious life these new national churches had no share in an international and cosmopolitan life of the kind the old medieval church had possessed. Calvinist Protestantism in particular encouraged among its faithful a paradoxical mixture of other-worldly longing for union with God, a longing that stands out in all Puritan living, and a very this-worldly respect for the man who worked hard and prospered materially. But the first Protestants made no new universe; they believed in original sin, in the inspiration of the Bible, in an authority not, to be sure, invested in the pope of Rome, but still an authority above the trial-and-error processes of ordinary living. The Protestants believed in an immanent God not at all like the laws of mathematics. They believed in hell-fire and, for the elect, in heavenly bliss.

Humanism, the second force making for change, was much more than the application of some vague Protestant or libertarian spirit to the secular life. It had in common with Protestantism a corrosive effect on what was left of medieval standards. It questioned the authority of immediate custom and of established scholastic philosophy. It was an active rebellion of artists and scholars. Some of its artists mastered their media magnificently (with the help of methods worked out by generations who had been trained in medieval methods) and produced very great art. Many of them were adventurous, free-living, romantic, and exciting people who helped set our modern standards of the artist and writer as necessarily unconventional, impractical, selfish, but rather winning. Its *virtù* was in no clear sense a very Christian ideal, but rather the ideal of a handsome, athletic, though also intellectual, man. Humanism, like Calvinism, had its own deep-seated paradox. The humanists rebelled against clerical authority and the weight of tradition; they seem at least in their practice to hold the modern notion that men *make* their standards, *make* their truth, and do not merely discover it. Yet as a group they fell into a most pious attitude of respect for the masters of antiquity, whom they set up as authorities quite as absolute as any the Middle Ages worshiped. They had little awareness of the coming spread of ideas and aspirations to the masses; they were a privileged group of educated men, rather inclined to aristocratic and monarchical ideals, in no sense democrats. They did not think the world could be a very much better place, except perhaps for themselves.

Rationalism, the third force, was also an agent of destruction, less obvious and less powerful in the early years of the modern age than Protestantism or humanism, in the long run more important and more powerful. The rationalist threw overboard far more of traditional Catholic Christianity than did the Protestant or the humanist. He not merely banished the supernatural from his universe; he was prepared to place man himself wholly within the framework of nature or the "material universe." He thought indeed that man had to guide himself by standards of right and wrong. The rationalists of the earlier centuries of our modern era thought these standards were fixed and certain, and that men *found* rather than made them. But where the medieval Christian found these standards in custom, in authority, in what had been so time out of mind, the rationalist sought to find them beneath appearances, custom, and apparent diversities, and to find them by a patient investigation in which the rational mind found the mathematical reality behind the vulgarly varied and colored appearance. Rationalism has none of the obvious paradoxes of Protestantism and humanism—unless, indeed, you are so far a real skeptic as to hold that it is a paradox to try to think any kind of orderly system into human experience of this world. Rationalism even in these years owed much of its slowly growing prestige to the achievements of natural science. Finally, when with Newton science succeeded in attaining to a marvelously complete scheme of the universe, one that could be tested mathematically and that worked in the sense that it enabled successful prediction, the stage was set for the new rationalist worldview, for a cosmology as different from that of St. Augustine or St. Thomas Aquinas as theirs was from that of a Greek of the fifth century B.C.

CHAPTER FOUR

THE EIGHTEENTH CENTURY

A NEW COSMOLOGY

The Agents of Enlightenment

With the eighteenth century the intellectual historian finds himself faced with a difficulty that faces all historians of the last few centuries: He is overwhelmed with materials. You can make exhaustive lists of medieval thinkers; and a conscientious scholar could master, or at least read, all the Greek and Roman writings that have survived. But with the invention of printing, with the proliferation of writers of all sorts who could be supported by a society with increasing command over its material environment, the mass of writings in all fields is too much for any single scholar, and indeed for any organized company of scholars. Moreover, there seems to be an increasing range of taste and opinion. A process like that which multiplied Protestant sects multiplies opinions of all sorts in all fields of *noncumulative* knowledge; and *cumulative* knowledge continues to pile up in something like geometric progression. Now possibly this range and complexity can be explained by the printing press and good rag paper (unlike our modern newspapers, which will disintegrate into unusable shape in less than half a century, even the periodical and fugitive writings of the eighteenth and early nineteenth centuries have survived in full legibility). The Middle Ages may have been as many-minded as our own. But we have to go by what we have, and what we have is—well, all but a tiny fraction of the over *eleven million* books and pamphlets in the Library of Congress were published since 1700.

Our generalizations must, then, be based on but a small sampling of the immense amount of information available. We cannot even pay as much attention to the great seminal minds as we have been able to pay hitherto, for we must concentrate on ideas as they get to work among the nameless many. We can but suggest that the reader go himself to the work of the men and women who put the last touches on our intellectual inheritance, who gave our Western culture its characteristic modern form or, if you are a certain kind of pessimist in these matters, its modern formlessness.

Here we may deliberately put the new world-view of the Enlightenment in its extreme form, a form in which it was definitely *not* held by most of its most famous exponents, a Locke, a Voltaire, a Rousseau, a Kant. This is *the belief that all human beings can attain here on this earth a state of perfection hitherto in the West thought to be possible only for Christians in a state of grace, and for them only after death.* St. Just, the youthful French revolutionary, put it with deceptive simplicity before the Convention: *le bonheur est une idée neuve en Europe*—happiness is a new idea in Europe. Not new in heaven, of course, but new in Europe, pretty new even in America. Another Frenchman, Condorcet, put the matter even more extremely: he hints at least at the doctrine of "natural salvation," immortal life for the individual in this flesh, on this earth, forever.

This perfectibility of human kind had not been brought about by nearly two thousand years of Christianity, nor by the preceding paganism of other millennia. If it were to be brought about in the eighteenth century, obviously something new—some invention or discovery—had to be made. This something new is best summed up in the work of two late seventeenth-century Englishmen who brought to a focus the preparatory work of the early modern centuries, Newton and Locke. Newton's life work, and especially his perfection of the calculus and his grand mathematical formulation of the relation of the planets and the laws of gravity, seemed to contemporaries to explain all natural phenomena, or at least to show how all such phenomena—including the behavior of human beings—could be explained. Locke, taking the methods of clear simple reasoning out of the bewildering metaphysics where Descartes had landed them, seemed to make them a nice extension of common sense. He seemed to show men the way Newton's great successes could be applied to the study of human affairs. Together, Newton and Locke set up those great clusters of ideas, Nature and Reason, which were to the Enlightenment what such clusters of ideas as grace, salvation, and predestination were to traditional Christianity.

Nature became to some of the true believers of the Enlightenment wholly a benign concept. To the Christian, even to the Thomist Christian, Nature had been always somewhat suspect, and certainly always inadequate without the help of the divine. From the time of the Enlightenment on, however, those who used the term Nature to try to influence human beings enjoyed to the full the benefits of the ambiguity exploited in the natural law of the Romans. Nature, to the man of the Enlightenment, was the external world he lived in, a world that clearly existed but in which by no means everything that happened was "natural." In fact, to the really ardent eighteenth-century partisan of the Enlightenment almost everything that happens, that exists at the moment, almost everything in the *actual* external world of Nature—or at any rate, of *human* nature as organized in society—was *unnatural.* Class distinctions, the etiquette of society, the privileges of clergy and nobles, the contrast of slum and palace—these did exist, but they were unnatural. Of course our partisan was thinking of *natural* in the sense of "good," or "normal," *unnatural* as "bad" or "abnormal." The point is that the Nature of Newton as the concept of it filtered down into the educated and half-educated was the orderly, untroubled, beautifully simple working of the universe *properly understood.* Once we understand this Nature in human affairs, all we have to do is to regulate our actions accordingly, and there will be no more unnatural behavior.

We understand the workings of this immanent (but not to the *untrained* obvious or indeed perceptible) Nature by what the Enlightenment loved to call Reason—often, as here, with a capital R. Reason is at its clearest, and indeed first showed itself among men, as mathematics. Reason, argued the agents of Enlightenment, enables us to penetrate from appearances to reality. Without Reason, or even with the faulty kind of Reason that, as common sense, men got along with for so many centuries, we should believe that the sun actually "rises" and "sets"; with Reason, we know the true relation of earth and sun. Similarly, Reason applied to human relations will show us that kings are not fathers of their people, that if meat is good to eat on Thursdays it is good to eat on Fridays, that if pork is nourishing to a Gentile it is nourishing to a Jew. Reason will enable us to find human institutions, human relations that are "natural"; once we find such institutions, we shall conform to them and be happy. Reason will clear up the mess that superstition, revelation, faith (the devils of the rationalists) have piled up here on earth.

With the validity of this leap, or series of leaps, from the law of gravity to human relations we are not at the moment concerned. The point is that the generation that read Newton and Locke made the leap. Neither Newton nor Locke went as far as the men of the next two or three generations who appealed to their authority. Outside his own work as a natural scientist, Newton was no innovator, and indeed is best known in such fields for a most unmodern and unenlightened excursion into Biblical literature. Locke, whose main concern was indeed psychology, ethics, and political theory, was a cautious person, a middle-of-the-roader, for whom the new methods served in part at least to confirm ancient wisdom.

Nor is the first generation to spread the new gospel of Reason radical in a simplifying, extremist fashion. This generation did indeed popularize and make available for ordinary educated men—and very definitely by this time, women—the ideas of the seventeenth century, which Alfred

Whitehead has called the "century of genius." They are mostly French-men, and indeed if on the whole England had rather more than her share of the seminal minds that produced the ideas of the Enlightenment, it was above all the French who transmitted these ideas throughout Europe and into Russia, even into the growing outposts of Western society all over the world. The greatest of these Frenchmen is Voltaire, in whose ninety-odd volumes you will find neatly and often wittily expressed almost all the ideas with which the Enlightenment started.

Started, not finished. For Voltaire, with Montesquieu, Pope, the English deists, belongs to the first or moderate generation of the Enlightenment. They are still greatly influenced by the current of taste we analyzed as that of the "spare humanists" of the Age of Louis XIV. They still believe in restraint, in decorum, in those "rules of old discovered, not devised" which preserve a social as well as an aesthetic equilibrium. They don't like the stuffy old ways, especially when the stuffiness is applied with compulsion, and in particular they dislike the old churches, Roman Catholic and Anglican. They make fun of what they don't like. The next generation will find the old ways much too objectionable to joke about.

Montesquieu's *Spirit of the Laws* (1748), the great sociological work of the moderate first generation, marks a kind of turning point. Though Voltaire lived until 1778, an object of hero worship in his final years, the new men after 1750 are mostly radicals. Like most radicals, they tend to be one-sided, to push a particular idea into the ground, to be, in short, sectarian. If their main interest is in religion, they go on from a mild deism to outright materialism and atheism. This atheism is not in any sense a form of skepticism, but a positive belief that the universe is a great machine. If they are psychologists, they go on from Locke's innocent distinction between primary and secondary qualities to construct a whole man on the basis of sensations impinging on an automatically recording psyche; that is, they have already the essence of twentieth-century notions of behaviorism, conditioned reflexes, and the like. Holbach and others are already at the point of view neatly summarized in the title of a book by a lesser colleague, La Mettrie's *L'homme machine,* "Man the Machine." If they are economists, they go on with the French physiocrats to coin one of the great simplicities of our world—and a powerful one—*laissez-faire, laissez-passer*—or to such long-popular slogans as "that government governs best which governs least, and least expensively." Adam Smith, whose *Wealth of Nations* was first published in 1776, and the Scottish group generally are exceptions to our rule. Smith is a moderate, a man temperamentally of the first generation of the Enlightenment, by no means a doctrinaire believer in absolutely free economic competition; it was his followers who simplified his doctrines into "rugged individualism." Or finally, with the followers of Rousseau this second generation could plunge into complete emotional rejection of their social and cultural environment and seek to make it over wholly in accord with the dictates of the Nature that spoke so clearly to simple peasants, primitive savages, children, and literary men like themselves.

By the time a third generation had grown up, the two elements of the later Enlightenment, the rationalist-classical and the sentimental-romantic, had been fully developed. In the critical years before the French Revolution, these two attitudes, these two clusters of ideas, worked together at least to the discredit of the old regime. We shall attempt in a later chapter a more detailed analysis of the importance of the Romantic Movement, which exists almost full-blown in Rousseau himself. Here we may note that rationalism and romanticism are inseparably woven together in the minds of most eighteenth-century Western men of the Enlightenment. Reason and sentiment not merely agreed to condemn the old ways of nobles, priests, and the unenlightened generally; in many minds, they combined to approve the new, the rule of the *intelligent and kind-hearted* majority of unspoiled men. Indeed, the *natural* man of the simpler followers of the Enlightenment was *both* naturally virtuous and naturally reasonable; his heart and his head were both sound.

It is not here maintained that differences between Rousseau and the rationalists did not exist. They were real, they were picturesquely expressed, and they are worth studying. Romanticism was a *revolt* from rationalism. But it is much more important for us to note that the revolt was the revolt of a child from its parent—a child that greatly resembled the parent. The resemblance lay in a fundamental: Both rejected the doctrine of original sin, and both held that man's life on earth can be almost indefinitely improved—that he can lead the good life—if certain environmental changes are made.

A third generation listened to both rationalist and romantic and made the American and the French revolutions, remade Britain without a revolution, and set the foundations for the developed cosmology of the nineteeth century. These men were of varied kinds, by no means in agreement. Indeed, at the height of the French Revolution they set a classic example of quarrels to the death—for power, no doubt, but power embodied in ideas. To seek a least common denominator among John Adams, Sam Adams, Thomas Jefferson, Tom Paine, La Fayette, Danton, Robespierre, Francis Place, Lord Grey, and the other leaders of this movement would be difficult and unprofitable. We shall here attempt only to indicate the broad lines of the attitude toward human relations, toward society in the broadest sense of the word, which might be that of an ordinary, educated, forward-looking young person of the later eighteenth century in the Western world.

He must of necessity be a fictitious person. Even in the cosmopolitan eighteenth century there would be firm national and regional imprints;

the young Westernizing Russian aristocrat reading Voltaire in French
was not much like the Yankee lad discovering in Locke and the English
deists how wrong his Congregational minister was about hell-fire. The
young German, especially, was even by 1780 the soulful, deep, questing
German never content with the shallow rationalism of his French neigh-
bors and enemies. He was already on his German way to something more,
something greater, something immeasurable, something impossible. We
shall, however, have much to do later with nationalism. Here we must
attempt frankly a process of simplification and abstraction.

One further word is needed before we attempt to see what the new
cosmology was. With the eighteenth century we are in many ways in
modern times. Certainly we have no longer any serious question about
the *fact* of the spread of ideas in some form among many thousands, indeed millions, who cannot be numbered among the intellectuals, nor
among the ruling classes in any restricted sense of the term. There are
many and unresolved problems regarding the nature of their spread, indeed there are in essence all the problems that face us today in the study
of public opinion. But at least we know there *was* a public opinion, and
we have some clues to what it believed.

The newspaper was in its infancy at the beginning of the century,
though by the end it had attained something like its modern form, especially in England, the United States, and France. Throughout the
century, however, the cheap pamphlet or broadside meant that the
printed word could circulate very widely. Books remained relatively expensive, but there were the beginnings of the circulating library in many
social clubs and other voluntary groups. Literacy now began to extend
to a considerable part of the population in the West. The masses did
not yet read, though by the end of the century the skilled workers in the
more advanced countries could and did read. Only the rural masses were
still completely illiterate, and the French Revolution made a beginning
of literacy even for them. The important thing, however, is the existence
in all these countries of a strong, literate middle class, numbering all told
several millions, and devoted to the ideas of the Enlightenment.

Finally, the eighteenth century saw the ripening of those characteristically modern agents of the spread of ideas for which we really have no
good single name—they were voluntary groups organized sometimes for
a specific goal, like the later Anti-Saloon League in the United States,
sometimes for social ritual and insurance, like the many fraternal societies, sometimes purely for amusement, like the informal conversation
groups the French call *salons*. Western society in the eighteenth century
had a very rich group life indeed. As the century wore on, especially in
France, all these groups, even those that seem as remote from the history
of ideas as a *tabagie* (i.e., smoking club, from *tabac*, tobacco) became in
fact agents for the spread of the new, and by then actually revolution-

ary ideas. Of course, these bourgeois flirted, danced, played cards, and indulged in small talk; but they probably mixed in more serious intellectual effort than is usual in such circles. Even their pleasures took on a tinge of what they fashionably called *patriotisme,* which is not what we call patriotism, but rather loyalty toward the Enlightenment. The French have a game of cards, a variant of whist, which they call *le boston,* after the town that stood up so valiantly in the 1770's for the new ideas.

The Faith of the Enlightened

In the widest terms the change in the attitude of Western men toward the universe and everything in it was the change from the Christian supernatural heaven after death to the rationalist natural heaven on this earth, now—or at least very shortly. But the clearest way of realizing the greatness of that change is to start off with a very basic modern doctrine that is unquestionably new—the doctrine of progress. Belief in progress, in spite of the two world wars of our generation, the constant threat of a third and worse one, and the grave economic crisis of the thirties, is still so much a part of the way young Americans are brought up that very few Americans realize how unprecedented that belief is. Of course, men have long felt that one way of doing something is "better" than another; they have known specific improvements in techniques; above all, they have been aware as members of a group that their particular group was in a flourishing state, or the reverse.

But remember fifth-century Athens. Here were men in the flush of a very great corporate achievement, men who were quite aware of the fact that they were doing many things better than their ancestors had done them. Thucydides almost calls his Peloponnesian War a "bigger and better" war than any that had been fought before. There is in the funeral speech of Pericles a touch of the Chamber of Commerce of today. Yet you can find no clear notion of progress as a part of the cosmos, as a process of development from lower to higher, in these confident years of Athenian culture. And you find even less that resembles the doctrine of progress if you look at other phases of ancient and medieval history.

You find, indeed, several organized schemes of man's destiny as seen in history. The popular pagan legends of the Mediterranean put the happiest and best age of mankind in the distant past, in a Golden Age, an age of heroes, an age of which the Hebrew version is our familiar Garden of Eden. Among the intellectuals of the Graeco-Roman world there were various sophisticated ideas about the course of history, and notably a series of cyclical theories. Such for instance is the most widely accepted one of a Golden Age followed by a Silver Age in turn followed by an Iron Age, after which there was to be a catastrophe, a new Golden

Age, and then the cycle all over again, world without end. It seems quite likely that some of these ideas are related to Hindu ideas about trans-migration of souls, eternal recurrences, and the like, and that they mark an otherwise unrecorded meeting of the East and West. They are, of course, quite unlike our ideas of progress. And notably, they are held by men who usually think of themselves as living in an Iron Age. They are, in short, for those holding them, like the notions of a past Golden Age, based on a belief in *regression* or decadence, not on a belief in progress.

We have already noted that traditional Christianity did not have a theory of progress in nature on this earth—certainly not in the clear form this theory took in the Enlightenment. We shall return at the end of this chapter to the subtle and difficult problem of the relations between traditional Christian belief and the Enlightenment. We may note here in passing that the relation is a very close one indeed, that in fact the Enlightenment is a child of Christianity—which may explain for our Freudian times why the Enlightenment was so hostile to traditional Christianity. There is even in Christianity a certain emotional basis not at all incongruous with belief in progress. The formal cosmology of traditional Christianity is, however, clearly closer to pagan notions of man's course on earth than to those of the Enlightenment. The best was first—the state of innocence before the Fall; man has *lapsed;* he cannot reconstitute Eden on earth; he can better himself, it is true, but not ac-tually by any *process,* not even by actions that are properly speaking his-torical, but only by a transcendental miracle, that of salvation through grace; heaven is quite definitely not to be achieved on earth.

We noted in the *quérelle des anciens et des modernes* of the late seven-teenth century the beginnings of public debate among intellectuals on these matters. The doctrine, in broad lines much like our own Ameri-can folk notions of progress, gets itself very quickly accepted in Western culture of the eighteenth century, though by no means unanimously, and by no means without opposition. You can get from Voltaire, for in-stance, as much evidence for the thesis that he believed in cycles, with 1750 *lower* in a cycle than the Age of Louis XIV, as for the theory that he believed in progress, and in his own Age of Enlightenment. At the very end of the century, however, Condorcet's *Progrès de l'esprit humain* gives a complete, full-dress account of the ten stages by which men had lifted themselves from primitive savagery to the brink of perfection on earth. Fifteen hundred years after St. Augustine comes this philosophy of history in which the *civitas Dei* and the *civitas terrena* are melted in-distinguishably together.

Condorcet is rather vague about the way in which all this happens, about the moving force that pushes humanity from one stage to a higher one, and in general it can be said that until in the next century Darwinian ideas of organic evolution were drawn upon in the social sciences, there is hardly a satisfactory general theory of progress that attempts to explain why and how detailed progressive changes are made. The favorite explanation among the intellectuals in the eighteenth century was that progress is due to the spread of reason, to the increasing enlightenment (*les lumières*) that enables men to control their environment better.

Here is already seen most clearly the historic association of scientific and technological improvement with the idea of progress in the moral and cultural sense. By the eighteenth century the work of scientists from Copernicus through Newton had produced a very broad set of generalizations about the behavior of the material universe—generalizations by 1750 known to laymen at least as well as we know those of relativity and quantum mechanics. Moreover, it was clear that these Newtonian generalizations were better, truer, than those of his medieval predecessors. Still more, by mid-century there was evident the kind of material progress that is with the unreflective perhaps a much firmer source of belief in progress than is pure science. There were better roads along which coaches traveled each year a bit faster; there were obvious, homely improvements such as water closets; there was even, at the end of the century, the beginning of the conquest of the air. The conquest was an imperfect one in balloons, it is true, but even so, in 1787 a Frenchman achieved a very modern death attempting to cross the English Channel in the air. In short, a very old man in the eighteenth century might look back to his childhood as a time when men had fewer conveniences, a simpler material environment, fewer and less efficient tools and machines, a lower standard of living.

The theory of progress, however much it owes to the growth of cumulative knowledge and to the increasing ability of men to produce material wealth from their natural environment, is a theory of morals and indeed metaphysics. Men are, according to this theory, becoming better, happier, more nearly what the ideals of the best of our cultures have aimed at. If you try to pursue this notion of moral improvement into concrete details, you will come up against something of the same kind of vagueness that has always clung to Christian notions of heaven—in itself, perhaps, some evidence for the idea that the doctrine of progress is no more than a modern eschatology. Progress will lead us—and in the original, eighteenth-century notion of progress, will lead us very quickly, within a human generation or two—to a state in which men will all be happy, in which there will be no evil. This happiness is by no means just physical comfort. It is not inaccurate to say that in the eighteenth century most of those who talked of progress and the perfectibility of man were thinking in terms close to those of Christian, Greek, and later Hebraic ethics, of peace on earth to men of good will, of the absence of all the traditional vices, of the presence of the traditional virtues.

So much for the broad basis of a belief in progress on this earth. This progress was to be brought about by the spread of reason. Reason, to the ordinary man of the Enlightenment we are attempting here to follow, was the great key word to his new universe. It was reason that would lead men to understand nature (his other great key word) and by understanding nature to mold his conduct in accordance with nature, and thus avoid the vain attempts he had made under the mistaken notions of traditional Christianity and its moral and political allies to go contrary to nature. Now reason was not quite something that came suddenly into existence about 1687 (this is the date of the publication of Newton's *Philosophiae Naturalis Principia Mathematica*). It must be admitted that there were intolerant modernists who came very close to holding that everything prior to about 1700 was one huge series of mistakes, the blundering of an awkward man in a darkened room; but our average enlightened intellectual was inclined to credit the old Greeks and Romans with having done good spade work, and to believe that what we call the Renaissance and Reformation had begun once more the development of reason. It was in the Church, and especially in the medieval Catholic Church and its successors, that the enlightened found the source of darkness, the unnatural suppression of nature—in short, the Satan every religion needs. To this matter we shall return, for it is of great importance. For the moment, we can register the fact that the man of the Enlightenment believed that reason was something all men, save a few unfortunate defectives, were capable of following; reason had been suppressed, perhaps even atrophied, by the long rule of traditional Christianity. But now, in the eighteenth century, reason could once more resume its sway, and do for all men what it had done for men like Newton and Locke. Reason could show men how to control their environment and themselves.

For reason could show men how nature worked or would work if men ceased impeding that work by their unnatural institutions and habits. Reason could make them aware of natural laws they had in their ignorance been violating. For instance, they had been trying by tariffs, navigation acts, and all sorts of economic regulations to "protect" the trade of their own country, to secure for their country a larger share of wealth. Once they reasoned on these matters, they would see that if each man pursued his own economic interest (that is, acted naturally) to buy most cheaply and sell most dearly there would be established by the free (natural) play of supply and demand a maximum production of wealth. They would see that tariffs, and indeed all attempts to regulate economic activity by political action, made for *less* production, and could benefit only a very few who thereby got an *unnatural* monopoly.

Or again, men had been trying for generations to drive out or exorcise the demons they believed had somehow got into the insane. They whipped the poor insane people, they tied them down, they went through all sorts of ritual performances to drive out the demons. But reason, working on the problems of religion, could show men that there are no such things as demons; and working on the level of medical and psychological research, it could show that insanity was a natural (if regrettable) disturbance of the mind (and perhaps body), a *disease*, in short, which might be cured or at least alleviated by further use of reason.

Or finally, men and women had for centuries joined monastic orders, taken vows of chastity, obedience, poverty, and lived out their lives as monks and nuns. Reason would show that, though originally monks had perhaps cleared fields and drained swamps, though still perhaps they occasionally did some useful work, on the whole monasticism meant a great waste of human productive power; even more clearly, reason would show that it was most unnatural for healthy human beings to abstain entirely from sexual intercourse, and that theological justification for such unnatural behavior was as much nonsense as was the idea of demons possessing the insane. When reason got through with monasticism, that institution was seen as a typical example of bad beliefs, bad habits, bad ways of doing things; monasticism would disappear in the new society.

All this added up to the enlightened man into a system that explained the universe. For that system we have already noted the useful term "Newtonian world-machine." It was a machine which, especially as it concerned human relations, the enlightened were only beginning to understand. Thanks to Newton and his predecessors, they understood the solar system, gravity, mass, and in fact in its broad lines all natural science; research was needed only to fill in the details. But as to human relations, though they knew enough to know that their unenlightened predecessors, under the influence of traditional Christianity, had been all wrong about human relations, had indeed built up a system of laws and institutions inadequate at best, vicious at worst, they had as yet not quite attained their Newton. He was, however, just around the corner, this Newton of social science, the man who would sum up our enlightened knowledge into a system of social science men had only to follow to ensure the *real* Golden Age, the *real* Eden—the one that lies ahead, not behind.

Traditional Christianity could no longer provide a cosmology for the enlightened. There was beginning to be enough geology so that the date of creation—4004 B.C. according to Archbishop Ussher—and the story of the flood came to seem more and more unlikely. But there was no need to wait for the growth of geological knowledge. Take the Christian doctrine of the Trinity. Mathematics was against that: In no respectable arithmetical system could three be three and at the same time one. As for miracles, why had they stopped? If you could raise the dead in the first century why not in the eighteenth? And so on, in arguments nowadays familiar enough, but then fresh and daring.

Those whose faith in traditional Christianity was shaken, however, did not at once do away with the idea of God. Most of the enlightened in the first half of the century, including such great figures as Voltaire and Pope, were, at least publicly, deists. Now deism is a fairly definite and concrete belief about the universe, and save in some polemics of the time and since, is not a synonym either of atheism or of skepticism (agnosticism). *Deism* needs to be distinguished from *theism,* which involves a more personal God, a God not necessarily anthropomorphic, but at least in some senses immanent, capable of being prayed to; from *pantheism,* which has God penetrate every particle of the universe; and from *philosophical idealism,* which talks of spirit (*Geist*) rather than God. Actually your deist is very firm about the existence of God, remote and chilly though this God be. The deist's belief is the neatest possible reflection of Newton's orderly universe, spinning around according to law. The deist's God is the person responsible for planning, building, and setting in motion this world-machine: for how can one have a machine without a maker, a result without a cause? In technical terms, the deist proved the existence of his God by two very old arguments, the argument from a First Cause, and the argument from Design. But once this necessary God had got the world-machine to running, he ceased to do anything about it. This clockmaker God had made his clock-universe, wound it up for eternity, and would let it run for eternity, according to the laws Newton had just made clear. Men in this universe are on their own. God has designed them as part of his machine, and has arranged for them to run on, but with the special gift of getting to know by the use of their reason just how they run. Clearly there is no use praying to this clockmaker God, who could not if he would interfere with his own handiwork. Clearly this God never showed himself to Moses on Sinai, never sent his only begotten son to earth to redeem sinful men—couldn't possibly have such a son.

He seemed, in fact, a by no means necessary God, a sort of do-nothing God. That men should have set up so emotionally unsatisfactory a God at all is an interesting example of the way intellectual changes have to proceed slowly. The jump from a Christian God to no God was simply too great. But deism was one of the unsatisfactory kinds of compromise, as inadequate intellectually as emotionally. Voltaire's own famous epigram about his God—"if God did not exist, he would have to be invented"—betrays a fatal weakness. The radicals of the next generation saw no need to invent him. They were already familiar through mathematics with the concept of infinity. The world-machine had always existed and would always exist, at least as far as mere men could tell. How could anyone possibly know that a God as remote as that of the deists existed? If he was altogether outside the created universe, how could he be inside, even inside our minds as a conception? Clearly he was not necessary. Nature was enough—this great universe we should never have enough time to study in its entirety. Let us stop worrying about God, and make ours a religion of reason, a system of ethics without all the nonsense of theology.

Such at least was the view of the milder rebels, materialists who found God unnecessary. Others went beyond them, and found God a positive evil, especially if he were the God of the Roman Catholic Church. They proudly called themselves atheists, men without a God. Theirs was no longer a doubt. They knew the Christian God did not exist; they knew the universe was a system of "matter" in motion, which could be fully understood by the use of human reason along lines established by the natural sciences. Their materialism, their atheism was a positive belief, not a form of skepticism; it was a definite form of faith, a kind of religion. This positive belief in a knowable universe ultimately composed of particles of matter has remained ever since an element in Western culture. And yet no one knows at all accurately how many people have accepted, and still accept, some form of this belief.

Deist and atheist both rejected the organized Christianity of their day. The eighteenth was the great century of anticlericalism, the century when all kinds of hostilities and grievances against Catholic and Protestant Christianity could come out in the open, thanks to the "spirit of the age" of the Enlightenment, to cheap printing, to lax censorship, to inefficient police, to the amused approval with which the old ruling classes greeted these attacks on the established religion. What was legal in those two amazingly free countries, England and Holland, was readily bootlegged into France and the Germanies. For the first time since the Roman Empire, Christianity felt itself under heavy attack within its own culture. By the time of the French Revolution, that attack was to attain an extraordinary bitterness, especially in continental countries, and Christians were once more to suffer martyrdom for their faith, this time on the guillotine.

All the faithful of the new religion of reason, deist and complete materialist alike, even though they dismissed the Christian God, had to contend with the problem of evil. It was a very knotty problem for them. They postulated a world-machine, of which man is definitely part, which runs according to the laws of nature. They further postulated a faculty in men, which they called reason, by the exercise of which men could understand these laws of nature, orderly and just laws, and by conforming in their conduct to these laws of nature could live together peaceably and happily. Yet as they looked about this world of the eighteenth century they saw strife and misery everywhere, they saw all sorts of evils. Were these evils in accord with the laws of nature, benign nature? Of course not, they were most unnatural, and the enlightened were naturally at work rooting them out. But how did they get there? How did the unnatural get to be the natural? How did the higher become the lower? This difficulty had already been encountered in Christianity. But

Christianity has at least its Satan, however difficult it may be to reconcile Satan's existence with God's goodness and omnipotence. Those who accepted the cosmology of the Newtonian world-machine had still graver difficulties in introducing, or at any rate in justifying, their obvious desire to change, to improve, something that was already perfect, automatic, determined. In fact, in no monistic naturalism is it easy to slip in the unnatural. Rousseau himself was no admirer of the Newtonian world-machine and of reason. The nature he found at the bottom of all things was the spontaneous, outgoing, loving-kindness of the heart as displayed by simple and uncorrupted persons, such as children, savages, and peasants. Above all, he found this state of nature in the past, before civilization brought corruption. In his *Discourse on the Origin of Inequality* Rousseau attempts to describe the origin of evil. The first man who dared to take from the common ownership a plot of ground, fence it in, and say "this is mine!"—he is the villain responsible for the end of the state of nature. Rousseau does not explain *why* this child of nature acted so unnaturally.

If the enlightened could not solve the problem of the origin of evil, they had very firm ideas about good and evil in their own time. Evil they considered to be a historical growth embodied in customs, laws, institutions—that is to say, in the environment, especially in the social environment, in what man had made of man. The physical environment they realized, especially after Montesquieu's *Spirit of the Laws,* was often harsh and barren, or too easy and luxurious; and they knew that certain diseases were apparently not wholly the result of the social environment. But they hoped they could master the physical environment; indeed they hoped they could master the social environment. The social environment of their own time they thought was almost wholly bad, so bad that perhaps it would have to be destroyed root and branch. They did not, for the most part, believe that this destruction would be violent. They foresaw a French Revolution, but not a Reign of Terror.

In a general view, the "average" enlightened person (not, we repeat, such complex and subtle persons as Voltaire, Diderot, or even Rousseau) equated evil with the environment, and good with something innate in human beings, with human nature. Man is born good; he is made bad by society. The way to make him good again is to protect this natural goodness from the corruption society brings with it. Or more tangibly, the way to reform individuals is to reform society. Reason can show us how; every law, every custom, every institution must be submitted to the test of its reasonableness. Is a hereditary nobility reasonable? If it is not, we must abolish it; if it is, we must retain it. Hereditary nobility when examined by reason as reason worked in the minds of most enlightened men at least by the 1780's turned out not to be reasonable. One of the first acts of the French National Assembly called to remake France was to abolish nobility.

We have come up against one of the great forms in which ethical and political problems present themselves to modern men, the form we all know as environment versus heredity. Occasionally someone will announce firmly that he finds war and its attendant sufferings and cruelty a Good Thing, and someone else will complain that our physical comforts are a Bad Thing. But men in Western society are mostly agreed on the broad lines of what they find good and what they find evil. Where they differ is in their explanation of the persistence of evil. The Enlightenment and we ourselves as heirs of the Enlightenment push the emphasis over onto the side of environment; we tend to believe—most Americans tend to believe—that if we can only work out the proper "arrangements," laws, institutions, above all education, human beings will get along together in something pretty close to the good life. Christian tradition tends to push the explanation over onto the side of human nature; men are born with something inside them that makes them incline to evil; they are born in sin. It is true that Christianity sees a way out in the possibility of salvation Jesus brought us, but this is not quite environmentalism, not quite faith in the possibility of passing laws and working out educational curricula.

Now it is important to realize that even in its most hopeful early phases modern environmentalism did not usually go to absurd extremes. Only a madman would assert that any infant taken at random from a number of newborn babes could by the manipulation of his environment be made into anything at all—into a heavyweight boxer, a great musician, or a great physicist. Eighteenth-century psychology, taking its cue from Locke, did indeed think of the human mind as a blank receptacle into which experience poured the content of life; but not even the psychology of the *tabula rasa* interpreted human equality as human identity. More characteristic of eighteenth-century environmentalism is a statement by one of its younger sons, the socialist Robert Owen:

> Any general character, from the best to the worst, from the most ignorant to the most enlightened, may be given to any community, even to the world at large, by the applicaion of proper means; which means are to a great extent at the command and under the control of those who have influence in the affairs of men.

Here the key word is "general." Owen does not think he can achieve certain specific results with each individual; he does think he can do so for large groups. After all, is this very far from the notions that lie behind all efforts to influence and condition peoples today?

In fact, a belief in environmentalism is still essential for all who hope to bring about fairly rapid and *extensive* changes in the actual behavior of human beings on earth. There are few today who believe such changes can be accomplished by the intervention of a supernatural power, by religion in the traditional sense. And only the crank could believe that quick results are possible by any eugenical manipulation of the human organism. We cannot *breed* better men and women fast; we shall have to *make* better men and women from our present materials. Let Owen speak again with the optimism of the Enlightenment, undimmed in him by the horrors of the French Revolution and the Napoleonic world wars:

> These plans must be devised to train children from their earliest infancy in good habits of every description (which will of course prevent them from acquiring those of falsehood and deception). They must afterwards be rationally educated, and their labour be usefully directed. Such habits and education will impress them with an active and ardent desire to promote the happiness of every individual, and that without the *shadow of exception* for sect, or party, or country, or climate. They will also ensure, with the fewest possible exceptions, health, strength, and vigour of body; for the happiness of man can be erected only on the foundations of health of body and peace of mind.

The Program of the Enlightenment

The men of the Enlightenment were not quite so unanimous as they have seemed to be up to this point in our analysis. Indeed, it is just at this point that the great division in their ranks, a division still by no means healed, comes out most clearly. Not all of the enlightened would have agreed that reason was against a hereditary nobility, and certainly not all the enlightened would have wished to do away with all class distinctions. Reason turned out in practice to have different ways for different men.

The great bifurcation in the ranks of the enlightened may be put as that between those who believed that a relatively few wise and gifted men in authority could manipulate the environment so that everybody, manipulators and manipulated alike, would be happy and those who believed that all that was needed was to destroy, cancel out, the existing bad environment, and that then everyone would cooperate spontaneously in creating the perfect environment. The first group, whatever lip service they may have given to the ideals of democracy and freedom for all men, were in fact authoritarians; in the particular background of eighteenth-century thought and institutions, they tended to pin their hopes on wise rulers and trained civil servants, on what historians call the movement for "enlightened despotism." The second group tended to believe that the ordinary man, the common man, the man in the street or the field, was a sound and sensible fellow, as well as the most numerous of mankind; they wanted such men to be free to follow their innate wisdom; they tended to believe in democratic methods, in voting by head, in majority rule; the more extreme of them were philosophical anarchists who believed that any government is bad, that men must abolish all government.

There is a very clear example of the reality of these contrasting posi-

tions in the career of one of the most influential of the philosophers of
the Enlightenment, Jeremy Bentham. Already as a young man Bentham
had worked out the neat, and to many most plausible, formula for his
utilitarianism: Everything should be done to secure the greatest happiness of the greatest number. Since he accompanied this formula with a
method, satisfactory to himself and his followers, of actually *measuring*
happiness, he had what he needed to provide a good environment to take
the place of the bad old one. He had the blueprints for a wonderful
job of social engineering.

Bentham's first notion was that the ruling classes of Britain, the great
lords and merchants he knew so well—he himself was of prosperous merchant stock, and a frequent guest of the intellectual Lord Shelburne—
would do his work for him. After all, these gentlemen read and talked
and were fully up to what was going on in the enlightened world. But
they had certain privileges under the old system—indeed it was clear that
the old bad environment seemed to them subjectively rather a good one—
and Bentham found he was not able to persuade them to adopt his proposed reforms. So, early in the nineteenth century he began to turn
toward the people, and before long had become a convinced democrat,
holding for universal suffrage, frequent elections to secure rotation in
office, and the rest of the machinery of democracy. He now believed that
the masses would make the changes the privileged classes could not be
persuaded to make. Of course, the masses needed teachers, needed leaders, and these were to be provided by a relatively small group of educated but not aristocratic followers of Bentham, the "philosophic
radicals." But these were to be a spearhead for democracy, not a privileged group of wise men monopolizing the work of government.

We wrote a moment ago of a bifurcation in the ranks of the enlightened. Unfortunately for the understanding of these matters, the human
mind rarely confronts such a simple choice as that between two tracks.
Indeed, the human mind can jump lightly from one path to another, until its course seems a maze. Our distinction between the environmental-
ists who trust to the manipulation of the environment by the few
(*philosophes,* engineers, planners, technocrats, brain trusts) and those who
expect the many to provide the necessary changed environment by the
democratic process of majority vote—this distinction is worth making, and
is one that will give us a first approximation, especially for the eighteenth
century. But at least one other simple dual classification, not quite identical with the first, is necessary here. This is the distinction between those
who believe that the new environment will exercise over ordinary men
a kind of compulsion—one they will get to enjoy but still something in
part external that ties them together in a disciplined group—and those
who believe that the new environment will in fact hardly involve institutions and laws at all, that men under the new order will spontane-

ously live up to the Golden Rule. The one point of view is authoritarian; the other libertarian, or anarchical.

In most matters the believers in enlightened despotism took an authoritarian position; for them the *old* authority, the Christian authority, was bad, not the *principle* of authority; authority in the hands of men trained to use enlightened reason was all right—was, in fact, necessary. Yet in economic affairs many of these authoritarians held that businessmen should be quite free to handle their own business, free from the restraints of governmental or guild authority. Actually what they defended even in economics was not freedom for all individuals, but merely freedom for the economic enterpriser, the industrialist. Within the little realm of the factory or other business, there is to be that organization, efficiency, rationalization so consonant with the authoritarian side of the Enlightenment. The same Robert Owen who stated so neatly the theory of environmentalism had himself been part owner and whole manager of a profitable textile mill at New Lanark in Scotland. New Lanark was for those days a model factory, surrounded by well-kept company houses, with excellent working conditions, and with Owen's own favorite experimental progressive schools available for the workers' children. But there was no "industrial democracy" at New Lanark. Owen's word was law; Owen manipulated the environment; Owen was the father in a most paternalistic system.

Bentham provides an even more typical example of the carefully contrived environment—contrived from above by the wise, fatherly authority. Bentham's basic principles are that men seek pleasure and avoid pain (note the apparent similarity to such concepts of physics as that of gravity), and that since this is a fact we must accept it as a moral good. The secret of government is therefore to devise a system of rewards and punishment such that socially and morally desirable action on the part of the individual results for him always in more pleasure than pain; and that socially and morally undesirable action should always bring him more pain than pleasure. Bentham went into great detail working out his calculus of pleasure and pain, classifying, weighing, and measuring various kinds of pleasures and pains. Of course what he did was to assign values such as a kindly, philosophical, serious-minded English gentleman would esteem. His ethics, like those of most Westerners in revolt against Christianity, turn out to be most Christian. But Bentham would not trust the ordinary institutions of society to measure out pain and pleasure properly. Somehow society was rewarding the actions that did not bring the greatest good to the greatest number, penalizing the actions that would do so if given a chance. But mere freedom wouldn't bring that chance. Men like Bentham would have to sit down and work out new devices, a new society.

Thus reason tells us that crime—say stealing—has to be punished because it brings more pain to the victim and, in the form of fear and anxiety more pain to everybody who knows of the theft (they are afraid it may happen to them) than it does profit to the thief. But reason tells us that notions of sin, damnation, penitence, and the like in relation to the theft are nonsense. We are dealing with a simple matter of bookkeeping. The thief must be caught and so punished that pain brought by the penalty will just barely outweigh in the thief's mind the pleasure (profit) brought by the crime. If the pleasure is greater than a very light penalty, the thief will be tempted to repeat the crime. If the pain is very much greater—if the punishment is extremely heavy as in the then criminal law of England—the thief will feel martyred, or crushed, or rebellious, and will certainly not be reformed. And the whole purpose of the law is by reforming the criminal to prevent repetition of the crime. So the punishment must be made to fit the crime.

Bentham's psychological detail seems to us nowadays rather naive, and the elaborate plans he makes, unworkable. But the reforming spirit we know well. Much of what Bentham and his followers tried to achieve in the reform of institutions has indeed been put on the statute books. No one is now hanged for stealing a sheep. We cannot quite hope for the sweeping results Bentham hoped for, but we continue to use many of his methods; and we continue, good democrats though we may be, to pin much of our hopes on institutional changes planned from above. The New Deal and the New Frontier both had a good deal of old Bentham in them (and note the typical implication that new is good).

Those on the side of liberty show a clearer split than do the authoritarians. There is throughout the century a current of thought, culminating perhaps in the *Political Justice* (1793) of the English radical William Godwin, which is a kind of lay antinomianism. Godwin held that men did wrong only because they tried to obey, and make others obey, fixed laws; if everybody did freely what he really wanted to do at each moment—and if all had been properly emancipated from prejudices, fanaticism, ignorance—then they would all act reasonably. No reasonable man would injure another, or try to amass more goods than he could use, or be jealous of anyone who did something he could not do. Godwin carried this doctrine of philosophical anarchism so far that he objected to an orchestra conductor's beating the time for the orchestra as a form of unjustified tyranny over the players; the players left to themselves freely would hit a natural rhythm and do better without a leader.

Anarchism even as an ideal has always seemed absurd to most men, yet it must not be dismissed as of no importance. At its extreme it is clearly of the lunatic fringe, but it is an ingredient in many less extreme views. As a goal, and as a kind of half-rejected hope, it has had its part not only in many kinds of socialism, but in our own democracy. As an ideal, it somehow keeps alive in our much-governed world.

There is, however, a better-trodden path that most of those on the side of liberty have taken—a path that has many branches, some of which have a disconcerting way of taking sudden one-hundred-and-eighty-degree turns toward authority. We shall have to examine a little more closely one of the famous documents in the history of pure political philosophy, the *Contrat social* of Rousseau (1762). This little treatise has been disputed over for generations. Some readers find it basically a document on the side of individual liberty; others find it on the side of authoritarian collectivism, one of the intellectual antecedents of modern totalitarianism.

Rousseau is at bottom grappling with the problem of political obedience. His earlier work, the whole bent of his disposition, lay toward what we have just called anarchism. "Man is born free," he writes in a ringing first sentence, "and everywhere he is in chains." Why? Because, answers Rousseau, he has had to exchange the state of nature for the state of civilization (never mind *why* he had to leave the state of nature—we have noted before in this book that there is no good logical or "rational" answer to the problem of evil). In the state of nature man obeyed no one, or if you prefer, obeyed his own whims and desires. Now in the state of civilization he must obey commands he knows do not stem directly from within himself. If, for instance, he is a slave, he has to obey a person like himself, a most degrading and unpleasant experience, indeed an unnatural and inhuman one. Even in existing eighteenth-century societies he has to obey laws he never helped to make, men he never helped select as his rulers. What is the way out?

You may have noted that Rousseau is at once attempting to analyze the psychological factors of obedience and to persuade his readers what kind of obedience is good and what bad. To use an approach he might not have approved, but one suitable to our day, we may say that men do not actually obey even in ordinary political routine unless they have managed to feel that they are not obeying another *human* will, like the slave obeying the master, but are obeying a higher will of some sort of which their own will is a part. This will Rousseau calls the *general will*. To the out-and-out nominalist the general will is, of course, a mere fiction. But no one can have had any sort of emotional participation in any group, from family to college to nation, without catching a glimpse of what Rousseau is groping for. The general will of Rousseau is created by the social contract; the social contract for him follows the Hobbesian pattern in that each member of a society enters into the contract with everyone else; the resultant group, however, does not turn government over to an absolute monarch as Hobbes would have it, but treats any governing authorities as its mere agents, dismissible whenever the general will thinks such dismissal best.

But how does this general will make itself known? After all, an individual's will can be apprehended by watching what he does. But who ever saw the United States, or listened to it? What sense does "the will of the American people" make, for those who won't be fobbed off with idealist metaphysics, but want to see or hear or somehow apprehend? Well, if in a national election one candidate gets 55 per cent of the popular vote and another 45 per cent, can't you say that the elected candidate represents the "will of the American people"? Or if the Congress is duly and freely elected, do not its votes represent the will of the people?

Rousseau would have answered with a firm "No!" to that second question. He believed in direct democracy, as in the old Greek city-state or a small Swiss canton, and thought that a big country like France could not be a real commonwealth with a general will. This denial that a big country can be a true state is a mere twist of Rousseau's mind, an interesting example of an almost Renaissance devotion to classical forms, something always pointed at in comments on Rousseau, but not of great importance. To the first question, granting that he would admit a nation of 175,000,000 could be a nation at all, Rousseau would have had to give an ambiguous answer: Yes, if the candidate who got 55 per cent of the votes *really* embodies the general will of the United States; No, if he does not. Rousseau has often been carelessly interpreted as supporting the theory that the will of the majority is always right. Actually he does no such thing.

We must add one more of Rousseau's terms to "individual will" and "general will"; this is "will of all." When a group makes a decision in any way, voting or applauding or even rattling shields as in Sparta, the general will is present if the decision is *right;* whereas the will of all, the mere mechanical sum of the selfish, unenlightened individual wills, is present if the decision is *wrong.* But who decides what is right and what is wrong? We are at a point we have reached before, a point where many human beings feel hopelessly lost. Clearly there is no litmus-paper test of right and wrong. You can perform no scientific "operational" test to distinguish the general will from the will of all. Rousseau writes as if he held that in a small group, say a New England town meeting, after full and free discussion, a decision by majority vote will in fact reflect the "sense of the meeting," will be the exercise of the general will. But not necessarily. The ultimate test is a transcendental one, a matter of faith.

You may find this confusing and much too philosophical, in a bad sense. But even though you refuse to follow Rousseau into the metaphysics of the general will, you should see that he is groping for a profound psychological truth. He notes that in a free democratic society those who had at first opposed a proposed measure voluntarily accept it when it becomes clear to them that it represents the general will. That is, the 45 per cent accept the wishes of the 55 per cent as *in fact,* for practical purposes, the wishes of the whole 100 per cent. Though this sounds sentimental to many deliberately hard-boiled persons, there is no viable democracy unless something approximating this process goes on. We may not quite accept the election of the man we opposed as the fulfillment of our "individual will"; yet if we refuse to accept that election at all we have become rebels, and if there are a lot of us in the same position we have a Latin-American republic at its caricatural worst, and not a stable democracy. The imaginative acceptance of something like what Rousseau means—part of the time at least—by "general will" seems necessary for the stability of any free society.

Rousseau's great ambiguity, however, lies just a step further on. By signing (even metaphorically, so to speak, by being born into a society) the social contract I give up my natural, simple liberty, and in return get the very great liberty of obeying the general will. If I didn't I should be rebelling against the right, I should actually be a slave of my own selfish will. In such a case to force me to obey is in fact to make me free. Rousseau puts it clearly:

> In order, then, that the social compact may not be but a vain formula, it must contain, though unexpressed, the single undertaking which can alone give force to the whole, namely, that whoever shall refuse to obey the general will must be constrained by the whole body of his fellow citizens to do so: which is no more than to say that it may be necessary to compel a man to be free. . . .

We have come a long way from the libertarian bias with which we started. The argument (or metaphor) is indeed an obvious one, which stands ready for anyone who wants to defend a restriction on individual liberty. Through various intellectuals like Kant and Herder it has passed into ordinary German belief, and has been used in one form or another by German authorities to justify obedience. It has always seemed a little dangerous to Western Europeans and Americans, has seemed to sacrifice the individual too completely to the state. But that Rousseau should have pushed his analysis to the point where he makes his general will sovereign and unimpeachable is an interesting example of where the human mind can go along the track of abstract thought. Rousseau as a person was an eccentric, an individualist, a man whose basic emotional objections to the pressure of organization of any kind on the individual remind one of Thoreau's; and yet here he is, at any rate in the passage quoted just above, one of the prophets of modern collectivist society.

There lies behind this ambiguity of the *Contrat social* another of those polar distinctions that we can analyze out of the whole experience of these eighteenth-century people. The ardent young follower of the Enlightenment in the 1780's did not pull his own ideas apart as we are trying to do. He was against the established order, against convention, against what he called error and superstition; he was for nature, reason, liberty, common sense, for all that seemed new and hopeful in this progressive world. But what gave shape to the new, the hopeful better things that were to take the place of the old? The formula we have hitherto encountered is reason, the kind of thinking that Newton did, the kind the *philosophes* were doing. But as the century wears on we begin to encounter new words, or old words with a new emphasis: sensibility, enthusiasm, pity, the heart. With the great vogue of Rousseau after 1760, the heart comes into its own against the head. No longer will reason be the guide, the architect of the new world; sentiment, feeling, will tell us how to work together to build anew. Reason begins to be suspect:

> If abstract reason only rules the mind,
> In sordid selfishness it lives confin'd;
> Moves in one vortex, separate and alone,
> And feels no other interest than its own.

We shall leave until the next chapters a consideration of the Romantic movement which, heralded well back in the eighteenth century by Rousseau and such English writers as Shaftesbury, came to be one of the main elements in the nineteenth-century view of life. For an understanding of the later Enlightenment, it is necessary to note that this turn toward emotion gave to concepts like "nature" a quite different coloring from that of the "nature" of the Newtonian world-machine. Nature was no longer the neat, the orderly, the mathematical; it was what "nature" still suggests to most of us, the external world untouched, or little touched, by men, untrimmed, untamed, wild, spontaneous, and quite unmathematical. Here we are concerned with the political implications of this change of base from classical nature to romantic nature.

You may hold, and be quite justified in holding, that the dichotomy between reason and emotion, between head and heart, is just one of the clichés of bad thinking. Thinking and feeling are not separable acts of human beings; our thoughts and our emotions are fused in our opinions. Nevertheless, simply as a working tool for analysis, the distinction is worth making. Here is a good concrete instance from the late eighteenth century, involving a problem still with us. The professional economists, by this time an established group with a respected, if new, discipline, could "prove" that poor relief and charity that gave the recipients a home and family of their own was bad for everybody, even for the recipients. When Malthus published his *Essay on the Principle of Population* in 1798, the arguments of the economists were rounded out: the more you did to soften the lot of the poor man, the more children he produced, the less there was to go around among workers, and the worse off they all were. The utilitarians took this up, and helped bring in a system of workhouse relief in Britain whereby the poor who had to have relief were segregated by sex in most unattractive poorhouses. The full logic might have led to letting the poor starve if they could not earn a living, but the West has never quite carried out the logic even of its economists.

We need not debate whether the reasoning of the economists in this matter actually is in accord with what "reason" should mean in our tradition. The point is that they claimed they were following reason—and their opponents accepted their claim. Their opponents said something like this: "We can't see what's wrong in your chain of reasoning. Perhaps the race would be better off if the incompetent were weeded out. But we can't take your argument. We're sorry for the poor man. We know you're wrong because we feel you're wrong. Perhaps the poor man is lazy, untrained, awkward, incompetent; but. . . ." The defense could go on indefinitely, and even when conducted by the purest partisans of the heart would certainly lapse into arguments, into reasoning; that is, the poor would be defended as having a right to the good life, or as actually being poor because they never had a chance (the environmentalist argument). Or the very modern argument might be brought forth, as it was by Robert Owen, that to raise the standard of living of the poor is to raise the demand for industrial mass production and to make possible steady economic progress. But the basic argument remained: We *feel* that the workhouse treatment is cruel.

Now, once more very roughly, the partisans of the head tended in the later Enlightenment to bolster the side of enlightened despotism, planning, and authority; the partisans of the heart tended to bolster the side of democracy, or at least of self-government by a numerous middle class, "natural" spontaneity, and individual liberty. But, as we noted above in contrasting thinking and feeling, these two are not separate strands, but combine in various strengths in our political attitudes.

The kind of American we call "progressive" or "liberal" has long been torn by the difficulty thus presented. His emotions, backed by the American democratic tradition, are strongly on the side of trusting the people, letting them decide after free discussion, letting them bring out that quality of being right that ordinary men in groups possess. He would like to believe in the people, to trust their judgment. On the other hand, his reason, backed by American intellectual habits, tells him that the man in the street is superstitious, has low tastes, is incapable of objective thinking of any great complexity, is driven by ungenerous and unlovely impulses. Again let us try to be concrete by example: The liberal would like to think that a few wicked Tory politicians, rich men, and misled intellectuals are responsible for Jim Crow in the South, but something keeps telling him that the real enemy of the Negro is the mass of whites, especially the "poor whites." From there he may go on to argue that the poor white fears the Negro because of economic institutions. Even so, he is, in dealing with a specific problem, faced with a real question: Do I or don't I trust the wisdom and good will of the common man? He can't be sure. His hesitation has deep historical roots, at least as far back as the Enlightenment.

The Enlightenment and the Christian Tradition

The ideas of the Enlightenment, whether they sprang from the head or the heart, or from both working hard together, were clearly corrosive of existing institutions. If you agree with Bacon's aphorism that "the subtlety of nature is greater many times over than the subtlety of the senses and understanding," you will see that any human attempt to think about social institutions has to *simplify* them. There results a neat pattern, or blueprint, compared with which the reality is always more complex, and therefore to many kinds of thinkers, less perfect. To put it more simply: Almost anybody can think of a better way than the actual one 'of doing something—running a club, devising an educational curriculum, coaching a football team, administering a government department—and can, as critic, point out the imperfections of what is actually done. Notably, if you hold that all things human should be conducted with the orderliness and clarity of the best mathematical reasoning, if you have just steeped yourself in Descartes, Newton, and Locke, you can be a most devastating critic of what goes on—even today. In 1750 you could perhaps find even more inefficiencies, irregularities, irrational survivals of the Middle Ages. Not only would the doctrine of the Trinity seem irrational to you; the fact that the actual size of a bushel measure, the value of a piece of money, would vary from town to town would offend your reforming zeal.

The eighteenth-century thinkers have indeed a somewhat exaggerated reputation as "destructive critics." More especially, they are accused of devotion to abstract thought, at the expense of attention to empirical detail. After the French Revolution had come to shock the civilized world with its violence, it became fashionable in conservative circles, and even in popular circles, to blame the philosophers of the eighteenth century for destroying the old regime with their criticisms and leaving nothing in its place. Into this nothing came the passions and imperfections of the real human beings the eighteenth-century philosophers had neglected in their preoccupation with the rights of abstract man. Edmund Burke led the attack on the philosophers of the Enlightenment, and it was continued by many nineteenth-century writers like Taine, who blamed the French Revolution on the simplifying, abstract *esprit classique*. French popular wit summed it up neatly:

> C'est la faute à Voltaire
> C'est la faute à Rousseau

(It's Voltaire's fault, it's Rousseau's fault!).

We cannot here go into this very vexed question, which has become one of the classical debates over the place of ideas in history, of the relative effectiveness of the kind of thinking the eighteenth-century philosophers did. We are inclined nowadays to doubt whether their writings could ever have weakened a society in other respects strong and well-organized; we tend to see them as *symptoms* of social disintegration rather than primarily as causes. But there can be no doubt that their writing served to focus men's minds and unite them on troubles that might otherwise have given rise to more sporadic and occasional protests. The philosophers of the Enlightenment sharpened men's sense of grievance by referring them constantly to a standard of right and wrong, to a *Weltanschauung* that dignified and intensified these grievances.

What must interest us now is a very big question indeed, a question we cannot fully answer: How is this world-view of the eighteenth-century Enlightenment related to that of traditional Christianity? Again, it would be easy to answer with a sweeping assertion of the identity of the two, or of their polar difference. Such answers have been given. To men like Burke, Joseph de Maistre, to all who focus their attention on the eighteenth-century doctrine of the natural goodness and reasonableness of man as a basic heresy, the Enlightenment seems as anti-Christian at heart as it was on the lips of violent anticlericals like Holbach and Helvetius; but to men like the Christian socialists of the nineteenth century, to our contemporary American liberal clergymen—John Haynes Holmes, for instance—the Enlightenment is a prolonging, a fulfillment, of what Christianity was meant to be. Here again the truth is complex. The world-attitude of the Enlightenment, of which we Americans are now the chief heirs and representatives, contains both Christian and anti-Christian elements mingled in a whole that, as world-attitudes go, is new.

At this point, a brief word of caution may be necessary. The word *skeptic* is sometimes loosely applied to men like Voltaire, to the writers of the great French Encyclopedia, to the whole attitude we have called the Enlightenment. That is, of course, a misuse of the word. The temper of the eighteenth century is not skeptical. It is anticlerical, positivist, at its extremes materialist. But the *philosophes,* if they disbelieved in traditional Christianity, believed in their own brave new world. Of course, large groups of men, even of intellectuals, are never skeptics. Skepticism is never anything like a mass movement; the Enlightenment was an intellectual mass movement of considerable scope. There is a small trickle of true philosophical skepticism from the Greeks on, though it dries up in the Middle Ages; the trickle flows again with the Renaissance, and produces in Montaigne the most famous and most charming of literary doubters.

In the eighteenth century there was indeed a very well-known professional philosopher, the Scot David Hume, who carried the Cartesian dilemma of thought and matter to a point at which skepticism has certainly begun. Hume was one of the most urbane questioners of revelation—his attack on miracles is still one of the great weapons in the armory of the anti-Christian—and of deism or "natural religion." But he had much company in this activity. Where he is more original is in his questioning the truth—in the sense of fixed, absolute, metaphysical certainty—of the generalizations the scientists had arrived at. Reason, as well as our senses, is for Hume subjective, or at least in no finally verifiable way a transcript or report of reality. Hume, like many other doubters of men's mental and moral capacities, found in custom, habit, tradition a firmer ground for life on this earth. He thus ended up in a position singularly at odds with that of his time, a believer in the old instead of the new. Yet he reads like one of the *philosophes;* he has the eighteenth-century touch in style; and his is a singularly dispassionate recognition of the place of passion in human acts. Hume is at bottom not so much the skeptic as the rather tired rationalist.

We need hardly repeat what we have brought up in other connections. The spirit of the Enlightenment is hostile to organized Christian religion. "In every country and in every age, the priest has been hostile to liberty. He is always in alliance with the despot, abetting his abuses in return for protection to his own." Thomas Jefferson is here, of course, using "priest" in a general sense to denote any minister of religion. His statement is by no means extreme, but rather in the center of a spectrum that runs from Voltaire's "Let's eat some Jesuit"—and there are more ferocious extremes than that—to the "natural religion" or deism of professing Catholics like Alexander Pope. The corrosiveness of the Enlightenment is nowhere clearer than in its attacks on Christianity.

Yet before we go on to the key problem of how much Christianity is left in the Enlightenment, how far Christianity survives in this modern faith, we must note that then as now many groups of Christians continued along the old ways, sometimes actively counterattacking in press and pulpit, sometimes quietly living out lives untouched by the new ways. The literature of the eighteenth century in the West is overwhelmingly on the side of the new Enlightenment; the names we remember, from Bayle and Voltaire to Jefferson and Paine, are on the attack. But all through the century little groups like the Bollandist monks went on in their lives of the saints with their pious but critical work as historians; the established churches continued to educate and to carry on their usual services. The masses and a good number of the middle classes and of the aristocracy continued all during these years to observe the ways of traditional Christianity.

In Britain and her American colonies and in Germany, a new form of Protestantism, by no means rationalist in bias, rose in the Methodist and Pietist movements. These movements were evangelical in their desire to bring peace on earth and do God's work; they turned ultimately, as so many Christians have done in modern times, to humanitarian goals; but they retained the essential other-worldliness of Christian tradition, and they were by no means revolutionary in their social and political outlooks. Indeed, we may note here parenthetically, as an example of the kind of hazardous but suggestive generalization one can draw from intellectual history, that historians like Lecky and Halévy have held that the popularity of Methodism among the British lower classes was a stabilizing factor that turned them away from the kind of revolutionary attitude that spread to the masses in France.

We confront, in short, in the eighteenth century as almost always in the Western world that range of opinion, that *multanimity* so characteristic of our culture. That multanimity seems to increase as we approach our own age, for to old ideas organized in old groups come ever newer ones. And so little dies—and what does die takes a very long time to disappear completely. They say there are still Englishmen who believe seriously that the rightful heir to the throne of Britain is one of the House of Stuart, driven out in 1688 for good. The Enlightenment we are striving to understand is then no totally new belief that supplants a totally old belief. It is rather a series of experiments, hunches, and attitudes old and new, another and very important ingredient in what to the despairing lover of peace, order and simplicity must seem the stew— the hash—of modern culture.

You can see the subtlety of the problem of how Christian the Enlightenment is if you will compare the attitudes toward nature and natural law of St. Thomas Aquinas and Adam Smith. The comparison is well worth making, because at first sight and in accordance with conventional formulas it is so easy to say that Adam Smith as one of the fathers of laissez-faire economics is at the opposite pole from the authoritarian economics of the just price, prohibition of usury, and the rest of the medieval formulas for economic relations. Of course, it would be silly to say that there are no differences between Aquinas and Adam Smith. But Smith is no anarchist, no believer in the natural goodness of man. He makes many qualifications even for the kind of economic liberty for the businessman that is the backbone of his system; he would not let free trade go so far as to leave a country without its own necessary resources in wartime. The kind of economic controls he objects to are those he finds contrary to nature, and of these by far the worst in his mind, indeed the central vice of the mercantilist system he was attacking, is *monopoly,* the artificial control the capitalist or group of capitalists favored by laws can establish over a product which by the natural play of supply and demand would be priced at a level as advantageous to society as possible in this world of sweat and scarcity.

Smith, like Aquinas, believes in a "just price"; and like Aquinas he believes that behind the apparently chaotic processes of individual buying and selling there is a natural order, to which men ought to conform. If they do not conform, it is to both Smith and Aquinas basically because some men will perversely attempt to upset the natural order in their own shortsighted interest. But the natural order is there, and it is a permitted Christian hope that men may learn to conform to it. It is true that for Aquinas nature prescribed certain social controls, amounting at times to price fixing, which were repudiated very specifically by Smith. Both doctors believe in a *vis medicatrix naturae,* a healing force in nature; they disagree on the amount of help nature needs, and on the best way of administering that help. They disagree, but not so completely as appears on the surface, on the nature of nature. But for both the great *unnatural* thing is monopoly, through which an individual or group of individuals can control a market in such a way as to benefit personally from an artificial scarcity.

Of formal parallels between traditional Christianity and the Enlightenment there are no end, for both are efforts, shared by many men and women, to give some sort of systematized set of answers to the Big Questions; both are systems of moral values, of ends and means, or, if you prefer, both are religions. These parallels are skillfully brought out in Carl Becker's *Heavenly City of the Eighteenth-Century Philosophers.* Becker's main point is that the faith of the Enlightenment has an eschatology as definite as that of the Christians, a heaven that stands ahead as the goal of our earthly struggle. The heavenly city of the eighteenth century is indeed to be on earth; but the important point is that it lies in the future—the near future, it is true, for men like Condorcet, but still not in the here and now. Men are indeed to enjoy it in the flesh (but remember that the resurrection *in the flesh* and the enjoyment of heaven are parts of Christian doctrine). It is not profitable to try to make out the concrete details of life in the hoped-for heaven. Perhaps the heaven of the Enlightenment is more fleshly, less spiritual than that of the Christians. But the essential part of each is the absence of evil, of frustration; the soul—and body—are happy in both heavens. To many Christians—to the most spiritual Christians—the above is, perhaps, a caricature of their heaven. Theirs is an indescribable ecstasy, and no mere negation. Yet, as with all mystic goals, theirs must seem to an outsider, a man of this world, to be a subduing, a canceling out, of what makes life worth living. And for the run of Christians, surely, heaven is no more than vague happiness, cessation of struggling, of *wanting.*

In both faiths the outcome is determined by a power stronger than any single man. Men can understand and adapt themselves to the designs of this power—indeed they must if they are to attain heaven—but they cannot alter the designs. That is to say, both religions, that of Christianity and that of the Enlightenment, are deterministic. And though both are deterministic, both in practice temper their determin-

ism for the individual with an ethics of struggle for the good and against
the bad, an ethics that leaves the individual at least the illusion of personal freedom. The Christian grace is paralleled by the philosophic
reason, Christian redemption by philosophic enlightenment. Even in
such matters as organization and ritual, the parallel is by no means far-
fetched. This comes out most clearly in the early years of the French
Revolution of 1789, when the Jacobin Clubs that embodied the new faith
took to an almost caricatural copying of Christian religious practices:
There were republican hymns, processions, love feasts, catechisms, even
a "republican sign of the cross." One of the most remarkable examples
of the survival of religious forms is found when professed deists indulge
in prayer, as they occasionally did. After all, the whole point about the
deist's clockmaker God is that he has set the universe in motion according to natural law and has thereupon left it to its own devices. Prayer
to such a god would seem peculiarly inefficacious, but in the hearts of
patriotic French Jacobins he is readily transformed into an avenging
God.

Still, the most striking thing traditional Christianity and this new
faith of the Enlightenment have in common is a feeling that man is no
misfit in this world, which is a world in some sense designed for man's
good living, and that, though something in man—for the Christian,
original sin, for the enlightened man of the eighteenth century, ignorance, faulty education, poverty, privilege, bad social environment—keeps
him from attaining the good life on earth, he can yet by a serious moral
and intellectual effort attune himself to this good element of design in
the universe, to God, Providence, or Nature. Both Christianity and the
faith of the Enlightenment are intensely active melioristic faiths; both
want to clean things up. Both want to clean up pretty much in the same
way; both have essential ethical goals, peace, moderate bodily satisfactions, social collaboration and individual freedom, a life quiet but not
dull; and both have the similar conceptions of evil, which, since they
are both fighting faiths, they probably make more of than they do of
good—cruelty, suffering, jealousy, vanity, selfishness, self-indulgence,
pride, all the long list we know so well.

Yet we must keep the balance. If the faith of the Enlightenment is
a kind of Christianity, a development out of Christianity, it is from the
point of view of the historical Christianity of the Middle Ages a heresy,
a distortion of Christianity; and from the point of view of Calvinism, a
blasphemy. The faith of the Enlightenment has no logical place for
a personal God accessible to human prayer, a God not bound by any
limitations, by any rules of the kind men discover when they study themselves and their environment. It admits no supernatural above the
natural. Partly because of its close alliance with natural science and
with abstract thinking generally, the faith of the Enlightenment tends to

be more rationalistic than even the most extreme of rationalist Christians, tends to make the mystic self-surrender of Christian experience impossible. Do not mistake here: The difference is not between "emotional" Christianity and "cold" rationalism; very strong emotions indeed have gone into the faith of the Enlightenment, and many rationalists are very feeling people; the difference lies in the *quality* of the emotion, and to a degree, in its *object*. Though the term is somewhat old-fashioned and simple, you can begin to formulate the difference if you think of the Enlightenment as less consonant with the emotions of the *introvert* than Christianity.

Again, it is by no means unimportant that the heaven of the Enlightenment is on earth—in the future, but on earth. The Enlightenment made its own the doctrine of progress, with its corollary doctrine of the perfectibility of man. Now from a sufficiently remote point of view you can maintain that both Christianity and the Enlightenment are much concerned with man's place in history, that both indeed have philosophies of history, and that both provide for a happy ending. But the doctrine of progress both simplifies and hastens, at least in the form it was held in the eighteenth century, the moral pilgrimage of man; it gives great emphasis to the material aspect of progress; and above all it expects progress to come from the liberation of naturally good and reasonable human beings from the restraints of law, tradition, convention, and authority, from most of what traditional Christianity had been at work building up for seventeen hundred years. It is this doctrine of the natural goodness of man that is, to the traditional Christian, the fundamental heresy of the Enlightenment. Its logical consequence is philosophical anarchy—the abolition of all external restraints on the behavior of the individual. As we have noted, no important eighteenth-century movement really pursued anarchy as a practical goal. But the slant remained in most progressive or democratic thought: The individual is right, the group wrong; freedom is a good in itself, discipline an evil in itself, or at best, unnecessary.

The Enlightenment promised heaven on earth, soon, and by a process that meant for the individual a "natural" release of expansive, appetitive forces within himself, not self-denial and inner discipline. Or at least, this is the easy, optimistic, vulgar side of the Enlightenment, the extreme of the Enlightenment, the immoderate side from which we can learn something of its weaknesses and dangers. Not all the enlightened were so naively optimistic. Still, the Enlightenment clearly did not come to promise blood, toil, sweat, and tears. We shall see what happened to the dream of the Enlightenment under the troubles that followed those hopeful earnests of Utopia, the American and the French revolutions.

CHAPTER FIVE

THE NINETEENTH CENTURY

I. THE DEVELOPED COSMOLOGY

Introduction

Such was the optimism of the early days of the French Revolution that many intellectuals thought there would be no more history. For to them history had existed only as a record of struggles, of slow upward progress through suffering. Now the suffering was over, now the goal had been reached, and there would need to be no history, since there would be no struggle and no change. Heaven has no history. At any rate, the past with its horrors had been overcome, and no one need be reminded of it again. Mankind was starting afresh. Condorcet, therefore, felt obliged to apologize for having any recourse to history in his account of human progress.

> Everything tells us that we have come to one of the great revolutions of the human race. What is more suitable for enlightening us as to what we should expect from that revolution, for providing us with a sure guide in the midst of these movements, than an account of revolutions which preceded and prepared this one? *The actual state of human enlightenment guarantees to us that this revolution will be a happy one;* but is this not on condition that we be able to make use of all our strength? And in order that the happiness which this revolution promises may be less dearly bought, that it may be extended more rapidly over greater space, that it may be more complete in its results, do we not have to study in the history of the human mind what obstacles we must still fear and what means we have to surmount these obstacles?

The author of that passage died a few months after he had written it, probably a suicide, perhaps from mere exhaustion, in the prison of a suburb of Paris, renamed during the Revolution Bourg-Egalité—Equalityville. A moderate member of the Convention, he was fleeing the wholesale proscriptions the triumphant extremists had directed against their enemies the moderates (events not unlike those described by Thucydides in Corcyra 2,300 years earlier). At the time, the Western world had just begun what was to be a world war of some twenty-five years, war into which even the virtuous and isolated new republic of the United States of America was to be drawn in 1812. The war was the costliest and bloodiest the human race had yet indulged in.

Into the course of the French Revolution—which was in its repercussions Western, not merely French—we cannot enter here. To its makers, as well as to its enemies, it was a proving-ground for the ideas of the Enlightenment. Here the experiment of abolishing the old bad environment and setting up the new good environment was actually made. The experiment produced the Reign of Terror, Napoleon, and a bloody war. Obviously something had gone wrong. Yet the intellectual leaders of mankind by no means drew the simple conclusion that the ideas behind the experiment were wholly wrong. They drew indeed many conclusions, and from these conclusions much of the nineteenth and twentieth centuries is understandable. We shall in the following chapters make a very rough division into those who, though shocked by the Revolution, continued to hold, with the kind of modifications suited to respectable middle-class people, the basic ideas of the Enlightenment; those who attacked these ideas as basically false; and those who attacked these ideas, at least as incorporated in nineteenth-century society, as basically correct, but distorted, or not achieved, or not carried far enough. Putting the matter in terms borrowed from politics, we shall consider the points of view of Center, Right, and Left.

Adjustments and Amendments in the New Cosmology

The firm ground of nineteenth-century common belief in the West remained the doctrine of progress. Indeed, that doctrine in the developed cosmology seemed even firmer than in the eighteenth century. The human race was getting better, growing happier, and there was no limit to this process on earth. With some of the concrete values and standards of this process we shall shortly have to deal. Here we may note that if the tragic events of the wars and revolutions at the end of the eighteenth century suggested that progress was not uninterrupted, not a smooth and regular curve upward, in the comparative quiet from 1815 to 1914 there was plenty of material evidence to confirm the belief in some sort of progress, perhaps irregular and uneven, especially in the field of morals, but still clear progress.

In the first place, science and technology continued an apparently uninterrupted advance. We have reached a stage in the history of science where we need hardly attempt any sort of chronicle. By the end of the eighteenth century Lavoisier's "new chemistry" had become simply modern chemistry, though Lavoisier himself suffered in the French Revolution a fate like Condorcet's. Geology too had come of age, and in 1802, according to the French lexicographer Littré, the word *biology* was first used. Though much had yet to be done in the biological sciences, it is true enough that by 1800 the broad bases had been laid, especially in taxonomic and morphological studies. Just before the middle of the century Auguste Comte made his well-known list of the sciences in the order of their command over their materials, and their "ripeness" or perfection. The older ones were in his eye the more complete, since their materials were easier to master. They run from mathematics and astronomy through physics and chemistry to biology and psychology. The "life sciences" even to Comte were not yet quite what they should be. There is one with which he ends his list, a science not yet born, but conceived, at least in Comte's ambitious mind, and which he christened, in a mixture of Latin and Greek that has always offended the classicists, *sociology*. The science of man was to be the crowning science.

It is more important for our purposes to note that this growth of the sciences was accompanied by a growth of inventions and of the business enterprise necessary to put them to use. Thus was strengthened an attitude Westerners began to hold early in the eighteenth century, a state of mind that welcomed and expected material improvements, faster travel, bigger cities, better plumbing, more varied and more abundant diet. Moreover, these were not just improvements for the privileged few; they were improvements everybody, even the humblest, could hope some day to share. There was a common pride in these achievements, a common expectation that they would go on, measurably, statistically, an attitude we Americans sometimes rather parochially think of as typically American, whereas it is typical of the Western world since the so-called Industrial Revolution. There were go-getters in England as well as in the Middle West. Liverpool in England was to all intents and purposes as new a city as its transatlantic namesake in Ohio. Almost everywhere in the Western world, you could see "things" multiplying around you. Whether or not it is progress, the fact of increasing human ability to produce usable goods was so obvious that no one could fail to see it.

In the second place, one could in the mid-nineteenth century make at least a plausible argument that there was moral and political progress. From 1815 to 1853 there was no important war within Europe and merely routine colonial wars. Slavery had been abolished in English colonies, and was about to be abolished in the United States. The serfs were freed in Russia. All sorts of good causes, from temperance to chastity, seemed to be making progress. Herbert Spencer could hope that women would soon rise above the use of cosmetics. Human life was valued, or at least preserved, in a way it had never been before. Cruel sports, cruel punishments, no longer made public appeal in the West. The kind of human behavior found in the witchcraft scare of the seventeenth century, a scare that took some of its worst forms in new-world Massachusetts, seemed quite impossible anywhere in the Western world in 1850.

The great contribution of the nineteenth century to the doctrine of progress is to be found in the work of the biologists. Darwin reaps—and deserves—most of the fame, but a long line of workers had for several generations been building up the notion of organic evolution. Geological research made it evident that life on this planet had been going on for a very long time, thousands, and then as the evidence came in, millions of years. Fossil remains seemed to show that the more mobile and nervously complicated organisms like the vertebrates came comparatively late, and that the earliest forms of life were, roughly speaking, the simplest. It looked from the record of the rocks as though life were on a sort of ascending scale through time, with man on the top. Thus as early as the late eighteenth century there was in the air—the air the intellectuals breathed—an idea of organic evolution. Progress had gone from the seashell to man. Darwin, like Newton, tied together in a theory that could be communicated to the ordinary educated man a mass of facts and theories derived from detailed studies.

Here is by no means the place to attempt an analysis of Darwin's theories of evolution. To the layman, who does concern us, these theories meant something like this. All living organisms are constantly competing with their own kind and with other kinds of organisms for food and space to survive. In this struggle for existence the individual organisms best adapted to get plenty of food and other good living conditions live on the whole best and longest, get the most sexually attractive and capable mates, and beget fit offspring like themselves. This adaptation is at bottom a matter of luck at birth, for organisms reproduce in quantity, and in that reproduction the offspring vary ever so slightly and apparently quite at random—one is a bit taller, a bit stronger, has a single muscle especially well developed, and so on. These lucky variations tend to be continued in the offspring, however, and thus a line, a species, tends to get established, more successful and better adapted to the struggle for life than the one from which it evolved. The organism *Homo sapiens* developed not from apes, but from earlier primates. Man has emerged from the struggle as Evolution's major triumph. This process is going on constantly, though very slowly. Man, with his brain, his upright posture, his hand, is at present apparently the favorite child of Evolution, of this cosmic process, but like other organisms the geological record tells us about, he may well *regress*, may fail as the dinosaurs failed, and be replaced by a fitter organism. Such, briefly, was the popular Darwinism of the Victorians.

Darwinian ideas are thus by no means necessarily optimistic. But those who accepted them for the most part found them full of hope. They seemed to make it quite clear that what is called progress is just as real as what is called gravity. They gave the sanction of natural science to moral and political ideas, much as Newton's ideas had done a century and a half earlier. It is true that with the publication of

Darwin's *Origin of Species* in 1859 one of the great conflicts between religion and science came to a head. Darwin's work, especially when spread abroad by determined disciples, seemed to many Christians not merely to conflict with a literal interpretation of the Book of Genesis but to deny that man is in any way different from other animals— except that the purely natural development of his central nervous system has enabled him to indulge in symbolic thinking and have moral ideas and "invent" God. The conflict has not yet wholly died out. In our time, and among intellectuals at least, it seems to be taking another form, a struggle whose catchwords are *humanism* or *the humanities* on the one hand, and *science* on the other.

Our chief interest here, however, is not the struggle over man's place in nature as it was fought out in the nineteenth century, nor even in the warfare of science and theology. The influence of Darwin's work spread over into philosophy, economics, and all the nascent social sciences. We shall encounter it again. Here we may note that organic evolution as Darwin and his followers brought it out was a very, very slow process indeed, so that all history from Homer to Tennyson was to time since the first Cambrian fossils as a few minutes to a year. The struggle for existence and indeed the whole armory of Darwinian ideas were far from suggesting a future of peace, cooperation, and absence of frustration and suffering. In short, the implications of Darwinism for morals and politics would seem to be rather against than for the hopeful tradition of the Enlightenment, which emphasized the possibilities of *rapid* change for the better. Yet the results of the whole process seemed most uplifting, and it is probable that Herbert Spencer was merely epitomizing the point of view of the average European and American when he wrote that Nature's discipline is "a little cruel that it may be very kind." Evolution not only seemed to the believer to provide an explanation of the way progress took place; it made that progress clearly inevitable and good.

Moreover, there were ways of reconciling even the harsher aspects of the Darwinian struggle for life with the humanitarian and pacifist traditions of the Enlightenment. The struggle for existence among lower organisms could be considered as somehow sublimated among human beings. "Nature red in tooth and claw" could, especially for the prosperous city-bred businessman, easily seem to have become peaceful and cooperative in the cultivated fields of Victorian England. Men competed now in productivity and in high conduct, not in the crude struggle of warfare. Still another interpretation, by no means without its dangers for the optimism of the Enlightenment, considered the Darwinian struggle in human life to be a struggle among organized groups, more especially nation-states, and not, or not primarily, among individuals within these states. Within the organization, within this *political organism* as these thinkers liked to call it, there prevailed co-operation, not competition. The competition was between Germany and England, say, not among Germans or Englishmen. Interpretations of this sort, even before Darwinian ideas were developed, were favored by almost all German publicists of the century, from Fichte to Treitschke. Their implications, like the extreme nationalism they are based on, are hostile to the whole eighteenth-century outlook, and are no mere modification of it.

Darwinian evolution was, however, for most educated men of the nineteenth century a clarification and a confirmation of the doctrine of progress, a strengthening of their inheritance from the Enlightenment. But it probably helped, as the century wore on, to add to the hold over their imagination of increasingly powerful ideas of national or racial superiority. The relation between the ideas of nationalism and the ideals of the Enlightenment is a very difficult one to analyze. The Enlightenment held all men to be equal, all differences such as those of color to be merely superficial and of no effect on human capacity for culture and the good life, and was therefore wholly cosmopolitan in its outlook. The nineteenth century fell into the trap of nationalist doctrines, betrayed its intellectual ancestors of the Enlightenment, and allowed the growth of that divisive nationalism from which we still suffer.

Let it clearly be understood that this contrast between cosmopolitanism and nationalism rests on certain general ideas of the eighteenth-century philosophers and certain other contrasting ones of nineteenth-century writers—between Lessing, say, writing his *Nathan the Wise* against race prejudice, and Gobineau, writing his *Essay on the Inequality of Races* in defense of race prejudice. In actual practice there is very little difference in the international relations, the international morality, of the two epochs. Warfare was the final recourse in both centuries, and diplomacy was hardly more virtuous in one than in another. It is not even true that the professions of the nineteenth-century diplomatists were nobler than those of their predecessors.

Nationalism is at bottom no more than an important form the sense of belonging to an in-group took in our modern Western culture. That culture has from its beginnings in ancient Greece had a richness of group life, from the family up to so huge and catholic a group as the Church of Rome in the Middle Ages. One of these numerous groups has been consistently based on a territorial political and administrative area, and on the kind of sentiments anchored in the word *motherland* or, more commonly in the West, *fatherland*. It would be extremely useful for a qualified student of history and the social sciences to study as amalgamations of ideas, sentiments, and interests this particular in-group feeling in a series of contrasting areas in space and time—fifth-century Athens, for example, imperial Rome, the France of Saint Joan of Arc, the France of

Voltaire, the France of the Third Republic. The researcher would un-questionably find differences, in the intensity and purity of the senti-ments of belonging to the national group, in the distribution of these feelings among social classes, in the extent and intensity of hostile feelings toward other national groups (out-groups), and so on.

He would also find similarities. This needs to be said emphatically, for nationalism is no sudden and new thing, a villain or devil that sprang out of the otherwise progressive, democratic, and peaceful culture of the Enlightenment. Nationalism is an age-old way of thinking and feeling focused as the result, in particular, of the formative first three centuries of the modern Western era (1500-1800) on certain territorial units. These units are not absolutely fixed, though most of them have been relatively firm throughout modern times—France, for instance, or to take an "oppressed" nationality, Ireland. No single outward test of nationality exists. Actually language is usually an adequate test, for the policy of those who govern modern nation-states has been to try to bring to the members of a national group the obvious unity a single language affords. In bilingual states like Belgium and Canada there is an evident stress and strain not found in otherwise comparable states like Holland and Australia. Switzerland remains the classic, and almost sole, example of a multilingual state that everyone admits is a true nation, a fatherland for its members.

The nation has been made by a most complex interplay of actual human relations for many years, often for many centuries. Modern liberals are fond of insisting that there is no physical, no physiological basis for nationalism, that no innate "national" characteristics, psychic or somatic, exist except in normal random distribution among the indi-viduals who make up nations like France, Germany, the United States. Frenchmen are not born with innate skill at making love, Englishmen are not born law-abiding and full of political common sense, Germans are not born blonds, nor with an innate feeling for authority. All this may well be true; but education and many more powerful molders of human sentiment and opinion have been at work for many years con-vincing people that national traits are facts of life. Nationalism may be the product of environment, not heredity, but a cultural environment established by a long historical development may be quite as hard to change as any physical traits.

Nationalism was unquestionably reinforced, in fact was given its characteristic modern form, as a result of the ideas of the Enlightenment and their interaction with the complex of human relations we call the French Revolution. In terms unduly abstract, perhaps, you can say that notions of popular sovereignty, democracy, the general will ac-cording to Rousseau, got translated into political reality as a justification for the sovereign nation-state. We have noted already that there is

behind the eighteenth-century rationalist language of Rousseau's *Social
Contract* a feeling for a group will transcending the nominalist limitations
of most eighteenth-century reason, a feeling that the political whole is
greater than the sum of its parts, a feeling not unfairly labeled mystical.
Specifically focused on a given national group, this mystical feeling
clothes the idea of nationality in symbols, ideals, shared by all its
members. Nationality is for its real zealots substituted for Christianity
and often for all other organized forms of group life. No doubt for the
average man nationalism is no more than one of the faiths that live
together in actual if illogical partnership in his heart and mind
(illogical in the sense that some of these faiths, say Christianity and
national patriotism, may have mutually incompatible ethical ideals).
Yet it is hard to exaggerate the extent to which for many modern Western
men the worship of the nation-state occupies a major part of their
conscious relations with groups outside the family. At least this statement holds for the nineteenth and early twentieth centuries. Since the
end of World War II there are good signs, especially in Western Europe,
that nationalism can be transcended by a whole people.

Indeed, the religious parallel we drew in the last chapter between
traditional Christianity and the "heavenly city of the eighteenth-century
philosophers" can be made even more concrete for the religion of the
fatherland. Here instead of a vague humanity to be bettered, instead of
fairly abstract ideas of "liberty, equality, fraternity," you have a definite
territorial unit organized with the full benefit of political power
behind it. Citizens can be indoctrinated from the very beginning so
that they identify themselves emotionally with the fate of the national
group. The ritual surrounding the flag, patriotic hymns, the reverent
reading of patriotic texts, the glorification of the national heroes (saints),
the insistence on the nation's mission, the nation's basic consonance with
the scheme of the universe—all this is so familiar to most of us that
unless we are internationalist crusaders in favor of a world-state or some
other proposed means for securing universal peace we never even notice
it. But if you want to realize how far this nationalist religion has gone
even in the United States, where it is not stimulated by any sense of
being nationally oppressed, any sense of wanting pieces of land we
haven't got, read the fascinating chapter on the cult of Lincoln in Ralph
Gabriel's *Course of American Democratic Thought.* You will find that
men have actually prayed to the dead Lincoln.

Nationalism, then, is one of the *working forms* the new doctrines of
popular sovereignty, progress, the perfectibility of man took in the
world of reality. Nationalism is congruous with many of the elements in
modern Western group life. Psychologically, it is congruous with the
rise to power of a middle class that lacked the cosmopolitan experience
and personal knowledge of other lands of a nobility, a class that found

the abstract devotion of the intellectual to all humanity beyond its range, a class for whom the nation stood ready to provide the enduring if vicarious satisfactions of "pooled self-esteem" (this last is the harsh definition the English humanitarian Clutton-Brock gave for modern national patriotism). Nationalism is wholly congruous with the facts of economic organization of the early and middle Industrial Revolution. Indeed nationalism, like all other phases of human relations, has been explained by the fanatics of the economic interpretation of history as wholly the result of the economic organization of the means of production in the early stages of modern industrial capitalism. If you feel the illumination of being right from such statements as that Waterloo was a conflict between British and French capitalism, probably nothing you read here will take away the glow. From our point of view, the profits obtainable through the nation organized as an economic unit—profits furthered by all sorts of acts within the frame of the nation-state, from standardization of weights and measures to protection of the flag in colonial trade—such profits and their implications reinforced what we call nationalism; they do not "explain" it.

Finally, nationalism on the whole got adapted to the generally optimistic cosmology of the eighteenth century as this cosmology filtered down to ordinary educated Westerners of the nineteenth century. This adaptation seems most neatly done, most fitly part of the kindly hopes of the Enlightenment, in the work of the Italian nationalist Mazzini. For Mazzini, the nation was an essential link in a chain that might be described as individual-nation-humanity. If *all* groups that feel themselves nations were free, then there would be no difficulties, certainly no wars, among them. It is only because the Italy of the early nineteenth century was under foreign rule, was cut up into artificial little units, that Italians showed hatred of foreigners. A free Italy would never make war or harbor hatreds. As Mazzini himself put it:

What is true for one nation is true as between nations. Nations are the individuals of humanity. The internal national organization is the instrument with which the nation accomplishes its mission in the world. Nationalities are sacred, and providentially constituted to represent, within humanity, the division or distribution of labor for the advantage of the peoples, as the division and distribution of labor within the limits of the state should be organized for the greatest benefit of all the citizens. If they do not look to *that* end, they are useless and fall. If they persist in evil, which is egotism, they perish: nor do they rise again unless they make atonement and return to good.

These ideas sound somewhat unreal in our mid-twentieth century, when men of Mazzini's idealist and crusading temperament are rarely nationalist—except, perhaps, in lands still subject to Western imperialist control. But it is one way in which nationalism can be reconciled with liberal cosmopolitan ideals. In an attenuated form, the average English-man or Frenchman probably made some such adjustment as this: Men are ultimately to be equals and brothers, and in the meantime the men of our nation can lead the less civilized rest to better things. But nationalism could be readily pushed into an attack on, rather than an amendment to, the ideas of the Enlightenment. The various brands of nationalism that exalted one national group into masters, all others into slaves, or which aimed at peopling the whole earth with one chosen group, the others having been duly killed off, were not consonant with the ideals of the eighteenth century. Of these anti-Enlightenment nationalisms the German variety that culminated in the Nazi faith is merely the best known and the most nearly successful.

Darwinism, we have noted, strengthened in the popular mind a belief in earthly progress, and was readily enough accommodated to the optimistic attitude of the Enlightenment toward human capacities. Nationalism could also be accommodated, at least in theoretical works like those of Mazzini, with the idea of a peaceful world of free men living rationally in mutual toleration—indeed, in mutual love. There is, however, a third great current in nineteenth-century intellectual and emotional life which presents much more difficult problems in relation to the prevailing attitudes of the "Age of Prose and Reason." However, even this current—the great "romantic" movement of revulsion against the culture of the eighteenth century which is one of the characteristic attitudes of the early nineteenth century—is in the broad perspective of Western history not really a sharp break with the Enlightenment, but for the most part, and in its effect on the attitudes of ordinary men and women toward the Big Questions of man's activities on earth, a continu-ation of the Enlightenment.

First, there is no doubt about the fact that the generation of the early 1800's looked back at its fathers with more than the usual modern Western contempt of one generation for its immediate predecessor. The young man wrapped up in Wordsworth shared all Wordsworth's own contempt for a writer like Pope, who seemed to him shallow, conceited, prosaic, no poet at all. The young Frenchman of 1816, perhaps born in exile, and now an ardent Catholic, felt a strong disgust for his aged grandfather, a Voltairean unrepentant, a hater of priests, a lover of good talk, good food, and bad women.

Put more abstractly and in the conventional terms of cultural history, to the classicism or neoclassicism of the eighteenth century succeeded the romanticism of the early nineteenth; to the materialism, the nominal-ism, the atomism of the Enlightenment succeeded the idealism, the emphasis on organic wholeness, of the late nineteenth century; to the deism, ardent atheism, occasional skepticism, and frequent anticlerical-ism of the eighteenth century succeeded the widespread revival of

Christian forms in the nineteenth. In short, the shift to romantic tastes is one of the classic examples of a rapid change in many phases of culture.

Now we do not wish to deny the reality of this change, nor the value of studying it—and it has had a great deal of study, especially from students of literature. The differences between a painting of Watteau's and a painting of Delacroix's, between a poem of Boileau's and a poem of Lamartine's, between a baroque church and a Neo-Gothic church, are real and important. Even more important is the shift in philosophy from the nominalist to the realist position or, if you do not take the toughness too seriously, from the tough-minded philosophy to the tender-minded. This very basic philosophical dichotomy, of course, extends as far back as ancient Greece. Like most dualisms, it breaks down into a bewildering range of variables under close analysis, yet it has its uses. We must pause a moment to outline the steps from eighteenth-century head-philosophy to nineteenth-century heart-philosophy.

The temper of eighteenth-century thought in the field of epistemology can be taken from Bentham, who may be on the extreme side, but is especially clear. For him the objects of sense perception are so real as to be not worth debating about. At the level of human relations, our senses make us aware of the existence of human beings, ourselves and others. That's all there is. Each human being is an individual, a social atom. Any grouping of such individuals is just a group of individuals; terms like "general will," "soul of a nation," and the like are pretentious nonsense. No group can feel or think or do what an individual can do. The whole is hardly even the sum of its parts. The whole (as in medieval nominalism) is in this case a fiction, a convenient fiction, but still a construct of the mind.

The movement away from this position is usually considered as having begun with the German philosopher Kant, whose productive period was the last half of the eighteenth century. Kant is a very difficult professional philosopher, probably for the average cultivated person today still the most typical and most representative of philosophers. For what the distinction is worth, he is probably in temperament and influence an idealist, a tender-minded thinker. But like Adam Smith in another field, he is by no means an extremist. Just as it was the nineteenth-century disciples of Adam Smith who carried doctrines of economic individualism to an extreme, so it is such disciples of Kant as the early nineteenth-century German Hegel who are out-and-out idealists. Kant, in spite of his vagueness and long-windedness, in spite of being so obviously on the side of the angels, is quite as obviously a child of the Enlightenment. He was disturbed by Hume's logical development of the Cartesian dualism of spirit and matter into skepticism about the conformity of human reason with an external world. He set out definitely to rescue philosophical certainty and did so to the satisfaction of many people. Briefly, he agreed with Hume that receptor experiences (*Sinnlichkeit*) and understanding (*Verstand*) could give us only contingent, changing, uncertain judgments. But he found in reason (*Vernunft*) the certainty he was looking for. Reason he saw as of two kinds, *practical reason,* which tells us infallibly through our moral intuition what is right and wrong in a given situation, and *pure reason,* which somehow or other makes valid judgments in a way mere ordinary calculating cannot make. Obviously the distinction between *Verstand* and *Vernunft* is of a piece with the earlier ones between *dominium* and *proprietas,* or *substance* and *accidents*—that is, a distinction made on criteria different from those the scientist uses, probably different from those common-sense uses, and certainly different from those the nominalist uses.

Vernunft had a magnificent career in a line of German philosophers from Kant through Fichte and Schelling to Hegel. We may here concentrate on Hegel, who is the best known of them, in many ways a very typical specimen. Hegel's *Vernunft* is a communication from the world-spirit, from the immanent, almost Spinozist God or Supreme Reality that rules the world. Now Hegel, as you can judge from one of his most quoted principles, that the real is rational and the rational real, was caught in a difficulty other idealists had had before him. His countryman of the end of the seventeenth century, Leibniz, had come to the conclusion, so bitterly attacked by Voltaire in *Candide,* that this must be the best of all possible worlds. We have noted that for the theologian who posits a God all-knowing, all-powerful, and all-good, the problem of the origin of evil is rather tough. These philosophers, however, are not really theists, nor even deists, however much they use the word God; they posit a principle, a spirit, a *Geist* (nothing the senses of men can get at directly, as in seeing or smelling) which is, so to speak, the power that moves the whole universe, from mice to men. But they run into a difficulty much like that of the theologians; the world-spirit has to do what it does, and therefore whatever is, is right, or it wouldn't be. This sort of argument is very offensive to many men, and often annoying even to the thinker who makes it.

Hegel was no fatalist, but a patriotic German who wanted some things on earth different—wanted, for instance, French ways disesteemed and German ways esteemed. He got out of his logical difficulties—or thought he did—by having his world-spirit go to work historically, in time, on a plan that was perfect, but not static. The process, which Hegel's part-disciple Karl Marx made even better known, was called the *dialectic.* The spirit sets up a thesis, say Greek liberty. That *thesis* somehow rouses up its exact, polar, antithetical opposite, in this example,

Oriental despotism, the *antithesis* of Greek liberty. Thesis and antithesis, embodied in human wills and appetites, fight it out in a gorgeous set of struggles designed by the world-spirit, and out of these struggles finally comes the *synthesis,* in this example, German *disciplined liberty.* Here is a somewhat unfair specimen of Hegel's ideas and methods—unfair since it deals with concrete facts most of us assume are not really illuminated by the kind of thing Hegel does:

> The typical crystal of the earth is the diamond in which every eye delights, recognizing it as the first-born son [synthesis] of light [thesis] and gravity [antithesis]. Light is abstract, completely free identity—air is the identity of the elementary; the subordinate identity is passivity in respect of light, and this is the transparency of the crystal. Metal, on the other hand, is opaque because in it the individual itself is concentrated into an existence for itself through high specific gravity.

The synthesis is not a compromise between thesis and antithesis, not an averaging out of the difference between them, but a brand-new thing, born of exhilarating struggle. It is true that Hegel seemed to think that the Prussian state of his professorial maturity was the end of the process, the perfect synthesis. But for us the important point to note is that even formal philosophical idealism, which tends to emphasize the static over the dynamic, the unchanging over the changing, seemed in this nineteenth century to have to accommodate itself to strong feeling for time, process, change, progress, evolution.

What is more important for us than the details of these idealistic philosophies is the fact of their success. In Germany they had the dominant position from the start of the century. In England, and especially in academic circles, they gradually overcame the resistance of the strong tradition of British empiricism, and by the end of the century T. H. Green, Bradley, and Bosanquet, idealists all, were certainly the most conspicuous of professional philosophers. In the United States echoes of Josiah Royce's idealism sounded from hundreds of chairs and pulpits. Idealism had even invaded France, that land of simple, prudential logic, where the language couldn't readily distinguish between *Verstand* and *Vernunft.* (Neither can English, though S. T. Coleridge translated *Verstand* as "understanding" and *Vernunft* as "reason.") Naturally, in a century of so much intellectual freedom as the nineteenth, no philosophical school had things all its own way. Various forms of materialism, positivism, pragmatism, and other deliberately tough-minded philosophies flourished, even in Germany. Indeed, the English thinker Herbert Spencer attempted a kind of *summa* of nineteenth-century evolutionary, scientific materialism, and was for several generations a kind of culture-hero for "advanced" people generally.

Now it is clear that the ordinary educated person—and by the late

nineteenth century there were millions of them in the Western world—
had in the hundred years that followed the American and the French
revolutions changed his intellectual garments considerably. We have
just emphasized the change in formal academic philosophy, from say
Locke or Bentham to Hegel and Bosanquet. You may argue that formal
philosophy has never had great influence on even educated laymen;
and you can add to that argument the special fact that by the nineteenth
century philosophy was getting to be a very specialized and academic
subject, cultivated almost wholly by professors, and thus even more
cut off from ordinary educated people. But there are all sorts of other
tests, art, literature, religion, and in all these the men and women of
the nineteenth century tended to look down on their forefathers and
mothers of the eighteenth as shallow, prosaic, superficial people who
never really felt or thought deeply, who never lived life whole.

Yet these differences pale before the fact that both centuries shared
the essentials of the modern cosmology; both believed in progress here
on earth, both believed that something radical can be done about all
sorts of arrangements here that will increase happiness and diminish
suffering; both were at bottom optimistic and melioristic. The romantic
and idealistic elements in the nineteeth-century revulsion from the
eighteenth ought in strict logic, perhaps, to have made optimistic belief
in human perfectibility impossible. The revival of emotion, imagination,
of a feeling for organic wholes ought to have made laissez-faire individualism, simple, innocent attachment to schemes for reform, very
high expectations of radical change in human behavior, much less
common. Some did draw some such consequences from the revolt
against the age of prose and reason: there is a note of pessimism unmistakable in the work of most of the great Victorian writers. But the
man-in-the-street did not. Nature might for the nineteeth century stand
for wild scenery, savage joys, unplanned exuberance, instead of the quiet
fields, conventional art, order and uniformity that seemed "natural" to
the eighteenth. But Nature was in both centuries a comforting ally of
man, just on the point of overcoming once and for all his unnatural
enemies. Lewis Morgan, the American anthropologist, sounds in 1877
almost like Condorcet a century earlier:

> Democracy in government, brotherhood in society, equality in rights and
> privileges, and universal education, foreshadow the next higher plane of so-
> ciety to which experience, intelligence and knowledge are steadily tending.

The Victorian Compromise

There is, of course, a grave difficulty in attempting to outline the
world-attitude of the "average" Westerner of the nineteenth century in

the fact that averages don't live. Moreover, the multanimity we know in the twentieth century is also a fact of the nineteenth. Still, the nineteenth is the great century of English power and prestige. The Englishman set the tone even for those "lesser breeds" who hated him. The ordinary Englishman of the middle classes is the most successful, most hopeful, in many ways most representative of *Homo sapiens* in the last century. He is the obvious heir of the Enlightenment, but he has experienced to the full the various winds of doctrine hostile to the Enlightenment. He led the fight against the French Revolution. His poets, preachers, artists, all welcomed the new depths of feeling the romantic movement brought. His traditions were definitely not on the perfectionist side, not encouraging to those who hoped very much for rapid, planned change in human behavior. He was the great beneficiary of the Industrial Revolution, a member of the greatest and richest nation-state of a competing world of nation-states. His patriotism need show no touch of the inferiority complex, for the Englishman was on top of the world. What he did to the heritage of the Enlightenment is worth investigating.

The Englishman believed in material progress. Indeed, all over the Western world men now took it for granted that enterprise and invention would produce ever more and more conveniences. Utopias now came fully equipped with gadgets that often enough were ultimately put in production. Thus the American Edward Bellamy, whose *Looking Backward* (1889) is the best known of these mechanical paradises, has his Rip Van Winkle hero marvel at a device whereby a push of a button floods the room with music. The prophets were occasionally wrong, however; in the first flush of enthusiasm over railroads Macaulay predicted that in the twentieth century there would be no more highways or streets, for everything would move on rails. Our Victorian took material prosperity in his stride. He was not ashamed of being comfortable, and was not greatly worried over the aesthetic inadequacies of the products of the machine. He knew that there were artists like Ruskin and Morris who thought that these cheap, machine-made goods were deplorably ugly, but there is no sign that this knowledge lessened his buying.

The Victorian was quite sure he knew why this material prosperity had come to Great Britain. The British people, he believed, were especially gifted with initiative, hard-headedness, inventiveness, and love of hard work; they had, in short, the necessary human qualities to prosper. But they also had, he believed, a set of institutions, social and political ways of doing things, essential to giving these gifts free play. We have come to the great Victorian belief in the economic doctrines of laissez faire. It is not, of course, that businessmen were all economists. But Christians are not all theologians. We have here, in fact, one of the classic instances of popular adoption of doctrines worked out by the intellectuals. Economics is the most developed of the social sciences; it has its own history, which needs for coverage a volume larger than this. We have hitherto encountered it but casually; in the nineteenth century, however, notions of how properly to conduct the production and distribution of wealth, not merely common-sense or traditional notions about a given way of making a living, but a fully developed theoretical scheme with political and ethical consequences, come into general circulation. In short, there is in the Victorian cosmology a strong economic component.

The fundamental doctrine is simple. Individuals, or freely associated individuals in joint-stock companies or the like (but not, for the typically nineteenth-century man, in trade unions) should try to make, buy, and sell whatever they wish and in any way they wish. Prices and standards will be set by the free play of this competition in accord with the law of supply and demand (a law your Victorian thought was essentially like the law of gravity). From such competitive processes by a law of nature would come a maximum of goods distributed with a maximum of social justice, each man getting essentially what his talents and his work had earned. Economic activity should go on almost without any participation by governmental authorities. Businessmen do, however, need at least to have some fixed contractual arrangements, and, though their selfish acts are usually excellent in their effects on society, some businessmen do occasionally overreach themselves. Fraud must be combated, and agents of government are needed to enforce contracts. No positive regulation by government, however, such as the establishment of minimum wages, should be permitted to interfere with the harmony of nature. There is indeed a corollary in classical economics, clear already in the work of Adam Smith: Monopoly, the control of any market by any single business organization, is the greatest of evils. But many of the classical economists and their followers, good children here of the Enlightenment, believed that actually monopolies were the *creation* of governments, the results of licensing, chartering, and so on; they believed that businessmen left to themselves would not voluntarily create monopolies of their own, though Adam Smith, with his usual good sense, could not help noticing that whenever merchants get together they try to combine, to form a monopoly. When it became clear, especially in nineteenth-century America, that monopolies or trusts were being so created, pure laissez-faire economics came to extend its approval of government controls beyond the enforcing of contracts. Monopolies in restraint of trade may be forbidden by law; the state may *enforce competition*.

Such, at least, is the theory of classical economics as it filtered down in relatively simple form to nineteenth-century businessmen. Among some of the intellectuals, at least, the doctrine was met with opposition we shall study in the next chapter. Workingmen did not hesitate to attempt to violate the law of supply and demand for labor by organizing in trade unions from the very first part of the century. Yet some of the attitudes of reliance on self-help and individual initiative, and of distrust of government regulation of economic activities, seeped down into the working classes. Classical laissez faire is still the ideal, the credo, of the conservative American business and professional community—though this community has had to adjust its behavior to a real world very far indeed from that of classical economic theory.

Actually the theory of the laissez-faire state is an admirable example of the complex and by no means well-understood problem of the relation between theories about human relations and actual life on this earth. That relation, we have noted already, is not the same as the relation between the law of gravity and the work of the engineer. Indeed, many modern students of human affairs take a position something like that of the French political theorist Georges Sorel, who calls theories of this sort "myths." The believers in such myths are heartened by their belief, and find the myths useful in many ways. But the myths are not analytical generalizations about reality. We must return to this anti-intellectual explanation in a later chapter. It is difficult to reject this explanation altogether, especially in regard to the grand social theories. An American can perhaps best understand the problem from our familiar theory of states' rights. In 1814 at the Hartford Convention it was the New England states that appealed to the theory and threatened secession; only a generation later these same states fought to prevent the Southern states from making good *their* appeal to the same theory; and in general it can be said that the most varied American political groups have from time to time appealed to the theory of states' rights.

Now if the theory of laissez faire is as adaptable as that of states' rights, one would expect that businessmen would be against state intervention and for individual initiative at times when they found such a policy agreeable to their own interests as they saw them, but that they would be willing to accept state intervention in their own interest. And so they have been. Even the British business community, which by the mid-nineteenth century had won the country over to international free trade, accepted without too much ado a whole set of government regulatory acts relating to factories, child labor, chimney sweeps, trade unions, and the like, mostly of Benthamite inspiration. British telegraphs were nationalized almost from the first (1856). In other countries, and notably in Germany and the United States, the business community was never offended in principle and in general (though sometimes in detail) by a form of strict government regulation known as the tariff. In the United States the rugged individualists of the Western states were the loudest howlers for "internal improvements" paid for and put through by the federal government; and in general it can be said to be American experience that though the expected attitude an American must take is to denounce politics, politicians, and government spending, extremely few American communities have refused to let the federal government spend money in the community.

Yet when all these qualifications—and they are important ones— are made, when we recognize that the facts of social life never quite fitted the theories of classical economics, there remains a push of the ideal away from the pole of authority and toward the pole of individual liberty. Laissez faire fits in not as an absolute, but as part of a Victorian way of life that encouraged, especially in business life, men who could try new ways, men who could take risks. Such encouragement meant that some men tried new ways that were not successful; it meant that there were failures as well as successes. It meant indeed that more human beings wanted to improve their lot—their physical welfare, their social standing—than could actually so do. It meant, as we shall see, that some force, some kind of compensatory social belief and practice was needed to compensate for the extreme individualism, what the German idealists scornfully called the "atomism," of much of Western economic and social activity.

Most Americans are familiar with this ethical-economic core of Victorian belief; indeed we have our own pat phrase for it—"rugged individualism." It takes many forms. One is the general distrust of government, of politics and politicians, we have just noted. There are hosts of popular aphorisms—"paddle your own canoe," "God helps those who help themselves," for instance—that point out this distrust of "the government" as one of the persistent ingredients of Western culture, which merely takes on in the nineteenth century a greater emphasis and is spread among all classes.

All over the Western world the nineteenth century sees some degree of belief in individualism, a belief that has one kind of theoretical justification and backing in the very old doctrine of *natural rights.* In the Middle Ages natural rights were possessed by individuals, but not equally, not even absolutely, but rather as a part of the whole complex of custom and tradition in which they were brought up. Rights and reason were wedded in eighteenth-century thought, and by the end of the century the "rights of man" had become a commonplace. The concrete contents of such rights varied with the political thinker who was claiming them, but they did get codified in bills and declarations of rights, especially in the United States and in France. The Englishman of Victorian days was likely to feel that he had the rights without needing any explicit statement of them.

The essence of this concept of rights is that the individual—any and all individuals—may behave in certain ways even though other and stronger or richer individuals or groups of individuals do not want to let him behave that way. One of the groups that may not interfere with his behaving in certain ways is the powerful group we call the state. Indeed the *state* is the organized group against which the eighteenth- and nineteenth-century form of the doctrine of the rights of man is directed. The Italian political philosopher Gaetano Mosca refers to this concept as one of "juridical defense," for in practice one set of agents of the state, the judges, will defend the individual or group *against* another set of agents of the state, administrators or executives. Behind this defense lies the venerable concept of a higher law or "constitution"; but the institution, the "mechanism" of juridical defense is essentially new, modern, only faintly prefigured in such institutions as the ancient Roman tribune of the people.

The rights under juridical defense commonly included freedom of speech, freedom of business enterprise (usually put as "property"), often freedom of association, and, if only in the form of a right to life, at least an implied right to certain minimum standards of living. This conception of individual rights is essentially the modern equivalent of the Christian concept of the sacredness of the immortal soul in every man, the humanist conception of the dignity of man. Again, it is an equivalent from which most of the richness and mystery of Christian feeling has been stripped—a bare equivalent. But the common, even vulgar, concept of "rugged individualism" is recognizably in the Western tradition, as totalitarian denial of individual rights is not.

Americans need hardly be reminded that these rights are not in practice absolute and unchanging, that, for instance, the state can take anyone's property by eminent domain—though in our kind of society the state must recompense the owner—that the state and in fact various voluntary societies for guarding our morals can curtail an individual's freedom of speech, that, in short, the little area the individual can fence off for himself under the protection of this doctrine can sometimes almost vanish. Nor need we be reminded that in the last century or so since mid-Victorian times this little area has been cut down even in the United States. You cannot get a more representative definition of the areas a good Victorian liberal thought should be sacred to the individual than John Mill's essay *On Liberty* of 1859. Parts of Mill's writings sound today like the writing of a conservative defender of old-fashioned individualism against the New Deal.

But Mill is too much an intellectual. You can see better how the ordinary Victorian felt in a book all the social historians mention, but which no one reads, for it is in no sense a great book. This is *Self-Help*, by Samuel Smiles, published (1860) at almost the same time as Darwin's *Origin of Species* and Mill's *On Liberty*.

> . . . it is every day becoming more clearly understood that the function of government is negative and restrictive, rather than positive and active; be-

ing resolvable principally into protection,—protection of life, liberty, and
property. Hence the chief "reforms" of the last fifty years have consisted mainly
in abolitions and disenactments. But there is no power of law that can make
the idle man industrious, the thriftless provident, or the drunken sober; though
every individual can be each and all of these if he will, by the exercise of his
own free powers of action and self-denial. Indeed, all experience serves to
prove that the worth and strength of a state depend far less upon the form of
its institutions than upon the character of its men. For the nation is only the
aggregate of individual conditions, and civilization itself is but a question of
personal improvement. . . . In the order of nature, the collective character of
a nation will as surely find its befitting results in its law and its government,
as water finds its own level. The noble people will be nobly ruled, and the
ignorant and corrupt ignobly. Indeed, liberty is quite as much a moral as a
political growth,—the result of free individual action, energy, and independence. It may be of comparatively little consequence how a man is governed
from without, whilst everything depends upon how he governs himself from
within. The greatest slave is not he who is ruled by a despot, great though that
evil be, but he who is the thrall of his own moral ignorance, selfishness, and
vice. There have been, and perhaps there still are, so-called patriots abroad,
who hold it to be the greatest stroke for liberty to kill a tyrant, forgetting
that the tyrant usually represents only too faithfully the millions of people
over whom he reigns. But nations who are enslaved at heart cannot be freed
by any mere changes of masters or of institutions; and so long as the fatal
delusion prevails, that liberty solely depends upon, and consists in government,
so long will such changes, no matter at what cost they be effected, have as little
practical and lasting result as the shifting figures in a phantasmagoria. The
solid foundations of liberty must rest upon individual character; which is also
the only sure guaranty for social security and national progress. In this consists the real strength of English liberty. Englishmen feel that they are free,
not merely because they live under those free institutions which they have so
laboriously built up, but because each member of society has to a greater or less
extent got the root of the matter within himself; and they continue to hold
fast and enjoy their liberty, not by freedom of speech merely, but by their
steadfast life and energetic action as free individual men.

There is an extraordinary amount of conventional Victorian belief
in those short passages—including the typical nominalist denial that a
whole is anything but the sum of its parts. But Smiles puts even more
explicitly the factor that balances the apparently anarchic individualism
he preaches.

> . . . thus we come to exhibit what has so long been the marvel of foreigners,—
> a healthy activity of individual freedom, and yet a collective obedience to
> established authority,—the unfettered energetic action of persons, together
> with the uniform subjection of all to the national code of Duty.

This balance, this "solid foundation" of individualism as Smiles put it,
is of course the famous "Victorian morality," the "middle-class morality"
of Shavian wit, the thing the generation of the 1890's rebelled so vigorously against. Probably these rebels, who were also intellectuals offended

by Victorian tastes and Victorian successes, are poor reporters of actual Victorian practices. Yet go direct to the Victorian novelists, and especially to Trollope, and you will see that, at least in the middle and the upper classes, the ruling classes, the individual is held to a very strict code of conduct, and above all is trained from childhood on to conformity, to accepting discipline, to the willing merging of himself in a group. This conditioning is achieved by a subtle social training, and of course is to be found in some form or another in all societies. In Victorian society, economic life was supposed to be a scramble. Social life, however, was supposed to be orderly. The emphasis on liberty is balanced by the emphasis on authority.

We need not go into great detail about this code of behavior. It is worth close study in the records of Victorian culture itself, so near to us, so much a part of us, and yet in the mid-twentieth century so far away. Perhaps the modern American finds most remote the social and moral structure of the family—its relatively large size, the great authority of the father, the strict discipline undergone by the children, the subordination of the females to the males, the infrequency—indeed the horror—of divorce. The kindest of Victorian parents would hardly have thought of treating his children with the "permissiveness" that is the fashion in most American families. Samuel Butler's *Way of All Flesh* is the work of a very intellectual rebel and its picture of a Victorian father may well be false as well as exceptional. But Butler's father could hardly have been formed in any other society.

What the family had begun was continued in the boarding schools, the famous "public" schools that correspond to the American private schools, to which at least the boys of the upper and middle classes went. These schools were in some ways Spartan in their taming of the individual, in their molding him into a member of the team, the group. Adolescents are perhaps especially likely to want to conform. The English public schools made their boys into the pattern so familiar in English novels—the Englishman who knows his duty, who doesn't need a policeman because he has his conscience, the Englishman who can do what he likes because he couldn't possibly like to do anything very dangerous to society. There were, of course, always boys who couldn't be so molded. These were the rebels, some of whom drifted off to the far parts of the world, some of whom conformed just sufficiently to be classed as eccentrics, a group the Victorians tolerated on principle, and some of whom, like the poet Shelley at one end of the century and the poet Swinburne at the other, attacked the whole system, root and branch.

For the average Englishman of the ruling classes, then, the wild scramble, the Darwinian struggle for life to which his economic beliefs invited him, was balanced by the orderly world of decency and decorum that his education and family background prepared for him. Although there were many, many elements of instability in this Victorian compromise, still for the generation or two that it lasted it provided one of those rare periods of balance in Western history, a period peaceful but not lethargic, a time of change and experimentation that was not, however, a time of troubles, not an age of stomach ulcers and nervous breakdowns.

The compromise was in part a compromise with Christianity. All over the Western world, especially in Catholic countries, the anticlericalism of the Enlightenment lived on, taking firm roots in a Western culture where outward religious conformity had ceased to be prescribed by the law. But after the severe persecutions to which Christians were submitted during the "de-Christianization" movement of the French Revolution, there was a swing of the pendulum back toward Christianity, at least among the intellectual classes, a swing well marked by the French romantic writer Chateaubriand's *Génie du Christianisme* (1802). It would be unfair to say that Chateaubriand was unimpressed with the *truth* of Christianity, but its truth was certainly not what he brought out in his book; what struck him, and what he thought would impress his generation, was the beauty of Christianity, the moving quality of its liturgy, the haunting background of its Gothic past.

It will not do to leave the impression that Chateaubriand is typical of the Christian revival of the nineteenth century. Where that revival was markedly hostile toward the spirit of the age, toward the Victorian compromise we have here been attempting to define, it will be considered in the next chapter. Christian protest against the compromises Christian churches were making with the spirit of the age was firm and loud; no fair student in the nineteenth century will neglect that protest, whether it came from Maistre, from Newman, or from General Booth of the Salvation Army. But there can be no doubt that, especially in Protestant countries—though the Catholic peoples do not altogether escape it—this revival is in fact itself very much a compromise. The basic optimism toward human nature that is the mark of the Enlightenment penetrates nineteenth-century Christianity, along with a willingness to compromise with rationalism as well as with the comforts of the flesh. Were you merely to count Christian heads, were you to measure by the spread of missionary work in all parts of the globe, or by Bibles printed and by Sunday-school attendance, you might well conclude that the nineteenth was the greatest of Christian centuries. For all these indices show an upswing. Of course, the hopeful believer in human perfectibility can maintain that these indices are what count, and that this new synthesis of Christianity and the Enlightenment is a stage in attaining this perfectibility.

From the historian's point of view, the nineteenth century is not marked by any great new Christian sects, none, indeed, as successful as were in the full tide of the age of prose and reason the Methodist and Pietist groups of the eighteenth century. Numerically, two new American groups, the Mormons and the Christian Scientists, were the most striking. But probably the multiplication of religious splinter groups, of heresies against heresies, and in particular of cults variously compounded from Eastern brews, was greater than ever. Unitarian and Universalist groups that explicitly denied the sacramental character of the worship of Jesus, groups that showed a strong rationalist influence, flourished among the prosperous intellectual classes. At the other extreme, on the surface at least, were the High-Church movements in England and America with their appeal to ritual and tradition. Thus the Christian revival, whatever else it was, was not a revival of Christian unity. The nineteenth is as many-minded, as eclectic, a century in religion as in architecture.

But for the average middle-class person we are here concerned with, churchgoing was a necessary thing. The Victorian compromise meant that the leading elements in the community could no longer take the extreme anti-Christian position many of the enlightened had taken in the eighteenth century. Jefferson's hostility to organized religion had begun to be inconvenient to him when he became President in 1800. A Jefferson in the mid-nineteenth century would simply have had to deny himself a political career in most countries had he taken so outspoken a position against organized Christian churches. This does not mean that the Lancashire mill owner as he attended the service of the local Congregational chapel, the coupon-cutting bondholder as he went to his village church, were outright hypocrites. Some such hypocrisy must have existed in a community where so many social and business pressures pushed toward formal religious conformity, but we have every reason to believe that most of these churchgoers were undisturbed by the contrast between their lives and Christian ideals. After all, we have had worldly Christians for a very long time—if not from the start.

What makes these worldly Victorian Christians so conspicuous to us may be no more than the brilliance with which later intellectuals like Bernard Shaw have attacked them. Still, from a mid-twentieth-century point of view they do look too self-righteous, too unaware of the depths of human incapacity for comfortable adjustment to routine, too much at ease in Zion. Perhaps it is just that from our point of view they look too lucky. But their merging of eighteenth-century rationalism and nineteenth-century sentiment didn't quite come off. They seem at least as shallow as the pure rationalists, and much less convinced of the need for reform in the institutions of this world.

The forms of the political and social life of the Western world in the nineteenth century show a very great variation, from the traditional democracy of the United States to the traditional monarchy of Prussia. In a sense, the Western world is like the much smaller world of fifth-century Hellas; it has as national components its equivalents of Sparta, Thebes, Athens; the nation-state is the city-state on a grander scale. Yet in modern Europe even more than in ancient Hellas, one feels that there is a kind of pervading set of general attitudes, never quite the same in different countries, never quite in the same relation with other currents in different countries, but still not by any means a myth. There is a Western culture, a Western consciousness of kind in the nineteenth century. The Marxist does not hesitate to label the whole set of attitudes "middle-class," and if one understands that many of these attitudes were adopted by upper and lower classes as well, there is no harm in using the label.

In politics as in morals and religion there is a nineteenth-century compromise. We have noted that the Enlightenment itself was divided in its political hopes and program, that sometimes even the same man— say Bentham—believed in a benevolent manipulation of the environment by a wise minority and also in the ability of the mass of men to pick their own rulers by universal suffrage. The nineteenth century managed without too much frustration to hold inconclusive views on this difficult question. It believed in liberty for all, but. . . . The favorite way out was to believe in liberty but not in license. The distinction between liberty and license was a moral one: One was free to do right, but to do wrong meant license, and that should be stopped. Thus the politics of the Victorian ties in with his moral code.

Briefly, the Victorian had some such political credo as the following. First, there is the inevitable start in the doctrine of progress, according to which ultimately all men will be free, equals, and brothers, there will be no police and no taxes, work will be pleasant and voluntary and there will be no poor, and no violence in any form—in short, the kind of Utopia we have called "philosophical anarchism." This ideal society, though some distance off in time, is certain and will be achieved by education and the gradual extension of democracy. Democracy, though perhaps dangerous even in England in the 1860's, was for the man of the nineteenth century definitely the "wave of the future." The good liberal even in countries by no means in the center of the Victorian compromise, in Germany, in eastern Europe, held the view that the ultimate realization of democratic ideals lay in the course of events. For the present, the best fitted should rule as trustees for the slowly improving masses. The best fitted are not the old aristocracy, whose blood has run thin, but the men of any class who have shown by their success in business or the professions that they can cope with practical problems. The Victorian believed in liberty, but the kind of liberty that means competition; and he believed in equality, but the kind of equality of opportunity that gives all men an equal start in the race, not the kind that would have no race—or at least, no prizes for the winners, and perhaps no winners. He came to be increasingly aware that his society handicapped the child of poor parents, that the equal start was a myth; and he came in general as the century wore on to feel that though the big race of Life was a fine thing, though from it came ever better champions, still the course needed cleaning up, needed first-aid stations, needed firm rules against tripping, crowding, and other dirty tricks. He came to believe more and more in state intervention to help the little fellow, to lessen actual economic inequalities, to do the kind of thing we all know as the work of the "welfare state." Still, the typical man of the mid-century was clear that in a choice between liberty and equality, democracy if it were to be healthy should lean toward liberty.

We have been considering what the Victorian thought was right; it is a harder task to describe what he thought was beautiful. We had best attempt here no more than a few generalizations on this phase of Western culture, once more with the warning that there are not only grave differences among social classes and other cultural groupings, but that over all is the great difference of nationality, perhaps plainer in matters aesthetic than elsewhere. Yet there are at least one, and perhaps two, safe generalizations to be made.

First, this is a period of very great—unusually great—variations in standards of taste. You can put it unfavorably as a lack of standards, an anarchy of taste; or favorably as a period when in art and culture as in economic life there was free play of individuality and competition out of which came a rich variety, the best of which was very good indeed. At any rate, you can note the facts of the situation clearly in a matter like architecture. Hitherto in the West a man who set out to build any kind of building, from the humblest up, knew in what style he was going to build, for he would build as people around him had been building. It is true that the style had changed, most conspicuously at the time Gothic gave place to classical, and that there had been a slow variation within these styles. In cities like Paris and London the Middle Ages had left survivors that stood out rather strikingly in the midst of early modern buildings, most of them in, roughly, the style Americans call colonial. But as the nineteenth century wore on what is called eclecticism took complete possession of the builder, public as well as private. There is a short flurry of Neo-Gothic in the early part of the century, but not even Neo-Gothic was a universal fashion.

Ultimately there came the position we Americans still apparently take as natural. A man wants to build a good house; he consults his family and an architect, and the consultation revolves largely about the question of what style—Cape Cod, bungalow, ranch house, "modern," English Tudor half timber, French chateau, South African Dutch, adobe, mission, and so on. It is unfair to take the building on American motor roads as typical of anything, but they do put the matter with great force:

If you want to build a hot-dog stand there are no limits left—you may build a beaverboard Eskimo igloo, a derby hat, a large lion, an immense hot dog itself. At no other stage in human history has man built in the bewildering variety he has built in since 1800. In no other culture have his cities looked like an architectural hash.

Second, it is probably true that in the nineteenth century there developed, along with this very great variety of tastes, a widespread feeling among cultivated people that they were increasingly being surrounded with ugly things. One assumes that no Athenian found the buildings on the Acropolis ugly, for these buildings have unity of style and are built in a single tradition. You would hardly get anything like unanimity among Americans on the subject of the public buildings of the city of Washington—though Washington has much more consistency in planning than any other great American city. Perhaps we do not have a good enough record of past ages. Certainly the intellectuals in all periods of Western history have complained bitterly enough about the manners, morals, and intelligence of the many; no doubt that Plato found popular tastes as low as he found all other things popular. But one has the impression that the nineteenth century, and we ourselves as its heirs, have added taste to the many other elements that separate social groups, and that more especially set off an intellectual class in partial isolation.

Yet again, there probably is a sort of cross section or least common denominator of taste in the nineteenth century, and again it is the taste of the successful man of affairs—and his wife. The Victorian liked things solid and just a bit showy; he liked abundance, and disliked the spare, the austere. He was a romantic, an escapist, with a great interest in distant and exotic things; but he also prided himself on his hard-headed sense of reality, on his ability to record and report. The literature of the century has almost the full range of the spectrum, from the romantic writhings and ironies of lost souls like Byron and his European disciples to the calm but very decent common sense of Trollope and the crusading "naturalism" of Zola. Everything is there—again as in a hash.

It is, however, a well-blended hash with a flavor of its own. Looking back on that age from ours, one is struck by the fact that in spite of its diversity of tastes, its romantic escapism, its disputes over fundamentals, the nineteenth century does attain a parodoxical kind of unity, and is an age of balance, a "flowering." The man of the nineteenth century had a sense of *belonging* (deeper than mere optimism) that we lack. His universe had not, as ours seem to have, got out of hand for him. He did not need to take refuge in fantastic styles or unadorned, often inhuman, functionalism, as we have done. He did not need to try to escape from escape.

One hesitates to try to find a symbol of nineteenth-century culture, as one finds the Parthenon a symbol of Periclean Athens, the cathedral of

Chartres a symbol for the thirteenth century. A railroad station? A great factory? The great London exposition of 1851 with its Crystal Palace, the Paris exposition of 1889 with its Eiffel Tower? A bird's-eye view of Manhattan? These are all unfair, for the nineteenth century was not just an age of industry and material achievement. The nineteenth century invested heavily in public buildings of all sorts, but none of them seems a suitable symbol. Perhaps after all, since so much of the effort of the century was spent in making the lives of individuals more comfortable, more happy, more important, we can take as a symbol one of the better residential streets of a great citiy—London, Manchester, Lyons, Dresden, Baltimore, perhaps one of those streets dedicated to separate private houses, "villas" as they are called in Europe. Here you have comfort, plenty of room, greenery, quiet—and an anarchy of taste in architecture. If your sympathies are with the radicals, you will think that this street should be balanced with a street from the slums. But do not worry. That slum street was very much in the minds of the dwellers in the villas. They hoped that someday there would be no slums, though they did not think they could do much about it right away. But the slums worried them, even in mid-century. As a master class, the Victorian middle class had too brief and insecure a rule to acquire the serenity of self-confidence the feudal aristocracy had once had.

The slum street would have liked to transmute itself into the street of villas. We have insisted throughout this chapter that there are all sorts of groups besides the Victorian middle class we have chosen as a most typical specimen. And so there are: national groups, confident almost as the British, as for instance the Prussian or the American, or irredentist, complaining, full of martyrdom, like the Irish or the Poles; anticlerical, positivist, ethical-culture groups proudly not going to Christian churches, but very insistent that their ethics were at least as Christian as those of the orthodox; little groups of fanatics, mostly mild ones, devoted to one single crank device or social gadget, but otherwise conformist enough, the single-taxers, the theosophists, the vegetarians, the preventers of cruelty to children or animals, the prohibitionists, and so on through the long roster of nineteenth- and twentieth-century "good causes"; and, by no means the least conspicuous, the intellectuals, trying very hard to repudiate or remold the strange, chaotic society in which they found themselves.

What we have called the developed cosmology, then, was the basic belief of most Western educated men and women of the nineteenth century, the standard by which even the uneducated or less educated masses guided their aspirations. This cosmology accepted the belief of the Enlightenment in the progress, in the perfectibility of man here on earth, in the attainment of happiness here on earth. But the nineteenth century took away from these beliefs their sharpness and their immediacy, in some ways much as later Christian belief took away from primitive Christianity the frightening, if hopeful, possibilities of an immediate second coming of Christ. The Victorian compromised with the hope and the heroism of the Enlightenment. He was for gradual progress, for a slow, careful process of educating the masses, for a strict moral code enforced by the full social pressure of men in groups, for liberty to experiment but not at the expense of what he felt to be moral absolutes, for the career open to talents, varied but not of course "antisocial" or perverse talents, for peace on earth but not at the cost of his national honor and dignity—for democracy, even, but not for radical, not for socialist democracy, not for democracy that took literally "liberty, equality, fraternity." Surely, thought the Victorian, one can be a democrat, a liberal, an enlightened, modern person, and yet be prosperous, happy, comfortable even in this world where not all are yet prosperous, happy, and comfortable. The "yet" was a great salve to his conscience. Someday all men would be as well off as he was now; meanwhile, the lucky and the privileged should not jeopardize the possible by trying—or letting others try—to achieve the impossible. In this nineteenth-century world the existence of the rich man, or at any rate of the moderately rich *bourgeois,* should not inspire any silly metaphors about the difficulty of putting a camel through the eye of a needle.

Yet we should not take leave of the confident Victorians, envious as indeed we must be of their self-confidence, without recognizing the fact that we are the heirs of their faith in human beings—a modified faith compared with the wild optimism of the Enlightenment, a faith we have further vastly modified, have perhaps almost abandoned. You can see in John Stuart Mill that faith at its clearest, and in some senses at its best, as it is found among intellectuals. Most of the intellectuals parted company with the Enlightenment as reflected in the Victorian compromise. It is true that a Longfellow, a Tennyson, a Dickens, and many another imaginative artist is in some ways in tune with the triumphant middle classes, or at least not diametrically and bitterly opposed to all they stand for. But there are not many *politiques et moralistes* who stick to the colors of the Enlightenment. Of these, Mill is an admirable specimen.

He was the son of James Mill, a self-made Scot who was a favorite disciple of Bentham. John Mill is then a sort of grandchild of Bentham. All his life he maintained that he was true to the Enlightenment—anti-Christian in a theological, but not in an ethical, sense; a firm believer in the power of reason working on common-sense and empirical grounds; a distruster of philosophical idealism, of German idealism especially (Mill once said that he always felt slightly nauseated after trying to read Hegel); a reformer anxious to improve the material condition of the masses; a believer in liberty for all, in toleration of other people's ways even when they conflict with your own; above all, perhaps, a man who felt deeply that there is something profoundly necessary to human life expressed in that formal and all too often empty term, *liberty*. Yet this same Mill had retreated from, had modified in many ways what he had inherited from his spiritual grandfather. Under the influence of romantic poets like Wordsworth and Coleridge he had come, just like the ordinary folk of his generation, to qualify the stark rationalism of the Enlightenment with a feeling for the uncertainties, the emotional responses, the *irrational*, as an enrichment of life, not a delusion; he had even had, under the influence of Carlyle, a brief period when he thought he was attracted to mysticism, but he soon returned to a moderate rationalism; he believed in liberty, yet toward the end of his life he called himself not only a democrat, but in some senses a socialist, for he had come to believe that the government must interfere, not only to enforce contracts, but to make positively better the position of the poor and the handicapped; he was a utilitarian, the heir of the Bentham who had in his *Deontology* decided that the pleasures of belief in God were less than the pains of such belief, and had therefore decided against the utility of religion; and yet toward the end of his life John Mill embraced a sort of modern Manichaeanism of his own, in which a good God and a bad Spirit fought out the uncertain battle and sought to enlist us all. The successor of the school that believed in the perfectibility of man had a great fear of the possible tyranny of the majority, and wrote this revealing aside—"for ordinary human nature is such poor stuff."

Yet Mill stated as clearly as anyone has ever stated the central doctrine of nineteenth-century liberalism:

> . . . the only purpose for which power can be rightfully exercised over any member of a civilized community, against his will, is to prevent harm to others. His own good, either physical or moral, is not a sufficient warrant. He cannot rightfully be compelled to do or forbear because it will be better for him to do so, because it will make him happier, because, in the opinions of others, to do so would be wise, or even right. These are good reasons for remonstrating with him, or reasoning with him, or persuading him, or entreating him, but not for compelling him, or visiting him with any evil in case he do otherwise. To justify that, the conduct from which it is desired to deter him, must be calculated to produce evil to some one else. The only part of the conduct of any one, for which he is amenable to society, is that which concerns others. In the part which merely concerns himself, his independence is, of right, absolute. Over himself, over his own body and mind, the individual is sovereign.

This will sound to many intellectuals today remote, too simple, perhaps wrongly focused, perhaps wrong-headed. We distrust all kinds of sovereignty today, at least if we have been swept into fashionable currents of philosophical relativism; or if we still trust in absolutes, the absolute sacredness of the individual's sovereignty over himself is not one of the absolutes we hold. Yet some such beliefs as Mill here expresses are surely very widely held here in America in the mid-twentieth century. We still have that sympathy with the human individual trying to define, assert, and make appreciated his uniqueness, which is one of the traditions of the West. We still dislike regimentation, paternalism, deference to authority, even though we want security and are tired of the fine, free Darwinian fight. We still think of *Homo sapiens,* not as a member of a society like those of the bees and the ants, but as a free, roving, adventurous animal. In short, we are still living in part on the intellectual and emotional capital of the last century—and, indeed, of the whole tradition of Western ethics and philosophy.

CHAPTER SIX

THE NINETEENTH CENTURY

II. ATTACKS FROM RIGHT AND LEFT

The Role of Intellectuals

The nineteenth century sees the full development of a change in the sources of livelihood of that very important part of the intellectual classes, the writers; and it sees the final touches in the process of making the characteristic modern group we call the intellectuals. Both these topics must receive attention in any intellectual history of the West.

From the days of the Greeks to early modern times writers of all sorts, poets and storytellers and scholars, had either to have income from their own property, or to be subsidized by rich patrons, like the Roman Maecenas; by the state, as with the Attic dramatists; or by an institution such as a monastic order. They could directly "sell" their talents to consumers only rarely, and then as sophists or lecturers in the ancient world, as troubadours in the medieval, directly confronting their audience. With the invention of printing in the fifteenth century there came gradually to be a large enough market for books, so that slowly authors and publishers were able to work out a copyright system, and the writer became a licensed merchant selling his product in collaboration with a publisher who took much of the commercial risk. There came also to be a periodical—and by the eighteenth century a newspaper—press for which the writer worked for pay, sometimes on salary, sometimes at piecework rates. The eighteenth century is here a period of transition. Copyright is imperfect, patrons are still important, and journalism hardly offers prizes even for its most successful practitioners. The English "Grub Street" remains a set phrase for the struggling proletariat of the written word. Yet there grew up notably in England and in France a group of men who lived, however badly, by selling in a true market what they wrote. Although Defoe had done very well with *Robinson Crusoe* and other writings, Sir Walter Scott is perhaps the first man to make a fortune from his pen, which like Mark Twain later he proceeded to lose by unwise investments in the new business of big-scale publishing. Even Voltaire, a very good business man, did not make the bulk of his fortune from his writings.

By mid-nineteenth century authors have their full modern status; there are great prizes for those who write best sellers, and there is a livelihood dropping down to meager for the less successful. There is a full-fledged newspaper and periodical business, fed both by salaried reporters and staff men and by free-lance writers. The drama had begun to pay with Shakespeare, who was apparently a first-rate theatrical manager. By Victorian times the royalties from really successful plays had begun to be large. Still another opportunity for those who gain a living by putting words together on paper is commercial advertising. But in 1850 advertising was in its infancy, and not altogether a respectable profession; it still is not such for the pure intellectual, a revealing fact, at least for the sociologist.

Learned writing, including pure science, continued to be subsidized, chiefly by institutions. But the institutions that did the subsidizing were already by the nineteenth century secular rather than ecclesiastical institutions, and on the European continent were usually under state control. There developed in the textbook trade a welcome subsidiary source of income for members of the learned world. On the whole, however, the rest of the more purely intellectuals, those who preached and taught, continued to be supported by groups—state, church, college, and the like—on fixed and relatively low stipends. The law remained as it had been for centuries a learned profession as individually competitive as any business. Medicine, hardly a learned profession at all until early modern times, had by the mid-nineteenth century become one of the most esteemed of professions, though like the law it was, in terms of economic livelihood, almost entrepreneurial.

We cannot here go into that relatively neglected and fascinating field, the sociology of professions. We have made the obvious point that by the nineteenth century professional writers were fully in the current of economic competition as sellers of words, and that in a very broad way all those—now much more numerous than ever before, certainly absolutely, and *probably* relatively to the whole population—whose main job was some kind of deliberate thinking and planning, were more and more drawn into the currents of individual economic competition of the nineteenth century. Only preachers and teachers seem an exception, and they were not altogether so. Yet the intellectuals remained intellectuals, proud of it, and even in the more competitive ranges of, say, journalism, always conscious of some separateness of outlook from those who bought and sold material things. Great commercial success, especially in marginal fields like Hollywood, advertising, and publicity, tends in contemporary

America to give a bad conscience to the successful writer, and drive him leftward.

From our point of view, the importance of this change in the economic and to a certain extent the social status of intellectuals in the Western world is not that they get thrown into a vulgar commercial whirl, that they lose serenity and detachment. Intellectuals in the West have by no means commonly lived in ivory towers isolated from the dust and heat of the world in any age. What is new in the modern world is the process, clearly complete by the nineteenth century, that made the intellectuals dependent in part for their livelihood on a wide public, and did this notably for writers.

This dependency upon the custom of the many might be expected to have led most successful writers to flatter the public, to accept human relations as they found them—in short, to conform. And of the millions and millions of printed words, no doubt many *were* written merely to amuse or excite the ordinary man, to help him escape, to confirm him in his prejudices, to back up the Victorian compromise. Yet almost all the men we now study as part of our heritage, almost all the great writers, as well as a great number of writers of the forgotten and the incidental, *attacked* things as they were. The editorial writer, like the preacher, has in the modern world to be *against* something. The great writers of the nineteenth century and of the twentieth have belabored the race for its failures. Think of Carlyle, Emerson, Thoreau, Marx, Nietzsche. These, of course, were *politiques et moralistes,* and could hardly be such without finding their fellow creatures wrong, or wicked, or lazy, or stupid. But even the novelists are crusaders—some of them the more obviously crusaders when they avow they are scientific analysts of human behavior. Zola and Dreiser come to mind at once.

We are, however, edging over into a second point about the role of the intellectuals in the modern Western world, a central problem in a branch of sociology even less advanced than the sociology of the professions—that is, *Wissenssoziologie,* the sociology of knowledge, learning, ideas. We need make only one additional note on the modern position of the writer dependent on the wide popular market for his goods. Very often the most profitable occupation for such a writer is to abuse his customers, to tell them what fools they are, particularly in America, where the boobs of Mencken's *booboisie* used to read him with pleasure, where thousands of Babbitts bought Lewis's *Babbitt* to make it a best seller.

We by no means have for the three thousand years of Western history an adequate supply of facts about the attitude of the intellectuals—that is, the "intellectual classes" of Professor Baumer's definition—toward the accepted world-view and value-judgments of their societies; and we have not yet worked out any satisfactory interpretation or theory of the social role of the intellectuals. We have scraps of information and beginnings of theories, both of which have from time to time appeared in this book. We can say that as a group, except perhaps in the earliest and most consecrated days of Christianity, the intellectuals have been pretty well aware of their separateness from the bulk of their fellow men, pretty "class-conscious." At all times, even in the Dark Ages when the new ruling class was illiterate, or even in deliberately anti-intellectual Sparta, some members of the intellectual classes have been at the very top level of the social hierarchy. Some—the rural parish priest of the Middle Ages, the schoolteacher in most periods—have been in terms of real wages fairly close to the bottom.

Yet it is very hard indeed to make an effective generalization, even for a given period, to say nothing of the whole course of Western history, concerning the attitude of the intellectual classes toward the established order of their society. Rebels at the very top there have always been, though we know little of them in the Dark Ages. From Plato through the first Christian Fathers to Abelard, Wycliffe, and the innumerable intellectual rebels of today the succession is clear. Yet probably the great bulk of the intellectual classes, the great majority even of those who preach, teach, orate, editorialize, and comment have been conformists, supporters of things as they are, conservatives in the simple sense of the word, that of "keeping intact what we have." Certainly their listeners and readers have been in their conduct conformists and conservatives, or we should not be here to study the intellectual history of the West— there would be no West. It is probable indeed that even in the modern West the many readers of non-conformist writings, of writings attacking the established order, are not influenced at all to rebel themselves. They get a sort of catharsis or relief, much as our ancestors used to get relief through sermons on hell-fire.

At any rate, it is clear that since the beginnings of the Enlightenment, the *creative portion* of the intellectual classes have in general been dissatisfied with the world they saw around them, anxious to reform it, convinced it could be reformed. The eighteenth-century philosophers were agreed among themselves, in spite of certain differences over methods, that the job could be done fairly soon, that society could be made over according to standards (those of Nature and Reason) evident to all, once they were enlightened. These intellectuals of the Enlightened hated the *privileged* unenlightened—the priests, the conventional noblemen, the very few intellectuals who opposed them—but many, perhaps most, of them, especially in the late eighteenth-century after humanitarian "feeling" became fashionable among the intellectuals, loved and trusted the *unprivileged* unenlightened, the common people whom they were going to train for life in Utopia.

Now with the nineteenth century the creative intellectuals are still in rebellion, but they are no longer a united band. Some have moved in ideal toward the right, toward the old religion, toward the old, or a rejuvenated, aristocracy, toward some kind of authority, some definite design for making and keeping the many nice and quiet, and perhaps also happy. Some have moved left, toward some form of what now begins to be a word of fright to the conventional man of property—socialism. More important, the creative intellectuals come as the century goes on more and more into conflict with precisely the kind of people the eighteenth-century philosophers had cherished and nursed—the ordinary educated but not intellectual middle-class person. Most of the standards set up in the last chapter as those of the Victorian compromise were very largely repudiated by the nineteenth-century writers we still remember and read. These writers share some of the attitudes of the middle classes, notably a conviction that progress is real and possible; at the very least, they share a sense of history, of process, of flow. But they quite specifically dislike the middle classes, for whom they invent uncomplimentary names like "philistine." Even a writer who glories in the achievements of the middle classes, a writer whom the aesthetes and arty folk generally thought a philistine, the Herbert Spencer who wrote a nineteenth-century *summa,* is no conformist, no contented man, but a strong anticlerical, a man convinced that a lot is wrong with the world. Spencer, in short, protests, complains, bellyaches; he cannot for long describe or analyze without blaming—and very occasionally praising—without displaying annoyance or anxiety; he has, in short, the acid flavor we have come to expect from serious writers. Already in the nineteenth century the creative intellectuals are working up to the state they have reached in contemporary America, where one expects an intellectual to complain as naturally as he breathes, where one expects to open any serious publication and begin to read about what's wrong with our colleges, the crisis in the family, the destruction of our topsoil, the crossroads in international relations, the coming end of our culture. You will even find complaints about the role of the intellectual. Some years ago a distinguished French writer, Julien Benda, wrote a book called *La trahison des clercs,* which can be informally translated "What's Wrong With the Intellectuals."

We are, of course, exaggerating. Science, or cumulative knowledge, cannot in itself praise or blame, hope or fear; and there is a great deal of scientific writing in these times. Some artists may work with intent to please rather than to improve, though probably most art involves a judgment about the universe. Still, by and large it is true that roughly since the French Revolution the more creative and productive of the intellectual classes, and notably the writers, have rejected most of the way of life of the middles classes of the West, have rejected the values current among that class—and it must not be forgotten, the imitators and aspirants to middle-class status who make up the bulk of the working classes of this period.

Attacks from the Right

For convenience we shall classify attacks on the conventional ways of nineteenth-century life as from the Right and from the Left. These terms grew up out of French parliamentary practice early in the century, when the conservatives or monarchists took to sitting in a group to the right of the presiding officer, and the constitutionalists and radical reformers grouped themselves on his left. There is a certain symbolic fitness in this, since on the whole the Left wishes to push on to as full a realization as possible of the "principles of 1776 and 1789," the democratic aims of the American and French revolutions, and on the whole the Right wishes a much less democratic society. Of course, the simple linear differences suggested by these terms are inadequate to measure the complexities of opinion even in politics. For one thing, the center from which we measure Left and Right is not a clear fixed point, for there is always that democratic tension between the ideals of liberty and equality we have already noted. The ideal of security adds still another complication. Still, as a rough means of sorting out attacks on the position outlined in the last chapter, the division into Right and Left should be useful, especially if we note that the line is a curved line that can come full circle so that the extremes meet. In the last years of the Third French Republic it is striking to note how often the Monarchists and the Communists, in political terms extreme Right and extreme Left, voted on the same side of a given question. They both hated with virtuous ardor the vulgar conformists who did not want revolutionary change.

What the eighteen-century *philosophes,* with the sound instinct that makes us recognize our enemies, singled out for their bitterest attacks was the Roman Catholic Church. For if you hold, as the lesser but more numerous *philosophes* did, the doctrine of the natural goodness and reasonableness of ordinary men, then the polar opposite is the idea of original sin. But a great deal more of the cluster of ideas of the Enlightenment—naturalism with its denial of the supernatural; materialism; belief in assured progress on earth; dislike of tradition, of established hierarchies; belief in liberty or equality, and sometimes in liberty *and* equality—finds in traditional organized Christianity a cluster of antithetical ideas. We have already noted that in some senses the Enlightenment itself is a child of Christianity. We shall see that even the more conservative churches, the Roman Catholic and the Anglican, for instance, have by no means refused to adapt themselves in part to changes since the eighteenth century. It would be very wrong indeed to set up the formula: "Christianity" and the "modern spirit" are mutually exclusive systems of values. In fact, we have noted in the last chapter that conventional, churchgoing Christianity, Catholic as well as Protestant, was one of the elements of the Victorian compromise. Notably in the United States, where all but a crank minority believes in democracy, it follows that Christians have to believe in democracy.

Nevertheless, the established churches have from time to time produced thinkers who have been the most determined and absolute of opponents of democracy. Of these, there is surely no more eloquent, able, and one fears, at bottom unrealistic, thinker than Joseph de Maistre. This Savoyard civil servant exiled by the French Revolution sought to bring his fellows back to what he held to be eternal verities. With a good deal of insight he picked on Francis Bacon as one of the founders of the modern evil, which is precisely the notion that *something new and good is possible*. Few Americans can read a passage like the following without amazement, and usually indignation; yet it is important that we realize men in our own culture have held these beliefs:

> The very title of his [Bacon's] main work is a striking error. There is no *Novum Organum* or, to speak English, *new instrument,* with which we can reach what was inaccessible to our predecessors. Aristotle is the true anatomist who, so to speak, took apart under our eyes and showed to us the *human instrument.* One can only smile somewhat scornfully at a man who promises us a *new man.* Let us leave that expression for the Gospel. The human spirit is what it has always been. . . . Nobody can find in the human spirit more than is there. To think the thing possible is the greatest of errors; it is not knowing how to look at one's self. . . . There may be in particular sciences discoveries which are true machines very suited to perfect these sciences: thus the differential calculus was useful to mathematics as the toothed wheel was to watchmaking. But as for rational philosophy, it is clear that there cannot be a new instrument just as there are none for mechanical arts in general.

Maistre's big work, *Du Pape,* is a defense of papal authority, indeed, papal infallibility, and in general of an authoritarian system in a world he felt was falling into an anarchy of belief and practice. "Protestantism, philosophism," he wrote, "and a thousand other sects, more or less perverse or extravagant, having prodigiously diminished the truth among men, the human race cannot remain in the condition in which it now finds itself." Yet he apparently was realistic enough not to hope for any sudden mending, especially among peoples as far gone as the Anglo-Saxons. What he did hope was that a nucleus of wise and disciplined men in countries still Catholic at heart could hold fast during the storm of materialism, unbelief, and scientific progress and be there to bring the world to its senses after the inevitable breakdown.

To Maistre a usually rhetorical term of abuse can be almost literally applied: He was a *reactionary*, a man who held that nothing new could be good and nothing good could be new, that the Catholic synthesis of the Middles Ages was valid for all time. Yet even Maistre could not escape history, and at least in his sharp, clear, epigrammatic style bears the unmistakable mark of the eighteenth century. More than that, in his dislike of sentimental enthusiasm, in his scorn for the humanitarians of his day, he shows signs of the slightly cynical Catholic authoritarianism that was to trouble gentler souls within the Church itself. Note the way in which he suggests in the above passage that expressions like "new man" had better be left to the Gospel. Moreover, if you read him carefully enough, Maistre will be found to have some of the notions about the "organic" nature of society, the saving strength of tradition and prejudice, we shall find in Burke; but Maistre's *manner* is even less conciliating that Burke's, and he leaves the impression that his good organic society is rather inconsistently an unchanging society.

Maistre can hardly be to most twentieth-century Americans more than a queer specimen from another world. Unfortunately, most Americans have almost as much difficulty in the sympathetic understanding of a much profounder critic of democracy, the Irishman Edmund Burke. Now Burke lived in the second half of the eighteenth century, and his greatest book, the *Reflections on the Revolution in France,* was published in 1790. He is, however, one of the most able thinkers to question the basic beliefs of the Enlightenment, and continued throughout the nineteenth century to be the great source of a certain kind of conservative opposition to the tendencies of the age. Burke was a Protestant, a sincere Anglican who had grown up under English influence and who made his career in the British House of Commons. He supported the cause of the American rebels in speeches that were long read in this country; but from the very start he detected what he thought were disastrous possibilities in the French Revolution, and early made himself a leader in an intellectual crusade against it. This step brought him into violent conflict with the advanced thinkers of the time, and in particular made most Americans of the age of Jefferson regard him as a benighted soul. Tom Paine's *Rights of Man* was a reply to Burke, and to this day most Americans are likely to feel that Paine had the better of the argument. Yet Burke is well worth the attention even of the convinced democrat of the Left, for he seems to many to have made some analyses of human relations that deserve to be considered additions to our slender stock of cumulative knowledge in the social sciences. It is hard to distill this from the mass of his rhetoric; moreover, there remains in Burke a solid core of Christian faith that is clearly not reducible to cumulative knowledge in the scientific sense.

To Burke the French Revolution was predominantly the work of a certain type of idealist educated in the great hopes of the Enlightenment. Burke did not maintain that everything was satisfactory in the France of the old regime, that nothing needed to be done to improve French social and political life. Burke was not that kind of reactionary, though as his polemic continued and the Terror came on in France, he was capable of an occasional passage in which he sounds almost as rigid as Maistre. The base of Burke's criticism of the leaders of the French Revolution is that, instead of going ahead and trying to repair a defective flue, rebuild a wall or so, tighten a roof, they proposed almost literally to tear down the whole building and then put up a brand-new one for which their philosopher teachers had given them the blueprints. But the old building was the only building in existence, and even if men could have agreed to build according to the theorist's blueprint, the building must have taken some time. But they were not in fact so agreed. All that happened was that the old building was pretty well torn down, and the French people left without shelter from the storms. The new one had finally to be pieced together largely with the old materials, for men cannot live in the modern world without shelter. But the philosophers didn't build the new-old building; it had to be built by a more ruthless master builder, a man who could get things done by authoritarian means if necessary— by a Napoleon Bonaparte, in short. It is quite true that Burke, writing in 1789-1790, foresaw and specifically predicted a dictator like Napoleon, who finally did come to power in 1799.

Now the above figure of speech does less than justice to Burke but it may help the reader to follow his analysis. Burke starts with a Christian pessimism about the animal man; indeed, one of his great hatreds was his hatred for the Rousseau who preached the natural goodness of man unsoiled by civilization, the Rousseau whom he called the "insane Socrates of the National Assembly." Ordinary men if left to the promptings of their desires, their passions, will, according to Burke, always *tend* to run amuck, to cheat, seduce, violate, to make beasts of themselves. Yet in daily life most of them do none of these things, and the criminal exceptions can always be coped with in a sound society. Civil society presents the striking spectacle of potentially, "naturally," bad men behaving like good ones, or at least quiet ones. We must conclude that just the opposite of what Rousseau said is true: Man is saved, not ruined, by his membership in society, by his obedience to convention, tradition, prejudices, law, and the like. His social and political environment is the one thing that stands between him and chaos.

It follows that you must never destroy the great bulk of arrangements, institutions, set ways of managing human relations that we call "civil society." It is true that any bright person with the right aptitudes can devise all sorts of new ways of handling these matters, theoretical improvements that if they would only work might well be real improvements.

But Burke holds that you must go cautiously along this road, attempt very few changes at a time, and never attempt to change *all* civil society. The French in 1789 did really attempt such a complete overthrow; they sought to change everything from the system of weights and measures to the election of bishops and the structure of the central government. They turned the job over to theorists instead of sticking by men of practical experience.

What keeps ordinary men on the decent road, however, is in part at least habit, and a kind of emotional identification the individual makes with the society of which he feels himself part. This feeling is not something that can be produced to order; it has to grow, slowly and naturally. Burke would *not* have appreciated the story about the American college campus where a notice was posted, "Beginning tomorrow it will be a tradition that freshmen remove their caps when they pass before the statue of the founder." For Burke, what holds society together is nothing rational in the simple sense of the word, nothing planned, nothing put down on paper as a new constitution. In fact, he would hold the term "new constitution" to be complete nonsense. At most, you can introduce new elements in a constitution, as you might make a graft on a tree, by an organic, not a mechanical process.

Burke does not, of course, use the kind of language we have used above. He uses the terms current in his own age, including the hallowed one of "social contract." But note what a very different emphasis he gives to this notion. We are no longer dealing with Lockian or Benthamite calculation of interests, but with concepts clearly in the medieval Christian tradition.

> Society is, indeed, a contract. Subordinate contracts for objects of mere occasional interest may be dissolved at pleasure; but the state ought not to be considered as nothing better than a partnership agreement in a trade of pepper and coffee, calico or tobacco, or some other such low concern, to be taken up for a little temporary interest, and to be dissolved by the fancy of the parties. It is to be looked on with other reverence; because it is not a partnership in things subservient only to the gross animal existence of a temporary and perishable nature. It is a partnership in all science, a partnership in all art, a partnership in every virtue and in all perfection. As the ends of such a partnership cannot be obtained in many generations, it becomes a partnership not only between those who are living, but between those who are living, those who are dead, and those who are to be born. Each contract of each particular state is but a clause in the great primeval contract of eternal society, linking the lower with the higher natures, connecting the visible and invisible world, according to a fixed compact sanctioned by the inviolable oath which holds all physical and all moral natures each in their appointed place.

One more passage may be cited to show how Burke takes still another famous—and explosive—phrase of the Enlightenment, "natural rights," and brings it around to conformity with traditional notions of authority and inequality.

Government is not made in virtue of natural rights, which may and do exist in total independence of it; and exist in much greater clearness, and in a much greater degree of abstract perfection; but their abstract perfection is their practical defect. By having a right to everything they want everything. Government is a contrivance of human wisdom to provide for human *wants*. Men have a right that these wants should be provided for by this wisdom. Among these wants is to be reckoned the want, out of civil society, of a sufficient restraint upon their passions. Society requires not only that the passions of individuals should be subjected, but that even in the mass and body, as well as in the individuals, the inclinations of men should frequently be thwarted, their will controlled, and their passions brought into subjection. This can only be done *by a power out of themselves,* and not, in the exercise of its function, subject to that will and to those passions which it is its office to bridle and subdue. In thise sense the restraints on men, as well as their liberties, are to be reckoned among their rights. But as the liberties and the restrictions vary with times and circumstances, and admit of infinite modifications, they cannot be settled upon any abstract rule; and nothing is so foolish as to discuss them upon that principle.

What happened in France, according to Burke, was that foolish if well-meaning men got a chance in the financial crisis that led to the calling of the States General to try to destroy the old French society, and did succeed in breaking down much too much of it. The average Frenchman, no longer able to rely on the settled ways of old, was thrown off balance, frustrated. He took his frustration out in aggression. The Reign of Terror was the normal result of trying to effect too big changes in society. Burke, had he been alive, would no doubt have argued that the gangster bootlegging era in the United States of the 1920's was the normal result of trying by changing the law to make men change very old drinking habits.

Burke was not, however, a reactionary. He did believe in the possibility, indeed in the necessity, of the new, the experimental. He would "reform in order to conserve." His proposed reforms seemed mere stop-gaps to impatient radicals like Paine and Owen, and indeed the real reforming temperament must find Burke fundamentally anti-pathetic. For he is at the very bottom a pessimist. He simply does not believe that all men can be happy here on earth, ever. He puts his objections to the rationalist planning of the eighteenth-century enlightened largely in terms that mark the so-called "romantic revival"—in terms of the organic nature of human groups (as opposed to the mechanical), in terms of tradition, sentiment, even *prejudice,* a word almost equivalent to *sin* to the eighteenth-century philosophers. Yet behind this there lies an older nomenclature for an older set of feelings, essentially those of Augustine and Aquinas.

One more Christian thinker must be noted. Cardinal Newman was an Oxford don who became one of the great figures in the High-Church Anglican revival of the early nineteenth century known as the "Oxford Movement." Newman was a sensitive, imaginative young man who felt acutely the need for certainty and for authority. He could not satisfy himself until, in 1845, he went over to the Roman Catholic Church. Newman, like Maistre and Burke and indeed all the Christian conservatives, found the enemy in the philosophy of the Enlightenment, though by the mid-nineteenth century Newman could use "Liberalism" to designate the cluster of ideas he hated.

> By Liberalism I mean false liberty of thought, or the exercise of thought upon matters, in which, from the constitution of the human mind, thought cannot be brought to any successful issue, and therefore is out of place. . . . [Liberalism holds that] no revealed doctrines or precepts may reasonably stand in the way of scientific conclusions. Therefore, e.g. Political Economy may reverse our Lord's declarations about poverty and riches, or a system of Ethics may teach that the highest condition of body is ordinarily essential to the highest state of mind . . . [that] there is a right of Private Judgment: that is, there is no existing authority on earth competent to interfere with the liberty of individuals in reasoning and judging for themselves about the Bible and its contents, as they severally please. Therefore, e.g. religious establishments requiring subscription are Anti-christian. . . . [Liberalism holds that] there is no such thing as a national or state conscience . . . [that] utility and expedience are the measure of political duty . . . [that] the Civil Power may dispose of Church property without sacrilege . . . [that] the people are the legitimate source of power . . . [that] virtue is the child of knowledge, and vice of ignorance. Therefore, e.g. education, periodical literature, railroad travelling, ventilation, drainage, and the arts of life, when fully carried out, serve to make a population moral and happy.

Newman's interest for us, however, lies less in his attacks on liberalism, less even in his profound emotional acceptance of traditional Christianity, than in the rather surprising efforts he clearly made to accommodate his thought to the spirit of the Victorian Age. Do not misunderstand. No one was ever less a time-server than Newman. He almost certainly made no conscious effort to put over a message in terms which might be taken to pervert it. He was simply too intelligent, too aware of what was going on around him, perhaps also a bit too much of a Britisher, to take the neat, dogmatic position Maistre took: i.e., that nothing new is good, indeed nothing new is possible. Newman in his *Essay on the Development of Christian Doctrine* (1845) goes so far as to insist that precisely because Christianity in its traditional sacramental form is true it is bound to change, to grow, to develop. He does indeed guard himself from a completely relativist position: In so far as the Church is a divine institution it is of course perfect, and therefore above change. But in so far as it is a human institution here on earth it *must* change, because that is a rule of life. "In a higher world it is otherwise, but here below to live is to change, and to be perfect is to have changed often."

Not all change is good—indeed, Newman holds that such a belief is one of the great Liberal errors. We must distinguish between development and corruption. For life, which has the promise of development, holds also the threat of corruption. We cannot use any simple scientific test to tell us when a given change is good or bad, a development or a corruption. For that we must rest on what Newman called our "illative sense." This notion, developed especially in his *Grammar of Assent* (1870), is one of the earlier anticipations of much of the anti-intellectual doctrine we shall study in the next chapter. Briefly, Newman is seeking for some psychological explanation (justification, if you prefer) of belief that will go beyond the sort of criteria of truth modern man associates with natural science, and perhaps with common sense. It would be unfair to say that Newman's illative sense is basically William James's famous pragmatic "will to believe"; certainly Newman does not say that we should believe what we want to believe. But he does insist that full human life on this earth has to be guided by something more than notions of truth that guide the experimental scientist in his laboratory; that something is a mixture of what we Americans call "hunch" and "know-how," of aesthetic sensitivity, of moral sensitivity, of concrete experience of actual problems. Knowledge we arrive at through the illative sense is to knowledge arrived at by pure logic as a cable of many strands is to a single bar of steel; each is strong, but only one is of a simple, single piece. The illative sense, Newman maintains, varies in different individuals, and in them is often stronger in, for instance, aesthetic than in moral matters. There can be in such matters no such universal test as logic applied to science affords, no way of proving a truth of morals or aesthetics to a person with an imperfect or an untrained illative sense. But this is not to say that there is no such thing as truth in these matters; on the contrary, the general opinion of mankind over the ages has not been cynical or skeptical in these matters of value-judgment, but has recognized saints, artists, and wise men when it met them. Only if we expect Christian truths as we find them at work among men to be perfect, unchanging, absolute, only, in fact, if we are dogmatic where dogmas do not fit, shall we feel that our judgments of value are inferior in validity to the judgments of fact of the scientist.

Newman's own exercise of the illative sense led him in the direction of conservative politics, toward sustaining the existing system of social and economic relations. But the theoretical scaffolding he drew up is one of the very best for what is sometimes called liberal Catholicism, the conscious adapting of Christian attitudes to a greater degree of democracy, toward a greater acceptance of some of the goals of the Enlightenment.

We have chosen Maistre, Burke, and Newman as examples of thinkers who attack from the point of view of traditional Christian cosmology and psychology the optimistic and rationalistic beliefs of the Enlightenment. It is difficult, of course, to draw the line between men like these and other conservatives whose articulate interests are perhaps secular

rather than religious. Inevitably, most conservatives are at least out-
wardly Christian, since Christianity is the established faith of the West.
There are indeed attacks on democracy from the Right, from the new
authoritarian or *totalitarian* positions that are not really Christian or
traditional, and to these we shall shortly come. Their great development
was in the twentieth century, though their roots lie in the nineteenth.
In the nineteenth century, the most important intellectual opposition
still came from thinkers who wanted to go back to something they thought
better, and once, at least, actually prevailing here on earth. At bottom, what they opposed to democracy was aristocracy, the rule of the
wise and the good, the classical tradition of the Greek or the Roman
gentleman as it had been modified by later Christian and feudal practice.

We cannot here attempt a systematic treatment of such thinkers,
who differ from men like Burke chiefly in their emphasis. By the
nineteenth century, many of them are convinced that some form of
popular government is inevitable in the West, and their main concern
seems to be that some kinds of excellence (other than the gift of making
money or that of swaying crowds) be made available for the coming
democratic society.

In a sense, two great political thinkers commonly classified as "liberal,"
John Mill and Alexis de Tocqueville, really belong in this class. Mill
was greatly worried about the danger of the "tyranny of the majority," and
was much interested in proportional representation and in other schemes
to protect the liberty of minority groups. Tocqueville was a cultivated
French nobleman who came to the United States in the early nineteenth
century to study our prison systems, and who went back home to
write one of the classic accounts of American society, *Democracy in
America* (1835-1840). The book is rightly enough considered as one of
the kind favorable to us Americans, as in some ways the work of a
liberal; but Tocqueville was worried about us, about our preference for
equality over liberty, about our distrust of intellectual and spiritual
refinement and distinction, about the danger to the future of Western
man he sees in our great strength and our great indifference toward,
indeed dislike of, the traditional excellences of the classical gentleman.
He was a generous aristocrat, puzzled by American hopes for immediate
perfection, put off by our frontier egalitarianism, alarmed by our faith
that the majority is always right. But he foresaw our coming greatness—
foresaw, indeed, in a passage of great insight, our conflict with Russia.
He has fears that in our greatness we may put material above spiritual
ends, but he does not miss the nobler aspect of the "American dream."
Unlike so many European commentators, he never takes a nagging tone of
superiority.

A later English writer, Sir Henry Maine, puts very clearly the aristocratic distrust of democracy. In his *Popular Government* (1885) distrust

has come very near to fright. Maine, who was by profession a historian, had specialized in early legal history, and did much work on the frontiers of anthropology. But his studies had convinced him that the line of evolution of mankind, working through Western man as its highest representative, ran from primitive shackling of the individual with definite obligations never consciously or voluntarily assumed to the modern freedom of the individual to decide for himself what he is to do and be. In Maine's famous phrase, man's progress is "from status to contract." What alarmed him in the 1880's was the evidence from trade-union activities in Britain, social-security legislation in Germany, rising socialist propaganda everywhere, that some men preferred security to liberty, the safety of status to the risks of contractual freedom. Maine is one of the first great writers in the West to make use of some eighteenth-century notions of human freedom as a *defense* of existing political, social, and economic arrangements instead of using the notions of individual freedom as an *attack* on such arrangements. Maine is the Tory of the 1880's preaching what the radical of the 1780's had preached. Laissez faire, once a threat to the established mercantilist system, was now threatened by socialism, and had become the conservative doctrine of a capitalist middle class. Actually, there is nothing paradoxical about this. In a changing society, successful changes once made are incorporated in the structure of the society. If the society continues to change, as Western society very definitely has, then those who promote the proposed new changes will find themselves opposing what was once radical. Radical Tom Paine in 1790 wanted a government that would govern very little, cost very little, and that would let nature take its beneficent course; if you want that in the United States in the 1960's, you are an old-guard Republican, not a radical.

Just as Newman seems a wiser man than Maistre because he sought to understand the facts of social change, so another group of conservatives seems wiser than Maine and the other frightened gentlemen. These are the Tory democrats, seen at their best in the England that gave them the name. It is not exactly that the Tory democrats are more practical men than the plain Tories; indeed, though they have in Benjamin Disraeli a man practical enough to rise to the position of prime minister, they are mostly confirmed idealists, gentle-minded people, often theorists like the poet Coleridge, clergymen like F. D. Maurice. They are often very self-conscious Christians and sometimes accept the label "Christian socialist." They believe with Burke that most men are unable to guide themselves in freedom to a good life, that, in short, men are sheep who need shepherds. The Industrial Revolution and the false ideas of the Enlightenment about human equality had in their opinion resulted in the rise of bad shepherds—factory owners, politicians, agitators, journalists. What the people need is good shepherds who will see that government inspectors keep factories clean and sanitary, that the workers have social security, that all runs well. These good shepherds are the natural leaders of the people, the wellborn, the educated, the classical gentleman again.

The favorite doctrine of the Tory democrats—and the justification for the second part of their name—is that if the people are really given free choice, if the press, schools, and all the organs of public opinion are open to all points of view, then in such free conditions the people actually will of their own accord, by democratic voting, choose the right shepherds, the men who have the gifts and the training to rule wisely. The really wise and good, they argue, are in the nineteenth-century West in danger of letting the struggle go by default. They are staying out of the political battle, leaving it to the demagogues, the socialists, the cranks. If they will only go before the people with the truth, the people will know them for their true leaders.

The Tory democrats objected to the disorder, the vulgar scrambling, the harshness of a money-getting society. Many of them objected also to the ugliness of their times. But those whose chief quarrel with democratic ways as they developed in the nineteenth century was aesthetic are worth a brief word in themselves. They are not very easy to classify according to their acceptance or rejection of the Enlightenment. Some of the really tender-minded, like the Englishman William Morris, called themselves socialists, and argued that the trouble with democracy was that there wasn't enough of it, that it hadn't gone far enough, that it had created around ordinary men and women a new bad environment, that you should change that environment and let the natural goodness and wisdom of the masses come out. But John Ruskin, who called himself a Tory, is perhaps a better example of the type.

From this "Tory" Ruskin was named a college at Oxford founded in the late nineteenth century to allow competent sons of laboring men to study in that university of the ruling classes. For years, Ruskin College was a center of opposition to the actual Tory party. Indeed it is difficult to disentangle and label the variants of political and moral opposition to things-as-they-were in the nineteenth century. Ruskin is here perhaps unfairly grouped with those whose main feeling of opposition to their age centers in matters aesthetic. His focus seems to be a dislike for money-getters, a dislike for those who measured success in terms of material success, or the honors achieved in a vulgarly competitive society. In such moods he sounds like Carlyle, and at times comes, like Carlyle, close to asking for a Leader to get us out of this morass of materialism. You may judge of his aesthetic social criticism by two quotations, "There is no wealth but life" and "Life is the possession of the valuable by the valiant."

The aesthetic critics of nineteenth-century democratic culture were united at least in their belief that it produced "cheap and nasty" things in quantity, that the machine had killed any pleasure in creative work of the kind the old craftsman used to feel, that it had made work an unalleviated burden, that it had poisoned the leisure of the workingman by leaving him only mass-produced mediocrity even in his amusements. They were not in agreement about the way out, but most of them held that the uncorrupted few, the men like themselves who still knew the beautiful and the good, must somehow take the lead and create here and there little cells of beauty and wisdom. The nineteenth century was the great century of little social experiments, of ideal communities designed to prove that a given social environment will remake fallen men. There was still a good deal of space available in the United States, which is one reason why so many of these communities were founded there. Brook Farm in Massachusetts, the Phalanx in New Jersey, New Harmony in Indiana, Icaria in Illinois—the list is long, a fascinating catalogue of human hopes and failures. Morris, who was a gentleman of independent means, founded various shops for handwork, preached faithfully before little groups of converts, and wrote a Utopia called *News from Nowhere* (1891) in which men have got rid of machines and great ugly cities and live once more in a green and pleasant land of arts and crafts.

In this classification of aesthetic opponents of democracy you will no doubt find the greatest concentration of cranks, of men with one-way formulae for heaven on earth, the kind of fanatic who in the sixteenth century went in for the wilder sects. They offend the settled bourgeois sometimes out of all proportion to their importance. It was not Morris or Ruskin, it was not the Utopian socialists of the little communities, but the Marxists who really threatened the comfort of the philistine in his little suburban castle-home. Nevertheless it will not do to dismiss the aesthetic criticism of democracy too lightly. The slums of Manchester or Liverpool, the hot-dog stands, filling stations, motels, and cabin slums that line major American motor highways are surely among the ugliest things man has ever built on this earth. If there really is progress, it has hardly achieved the elimination, or even the lessening, of the ugly. Moreover, these critics, impractical and soft though many of them seem, focused attention on aspects of the very important problem of the incentives and rewards of labor in modern society. Capitalist and socialist thought alike tended, and still tend unduly today, to consider the problem of labor solely in terms of wages and "efficiency" in the technical sense of factory organization. Men like Morris, or the French Utopian socialist Fourier, incompetent though they were in the ways of the world, knew better. They pointed out that the problem of getting people to do the necessary work of the world is a full, complex, human problem, not merely a problem of dollars and cents or of efficient motions. They pointed out that men do not like to be bored, that they like to feel they have made something useful or even beautiful, that they have pride of workmanship, that they enjoy being part of a team.

Morris in *News from Nowhere* has the outsider notice, in the lovely public forest—Kensington Forest—where ugly suburban London used to be, gangs of sturdy young men cheerfully digging ditches, and is told by his guide that they enjoy competitive ditch-digging. When the outsider expresses surprise, his guide remarks that he understands that in nineteenth-century Oxford and Cambridge eight-oared crews went through the hardest physical labor with pleasure. The sermon may seem rather silly and sentimental; and yet on reflection you will realize that the amount of "work" expended by a college crew or a football team would easily build a housing project. There is no magic that can turn labor into sport, and Morris does not persuade us that there is. But there is a real problem of using the abundant energies of men in socially effective ways.

You can make a pretty effective argument that the critics of democracy with whom we have so far been engaged in this chapter are of purely historical and intellectual interest (no slight thing) but that they have not in fact greatly influenced the world we now live in. The immediately effective attacks on democracy have indeed been made from some other base than that of Christianity or the classical ideal of the beautiful and the good; they have at times appealed to these and other strains in our Western tradition, but their major appeal, and the one we now classify them under, is that of an exclusive in-group, national, racial—at any rate, biologically determined. From these attacks there came in the twentieth century those totalitarian movements of the Right—Fascism, Nazism, Falangism, and the like—which were perhaps no more than scotched in World War II.

Now the problem of the intellectual ancestry of Rightist totalitarianism is a fascinating one, and one that has already attracted much attention. Once more, we must warn the reader that it is absurd to say that Wagner, for instance, is "responsible for," "to blame for," a "cause of," the German Nazi movement. The Nazis cannot be explained fully and completely, any more than cancer or polio can be fully explained. We do know that such movements always have a set of views about all the questions, big and little, and we can see where they got some of their answers. That should be enough for all but the most determined metaphysicians.

We have already noted that the cluster of ideas and sentiments called nationalism gave trouble to those who wished all men to be brothers. Even within national states greatly influenced by the ideas of the Enlightenment, even in the states at the heart of the democratic tradition —the United States, Britain, France, and the smaller countries of western and northern Europe—the demands for national unity, for conformity on the part of each citizen to a national pattern, served to lessen the personal freedom, the range of character and eccentricity, within these in-groups. Moreover, most of the great democratic states, including the United States, had in the nineteenth century careers of successful expansion in the course of which they came to hold as possessions lands inhabited by men of different color and different culture. Almost universally among the citizens of these democracies there prevailed in the nineteenth and early twentieth centuries the feeling that theirs were better, higher, ways, and that they ought, peacefully if possible, to impose their ways on these darker-skinned peoples. A whole literature of the "white man's burden" arose to justify what its authors for the most part considered the inevitable Westernizing of the rest of the world.

Even in the lands where the democratic tradition was strongest, however, there were those who held that these non-Western peoples could not in fact be brought up to Western levels, and that they ought for their own good to be kept in a perpetually inferior status, or even be helped to die out. Americans like Lothrop Stoddard and Madison Grant, Britishers like Benjamin Kidd, were alarmed at the "rising tide of color," and urged that something had to be done to protect the hitherto dominant great races of whites. The Englishman Cecil Rhodes, no theorist but a businessman who made a fortune in South Africa, believed that Anglo-Saxons (or rather, English, Scots, Welshmen, and Americans) had achieved standards of moral and political decency no other peoples seemed able to achieve, and that therefore they should unite, get as much of the earth as possible, and multiply as fast as possible to fill it.

But the clearest line of antidemocratic Rightist totalitarian thought and practice comes out in the German and Italian experience. Their nationalism, their later totalitarianism, does not prove the existence of an innate incapacity for political virtue among Germans or Italians. Their politics is a complex resultant of many historical factors. There are many variables of historical growth in the past two centuries that help explain the rise of totalitarian societies in the twentieth century in these states.

One strand is certainly the simple strand of historical nationalism we have already noted as universal in the West. To this must be added, especially for Germany, a very strong strand of "racism," the notion that Germans are biologically a special variety of *Homo sapiens*—blond, sturdy, clean-cut, virtuous, the destined master race. Racism gave a pseudo-rational ethical justification for nationalism, gave it a content of ideas. To outsiders, this is clearly an example of a social myth; the Germans aren't even in a majority blonds. But we today are pretty well used to myths which, though they do not correspond to scientifically established truth, clearly influence people and get them to work together.

The irony has often been pointed out: The first strong modern literary source of these ideas of Germanic caste and color lies in the writings of a nineteenth-century Frenchman, the Comte de Gobineau. Actually there is a long history in the West of prestige attached, if not to actual blondness, at least to lightness of color. Even among the ancient Greeks, legend made such gods as Apollo blond; the whole Hindu caste system depends on *varna*, color; even in the Christian artistic tradition you will note a certain tendency to make the saints rather more blond than the sinners. Scientifically speaking, we do not know whether or not blonds tend to be more virtuous than brunettes; the question is simply meaningless. It is, however, a fact that this and other beliefs of a similar sort entered into the antidemocratic faith of the Nazis. As early as 1842, a German historian could write:

> The Celtic race, as it has developed in Ireland and in France, has always been moved by a bestial instinct, whereas we Germans never act save under the impulsion of thoughts and aspirations which are truly sacred.

The American historian of the revolt of the Netherlands, Motley, could contrast Celtic "dissoluteness" and German "chastity."

A third strand, and probably in fact the strongest and most important in Nazism and Fascism alike, is the emphasis on the authority of a ruler and a small group of the party elite around the ruler. This concept too has firm nineteenth-century background, and indeed is in one sense merely a reappearance of very old notions like that of the divine right of kings. Perhaps there is no better nineteenth-century proto-fascist than the once-popular Victorian writer Thomas Carlyle, whose influential *Heroes and Hero-Worship* is full of the leadership principle, the necessity of the stupid many's subservience to the wise few, the need of permanence, status, subordination in our madly and stupidly competitive society. Carlyle at first was moderate in his demands:

> Aristocracy and Priesthood, a Governing class and a Teaching class; these two, sometimes separate, and endeavouring to harmonize themselves, sometimes conjoined as one, and the King a Pontiff-King:—there did no Society exist without these two vital elements, there will none exist.

But as the nineteenth century wore on with democracy still going forward, especially in his own country, he came to be more and more ferociously authoritarian in his demands, and in the end came to call for a universal drill sergeant, a military dictator, a man of deeds and no words—merely commands.

Toward the end of the century, Germany itself produced one of the most articulate enemies of conventional democracy, one of the real, if unintended, builders of Nazi ideology. This was Friederich Nietzsche, partly insane and wholly intellectual, at bottom a sensitive moralist who could not bear the ugliness, cant, stuffiness of the rising bourgeois empire of the Hohenzollerns. Nietzsche, with all his subtleties, is a fascinating example of the modern intellectual with his infinite capacity for feeling pain, his impatience of the herd-men around him, his horror at the machine-made ugliness of the middle-class world. He called for the "superman" (Uebermensch), for a transvaluation of values that would once more bring noble violence to play against ignoble bourgeois comfort, against the democratic way of life:

> Democracy has in all ages been the form under which organizing strength has perished. . . . Liberalism, or the transformation of mankind into cattle. . . . Modern democracy is the historic form of the decay of the state. . . . The two opposing parties, the socialist and the national—or whatever they may be called in the different countries of Europe—are worthy of each other; envy and laziness are the motive powers in each of them. . . . The equality of souls before God, this lie, this screen for the *rancunes* of all the baseminded, this anarchist bomb of a concept, which has become the last revolution, the modern idea and principle of the destruction of the whole social order—this is *Christian* dynamite.

In fact, Nietzsche wrote a whole platform for totalitariansm of the Right a generation before it came to power:

> The future of German culture rests with the sons of Prussian officers. . . . Peace and letting other people alone—this is not a policy for which I have any respect whatever. To dominate (*herrschen*) and to help the highest thought to victory—that would be the only thing that could interest me in Germany. . . . The same discipline makes the soldier and the scholar efficient; and, looked at more closely, there is no true scholar who has not the instincts of the true soldier in his veins. . . . Ye shall love peace as a means to new wars—and the short peace more than the long. . . . War and courage have done more things than charity. Not your sympathy but your bravery hath hitherto saved the victims.

We must in fairness note that Nietzsche, in this respect like Rousseau, Carlyle, even Emerson, was a thinker apparently unworried by need for consistency, that "hobgoblin of little minds"; you could draw from Nietzsche a series of quotations quite contradicting the series above. We may also note that many of Nietzsche's advocates insist that by "war" and "courage" Nietzsche means, never what military men mean by those words, but a pure, spiritual, existential soaring, the "transvaluation of values."

In summary, the attacks from the Right on the nineteenth-century way of life—on the "Victorian compromise"—are many, varied, and extremely difficult to range in an order. There is the attack from the vantage of traditional Christianity, an attack that centers on the great doctrine of the Enlightenment, the natural goodness and reasonableness of man; an attack that emphasizes the importance of tradition, "prejudice," and constituted Christian authority in an orderly society; an attack that accuses nineteenth-century society of neglecting in its love of competition and progress the essential fact that man is a political animal. There is the attack from the point of view of the older aristocratic ideals —ideals directly descended from the spare humanism of the classical tradition—an attack that centers on the tendencies of democracies to follow noisy, unsound leaders, to be jealous of aristocratic minorities, if not of all minorities, to tend toward the "tyranny of the majority." For these aristocratic critics, the "average" man of the majority is mediocre or downright inferior. There is the attack from the point of view of good taste and culture, the aesthetic taste, which finds the new society devoted to the production of the "cheap and nasty." There are other attacks, notably those that foreshadow totalitarianism, which can be described only in a much more thorough study of the nineteenth century than is here possible. No neat summary of these attacks is adequate. But if you must have a single word, what all these attackers find wrong in their time is its *materialism*.

Attacks from the Left

Very broadly, we may say that nineteenth-century attacks from the Left on what the Victorian compromise had made of the ideals of the Enlightenment bore as their gist the broadening out of political democracy into social and above all economic democracy. The formula is a simplification. Men on the Left had as much trouble with the eternal tension between the ideals of liberty and authority as did men on the Center.

There is in the nineteenth century a certain amount of writing and speaking which urges that the real trouble is that the men and methods of 1776 and 1789 have not really been followed, that we need to get back to the simple rights of man, that the cure for the troubles of democracy is more democracy of the old sort—bills of rights, written constitutions, universal suffrage, secret ballot, equal electoral districts, rotation in office, compulsory secular education for all, and so on. This is substantially the position of the people usually called "radicals," like the Chartists in the England of the 1830's and 1840's; they hold that if only political democracy is carried out fully, rights of man and all, there will result from the free interplay of human ambitions something like a rough social and economic equality. No one will be very rich, no one will be very poor, but there will be a healthy variety of reward within a broadly egalitarian society. As the century wears on, the radicals come gradually to feel that this equalizing process needs help from social legislation of the kind familiar enough to Americans under the name of the New Deal. The radicals become collectivists, or at least state interventionists, and to their opponents, socialists.

This process can best be seen in Britain, where by the 1880's the Liberal party has begun to back social legislation, and the Tories have been forced into something like the defense of classical laissez faire. John Mill's later career shows how a Benthamite can be prepared quite readily for a mildly collectivist political position. But an even better index is a man like T. H. Green, an Oxford don much influenced by German idealistic philosophy, who helped to form the young men who in parliament and in the civil service were laying the foundations for the quasi-socialist Britain we know today. Green's *Principles of Political Obligation* (1888) is an attack on the metaphysics and politics of conventional British radicalism. Green finds that utilitarian nominalist notions do in fact leave the individual a mere social atom, blindly struggling with other atoms, in no sense a true social animal. His own notion of the state and of other social groups emphasizes their emotional hold over the individual, their "reality" in something like the German idealist sense, but Green manages to preserve room for individual rights as well as obligations. His state will be more than an umpire in a fair game; it will help the weaker and less skilled to take better part in the game. But it will not abolish the game entirely in favor of a kind of mass drill.

The main point for us here is that toward the end of the nineteenth century a current of collectivist or interventionist thought and practice set in with varying strength in the different parts of Western society. Of the greater countries, the United States was the last to feel this current. It is still resisted by many solid Americans as the destruction of our traditional liberties, as "socialism," as "un-American." Dispassionate analysis of the problem of state intervention in business and other private affairs of the individual is still difficult for most Americans.

Admittedly, the kind of policy advocated by the Fabians and the Labour party in Britain, the Third Force in France, the New Dealers in the United States is not identical with policies of even fairly advanced radicals—say Herbert Spencer—a hundred years ago. There is no great harm in putting it that the difference represents the influence of "socialist" thought on the democratic tradition. But one must be very clear that this Fabian–Third-Force–New-Deal development differs sharply from what is still the best and most definite sense of the term *socialism*— the very specific religious sect founded by Karl Marx.

The differences between the modified democratic way of life, cosmology, culture, or even religion represented by contemporary Leftist trends in the West and by the orthodox Marxist position are great

indeed; here we can but indicate some of the main lines an analysis of
these differences should take. But first it must be said that both the
Marxist and the non-Marxist Left can legitimately claim common origin
in the Enlightenment, and that both are in important ways opposed to
traditional Christianity. Both reject the doctrine of original sin in
favor of a basically optimistic view of human nature, both exclude
the supernatural, both focus on the ideal of a happy life on this earth
for everyone, both reject the ideal of a stratified society with permanent
inequalities of status and great inequalities of income. It is only fair
to note that today it is possible for a non-Marxist Leftist to accept some
measure of traditional Christian pessimism, and indeed to consider himself a Christian; Marxism, a much more rigid creed, can hardly make
any open compromise with Christianity or any theistic religion, but
must remain firmly positivist and materialist.

, Indeed, this rigidity of doctrine is one of the main differences between
the two systems of belief. The democratic Leftist retains at his most
collectivist at least a minimum of the old liberal belief that there
must be intellectual freedom to entertain new ideas, to experiment, to
invent. Even when he is no longer moved by a feeling for "rights"
of the individual, he is committed to the notion of progress through
variation, and he knows that groups as such do not have new ideas.
You can tell much from the tags and clichés that even the intellectuals
cannot quite avoid; the democratic Leftist will still hold that the only
dogma is that there be no dogmas, or that the only room for intolerance
is for intolerance of the intolerant.

It is true that a very articulate, if clearly also a minority, group in
full nineteenth century claimed its inspiration and origin in the eighteenth-century Enlightenment, and yet came in the end to disparage
individual liberty, to use most of the slogans of the authoritarians, order,
discipline, faith, solidarity. These are the so-called "positivists." The
term positivism is sometimes used loosely, as the equivalent of materialism, to describe a belief that rejects the supernatural and stands on
the firm, "positive" ground of science. Historically, however, the term
means a follower of the French *politique et moraliste* Auguste Comte,
whom we have already met as the maker of a table ranking the natural
sciences in the order of their "maturity." But Comte did more than
call for a supreme science of sociology. In his later years, especially
after the failure of the revolutions of 1848, he sought to establish a
kind of church based on a formal belief in progress, natural science,
humanity, and a formal and very vehement disbelief in the Christian
God. Comte himself was the high priest of this positivist faith, which
had its own organized churches, and which spread out into various other
groups allied in their faith in man, science, and the future. These

religious positivists, not yet quite extinct, must not be confused with the "logical positivists" of our own day, to whom we shall come.

Save, perhaps, for these Comtean positivists and their likes (who are not really democrats) the democratic Leftist retains always, even in his most up-to-date form, something of the old distrust of any system of ideas that tries to sink the individual in the group, that seems to make the individual merely a cell of an all-important whole; he preserves at heart a genuine respect for a great deal of the apparatus of individual rights which, especially as they apply to property, he is likely to dismiss rather cavalierly in some of his moods; he does not believe in the inevitability of the class struggle and of revolution and hopes that he can attain greater social and economic equality, greater stability in society, better administration both in business and government, by a process of voluntary change effected through legislation put through in the usual democratic way; he is, in modern cant terms, a gradualist and a reformist; he is, especially in recent years, increasingly willing to pay some attention to critics of the basic ideas of the Enlightenment, critics of the sort we have here classed as attackers from the Right, and critics of the kind we shall study in the next chapter as anti-intellectuals; and, having observed the totalitarian societies of the Nazis, the Fascists, and the Russian Communists in our own time, he has come to conclude that uniformity, regimentation, and absolute authority are prices much too great to pay for order and security from the whirl of Western competitive society.

We come at last to Marxist socialism, or communism. From our point of view, Marxism—or Marx-Lenin-Stalinism, to give what was until the downgrading of Stalin under Khrushchev the canonical succession—is a very rigorous development of, or heresy of, the world-attitude of the Enlightenment. It stands toward the central democratic form of the Enlightenment in some ways as Calvinism stands toward traditional Christianity of the Roman Catholics, or perhaps better, toward the Anglicans who under one formal church organization run the spectrum of belief from unitarianism to high sacramentalism. Marxism is a rigorous, dogmatic, puritanical, determinist, firmly disciplined sect of eighteenth-century optimistic humanitarian materialists.

If you feel that the term "religion" should be limited to systems of belief that maintain the existence of a God, or gods, or spirits, or at any rate something *immaterial, supernatural,* then you have already been thrown off the track by our comparing national patriotism with religion. In this book we have applied terms taken from our Western religious history to any organized and articulate set of beliefs about the Big Questions—right and wrong, human happiness, the order of the universe, and so on—which for the believer did at least two things: gave him intellectual orientation in this world (that is, answered his questions) and gave him emotional participation in a group through ritual and other forms of common action. In such terms Marxism, especially as it has been worked out in Russia, is one of the most active forms of religion in the world today, and one that all educated persons must make some effort to understand.

Marxism clearly fulfills one of the simple requirements of a religion: It has its sacred books, its authoritative scripture—in the orthodox tradition the writings of Marx and Engels with the comments, exegesis, and additions brought by Lenin. It has also its heresies, of which the most important goes back to the nineteenth-century "revisionist" movement associated first of all with the name of Eduard Bernstein, and which substituted for the *violent* revolution and subsequent dictatorship of the proletariat of orthodox Marxism the *gradual* achievement of social and economic democracy (equality) by legal political action. Revisionism turned into gradualism, which is substantially the position of present-day *socialists* (in contrast to *communists*). Gradualism was to its defenders not merely a device to quiet some bourgeois fears and gain bourgeois converts; it was also, in the minds of leaders like Kautsky, a necessary historical emendation to meet the failure of Marx's predictions of an inevitable violent uprising of the proletariat in advanced Western countries. There are many other Marxist splinter-groups or heresies, for which we cannot here find space. The existence of such heresies is not necessarily, however, a sign of weakness of the movement; indeed, if one thinks of the rise of Christianity, it is possible that these heresies are an indication of vitality in Marxism, of a continuing intellectual fermentation that is a sign of life rather than of decay and dispersion.

We must here concentrate on the orthodox form of the doctrine. Marx's greatest work is *Das Kapital,* which is in form a treatise on economics. Obviously, however, even *Das Kapital* is no narrowly professional study of economic theory, but a philosophy of history, a system of sociology, and a program for political action. Together with the rest of the accepted canon, it gives a rather more complete and systematic cosmology than any *single* work in the orthodox democratic tradition of the Enlightenment. Marxism is a *tighter, neater* thing than conventional democracy.

Marxism bears the clear stamp of the nineteenth century in which Marx and Engels lived and wrote. It is based on a very explicit conception of change, of growth, of evolution as an ultimate fact of universal validity. (Whether or not Marx thought of this evolutionary process as due to come to an end with the achievement of the classless society is an interesting but not central question to which we shall return.) Now one of the central themes of all Western thought on these high matters has been the reality and importance of change. The Platonic type of mind has tended to try to escape from the flow of life and death of this world as we human animals experience it into another world above time and change; and more than this—worldly philosophers like the rationalists of the early modern centuries sought for categories of logic that would be absolute and changeless. Marxism, at least on the surface, glories in process, change, and tries to find in change itself the answer to the riddle of change.

The specific answer to the riddle Marx got from his master Hegel was the dialectic. But for Hegel the process of thesis-antithesis-synthesis went on under the impulse of what he called spirit, an immaterial something, force, idea, or soul, at any rate nothing human senses, common sense, or natural science could ever get at. Marx proudly proclaimed that he had taken the pyramid Hegel foolishly tried to poise on its point and placed it squarely and sensibly on its broad base; that is, *he made the idealistic dialectic into the materialistic dialectic.* Change for Marx takes place according to a plan, but not the plan of Hegel's silly world-spirit. Change takes place in matter, in the sense world that surrounds us, of which we too are wholly a part, just like all the other animals. The changes in this material world—it can be called simply our environment—determine our whole lives, our physical well-being, our institutions, our ideas of right and wrong, our cosmology. The key word here is "determine," a favorite with Marx, for whom "dialectical materialism" and "historical determinism" were almost equivalent phrases.

Some of these determining environmental factors are, of course, of the kind men have long recognized—climate, for instance. But Marx focuses on a to him much more fundamental aspect of the environment that he calls the "means of production," the way men make a living. From this fundamental set of material conditions everything else in a man's life, in the life of groups of men, must follow. Nomads driving their herds over the Asiatic steppes eat and drink, raise families, obey laws and customs, follow chieftains, fight, and believe in a certain religion all in accordance with inevitable developments from the means of production of a nomadic pastoral society. Marxist scholars have shown great skill and erudition in the concrete working out of these concepts for various societies.

Marx himself was interested primarily in his own Western society, for which he worked out a complete outline of social change in accordance with his dialectic. His base line is the means of production of a self-sufficient manorial economy in the Middle Ages. The society determined by this manorial economy has a serf class that support a master class of feudal nobles and their attendant priests, has a fairly rigid graded system of status, and holds the kind of beliefs about God and the universe typical of the Middle Ages in the West. This manorial economy and feudal society is the *thesis.* The principle of change is for Marx something "material," not an idea in anyone's mind—though actually even

Marx has to admit that the material change comes about because some men want it, conceive it. The change that began the modern world is in its simplest form money, trade, the beginnings of a capitalist economy. As this change slowly goes on, a new class, a trading or *bourgeois* class is formed. Between the old feudal nobility and the new moneyed middle class there follows an active "class struggle" (another very famous Marxist expression). The new class has its own philosophy, characteristically Protestant after a time, its own views of the goodness of competition, the legitimacy of profit, the need of political democracy to get around royal and noble power, in short a full philosophy of life. This trading economy and bourgeois democratic society is the *antithesis*. The long struggle between thesis and antithesis, after preliminary bourgeois victories in England and Holland, culminated in the American and French revolutions and the full victory of the bourgeoisie in the nineteenth century.

The class struggle was by no means over. The victorious bourgeoisie, amalgamated with the conquered remains of the nobility, formed a synthesis, a new thesis, and struggled with a new antithesis, the *proletariat*. This struggle itself, and the classes that made the struggle, were the material result of another change in the mode of production, the introduction of the factory system and the modern form of industrial and financial capitalism. To the old banking and trading bourgeoisie there is added the industrialist, the factory owner, and a new and more powerful capitalist class arises. The workers are now herded together in factories under the eyes of their oppressors, and held down by the iron laws of capitalist economics to a bare subsistence wage. But at least they can organize, if only in secret, and under Marxist leadership become fully class-conscious. Thesis bourgeoisie and antithesis proletariat are now (Marx first announced the outline of this theory in the *Communist Manifesto* of 1848) fighting the last class struggle. The victory of the proletariat is assured.

Marx assured it by a rather complicated economic analysis that we cannot attempt to follow closely. The upshot of his argument is that by laws of capitalist competition production is bound periodically to result in gluts that bring on business crises in the course of which the weaker firms go to the wall, their members get proletarianized, and the surviving firms get bigger and more powerful. But the working class, though it suffers in each crisis, gets more numerous and more desperate. In a famous phrase, Marx saw the inevitable working of economic law making the poor poorer and the rich richer. At last there will come a supreme crisis, in which the proletariat, fully organized and fully class-conscious, will rise in its might and take over the means of production. Thus will be achieved the dictatorship of the proletariat, in the course of which banks, communications, transport, and factories will be taken from their bourgeois owners and collectivized, put in the hands of the new proletarian government. Then comes the final stage. With the liquidation of the capitalist owners there are no more classes—or rather, there is only one class left, the victorious proletariat. There can thus be no class struggle; and since the whole apparatus of the state has, according to the Marxist analysis, been necessary only in order that the thesis class might hold down the antithesis class in the class struggle, there will be no need for the state with its police, its courts, its armies, and its taxes. The state will wither away and we shall at last have the classless society, the heaven on earth of Marxist eschatology. As a matter of fact, Marx himself did not dwell on the details of his heaven, and even Engels and the later commentators are vague on this point. As good nineteenth-century believers in progress, however, they do not like to think of even heaven as static. Perhaps we may say that the Marxist holds that cruel and inhuman struggles like the class struggle will cease with the classless society, but that progress will go on through decent, painless, gamelike competiton.

It is now over a hundred years since the *Communist Manifesto,* and the course of history has not gone as Marx planned. It is true that the capitalist business cycle of prosperity and depression has gone on, and that possibly depressions have grown worse. There has certainly been a tendency toward the concentration of capital in giant industry, but it has not been uniform even in the German, British, and American economies. The formula that the rich are growing richer and the poor are growing poorer has certainly not proved true. Government is intervening to regulate industry even in the United States, and in all industrial countries there has been a tendency to some degree of what is often called "state socialism." And, of course, there was in 1917 in industrially backward Russia—a country Marx himself disliked—the first great revolutionary movement to come to power under Marxist auspices. The Russians have established the dictatorship of the proletariat, but there are as yet not the slightest signs of the withering away of the Russian state. Marx, indeed, supposed that once the revolution was successful in a great nation—he apparently thought it would come first in the most advanced one of his day, Great Britain—it would spread at least to all the rest of Western society, and therefore throughout the world. Faithful Marxists can, of course, point out that until the revolution is worldwide, the state cannot possibly be expected to wither away in beleaguered Russia.

Our concern here is not, however, primarily with the question of how well Marx forecast the future. The movement he founded has come to power in two great states, Russia and China, and in their "satellites"; and his followers, though somewhat split by heresies, are strong in many parts of Western society. Marxism is one of the religions—or if that word is too strong for you, one of the great clusters of guiding principles—that compete today for the loyalties of Western men.

The Marxist God is the omnipotent if impersonal force of dialectical materialism. The Marxists themselves do not hesitate to use the word *determinism,* with all its overtones of St. Augustine and Calvin. For them the overtones are those of science, not religion. This system, they insist, is a scientific one, which is why it must be true. Theirs is not, to an outsider, the science of the laboratory and the clinic, but a hypostasized science that does for them what the hypostasized science of Newton did for the eighteenth-century philosophers. That is, it gives them the comforting assurance that they have the key to the universe.

Dialectical materialism, then, will for the Marxist bring about the inevitable world revolution of the proletariat. It will bring that about in spite of anything the capitalists can do; indeed, the more the capitalist, following the course of action dictated to him by the means of production under which he works, behaves like a capitalist, the quicker will come the proletarian victory. The Rockefellers and the Morgans are doing just what dialectical materialism wants them to do. This does not apparently make the Marxist feel any more kindly toward them and their like. Nor does the certainty that the stars in their courses are working for the inevitable triumph of the proletariat make the Marxist a fatalist. We have already seen that for the Calvinist the certainty that God's will must prevail seems to make the believer all the more ready to go out into the world and fight to help God's will to prevail; and we have noted that for the Calvinist there is always the saving uncertainty that the individual human worm, even though he is a good member of the church of Calvin, may not really *know* God's will. For the Marxist there is not even this remnant of Christian humility to provide some logical support for his actual conduct as a fighter for the right as he sees it. The Marxist—and Marx himself—knows absolutely that dialectical materialism will do its work in the foreordained way. But one does not see the convinced Marxist sitting back and letting dialectical materialism do its work without him. On the contrary, he is an ardent propagandist, an ethical meliorist, a man who to judge by his conduct believes that his own efforts can make a difference in human behavior. Once more, we can only note that *metaphysical* belief in determinism seems for the Marxist, as for the Calvinist, quite consonant with a *psychological* belief in the importance of the *will* to believe—and act—in the individual.

To continue with our religious parallel: The Marxist heaven, as we have already noted, is the classless society, a state men can achieve here on earth, and which has in common with the eschatologies of other advanced religions the concept of a state of things where no human desires will be frustrated. It is true that the Marxist prides himself on his materialism, and believes that in the classless societies all *decent* human appetites will be satisfied; he would deny indignantly that his paradise has anything in common with that mystical and among intellectual Christians predominant concept of heaven as a place in which *all* appetites are overcome, extinguished, spiritually sublimated. Yet the classless society is no gross place, no place for the kind of sensual delights the Marxist associates with the vulgar capitalist ideal. Indeed, there is, in almost the common acceptance of the term, a *puritanical* aspect of Marxism; the Marxist is as scornful as any Calvinist of the merely Epicurean side of life, of vulgar, gross pleasures and even more of their aristocratic refinements. Marx himself is a moralist, as indignant at the crassness and injustices of an industrial society as Carlyle or Ruskin. The Marxist tries hard to save a positive aspect of his heaven, to insist that in the classless society men will compete and make progress as good children of our culture should; but what really strikes one in the Marxist as in other heavens is the ideal of absence of conflict and frustration, of the extinction of desire.

The notion of the revolution and the dictatorship of the proletariat can be taken as roughly a parallel to the Christian notion of a day of judgment. Again there is the obvious difference that the Marxist believes his saving catastrophe will be brought about by "natural" rather than by supernatural forces. For the Marxist the state of grace, the thing that marks off the faithful from the heathen, is simply the ability to see the universe in Marxist terms, "scientific" terms as the Marxist would put it. His Marx is the rationalist Messiah set over against the spiritual —and to the Marxists, of course, false—Messiah, Christ.

Again as in most religious bodies, this awareness of belonging, of *knowing the truth,* of having the inner light, is balanced by performance of certain symbolic acts that bind the believer to the whole body of the faithful. In other words, the Marxist has his works as well as his faith: He reads his Marxist holy books, he goes to meetings, he has his party card and his party duties. He has a clue to everything, an answer to all his questions. There should be nothing surprising to an informed outsider that in Communist Russia there is Marxist music, Marxist history, and even Marxist biology.

It is probably true that there is no clear Marxist equivalent for the kind of religious experience that for the Christian is focused in the word *conscience.* One whole aspect of Christianity, as we have noted in an earlier chapter, centers on the plight of the individual soul of sinful man in its willful struggle with God; Christianity is a highly individualistic faith with a highly individualistic concept of salvation. Marxism is committed to the notion that the true fulfillment of the individual is, not of course in mere ant- or beelike automatic participation in the social whole, but at least in a thorough identification of the individual with the whole collectivity. Marxism is a collectivist faith, and its notion of individual salvation cannot be very closely paralleled in Christianity. Yet the Marxist has a conscience, and however ill the notion fits with dialectic materialism, can suffer the tortures of conscience. This you will see readily enough in the hero of Arthur Koestler's *Darkness at Noon;* and if you take the trouble to look into his career, you will see it in Mr. Koestler himself.

In pure theory—or in Marxist theology at its highest level—Marx and Engels did the great work. Though Soviet practice has canonized Lenin and, until 1953, Stalin as having made essential additions to the main body of Marxist beliefs, to an outsider their importance seems rather as organizers than as thinkers. Marxism has not yet combined the thinker and the doer as successfully as they were combined in St. Paul. Lenin indeed, faced with the fact that the wicked capitalist nations of the West seemed in the early years of the twentieth century to be prospering, that at any rate they were not going on the rocks quite as Marx had predicted, added to the Marxist analysis a corollary to the effect that having reached the limit of exploiting their own citizens English and other Western capitalists had postponed the evil day by colonial imperialism, by exploiting the rest of the world. But this in itself was, according to Lenin, a confirmation of Marx; imperialism was the inevitable overripeness of capitalism, the last stage before the revolution of the proletariat.

Actually Lenin's great service to Marxism came as an organizer of a successful revolution in a backward country. To do this at all, Lenin had to organize a violent revolution—which Marx had always preached, though rather academically—a revolution put through by a minority of disciplined and desperate characters with long years of conspiratorial experience underground, and with no "bourgeois-democratic" scruples about legality, humane decency, honesty, and the like. Marx, for all his testy dislike of mere reformers, had definitely not liked the conspiratorial professional revolutionist. To some of Marx's followers, then, Lenin is not so much the exponent as the betrayer of true Marxism. To the kindly, hopeful, other-worldly Marxists (there are such, illogical though their attitude may seem to an outsider) Lenin's ruthless and quite consciously realistic behavior meant accepting the wicked bourgeois world they wanted to transcend. To them, Lenin, and much worse, Stalin, had simply surrendered to such wicked illusions as common sense, practicality, success.

The standard of moral and aesthetic values for the Marxist on this earth is essentially bourgeois, capitalist, with a slightly soured puritanical twist. There are intellectual circles in Western countries where Marxism is combined with various kinds of moral and aesthetic rebellion against conventional standards of the eighteenth- and nineteenth-century bourgeoisie—but not in Russia. Marxism is, in fact, one of the most legitimate heirs of the materialist and rationalist cosmology of the eighteenth-century philosophers. Marx himself has a vision of the properly functioning society strangely like that of Adam Smith—an economy, and therefore a society, in which each individual by behaving naturally contributes to the well-being and smooth working of the group. The ideal, the end, of Marxism is the philosophical anarchism among free and equal human beings that is one of the persistent themes of the Enlightenment.

The means, however, is violent revolution and a transitional state of dictatorship in which there will be rigorous use of authority from above, strict discipline among the masses, the whole apparatus of a totalitarian society. Here Marxism breaks sharply with the tradition of the Enlightenment, which, though proud of revolutions like the American and the French, was also a bit ashamed of the tar and feathering and guillotining, and regarded political revolution as at best a necessary evil to be avoided if possible. Now in this world the means affects the end. So far, the Marxist effort to arrive at anarchy by the use of authority has not got beyond a very firm use of authority by a small ruling class. And even were the Russian experiment able to continue in a world not hostile to Russia as a political entity, it seems extremely unlikely that the Marxist heaven on earth would be achieved. Only in an Hegelian world of the pure intellect do you achieve an end by trying to achieve its opposite. In this world, if you set out to build a society in which human beings behave as much like ants as possible you are not likely to get a society in which they behave like lions. The Marxist attempt to solve the eighteenth-century tension between liberty and equality has on the whole been even less successful than the orthodox democratic attempt.

The Nineteenth Century—A Summary

The study of the nineteenth century has led us, perhaps unduly, into many considerations about the twentieth century. We have followed some phases of Marxism far beyond the century in which the doctrine was born. We may return briefly to summarize the doctrines, the tensions we have studied in the last two chapters.

There is a center—not a dead center—in the nineteenth century, which we have called the Victorian compromise. That compromise sought to retain a moderate political democracy, a moderate nationalism, and great individual economic freedom of enterprise balanced by a strict moral code and conventional, churchgoing Christianity. In a Western society based on that compromise there was great industrial and scientific advance, great material inequalities and yet for the lower classes a higher standard of living in a material way than ever before, and a lively and varied intellectual and artistic flourishing.

Yet this intellectual and artistic flourishing, if contrasted with that of the thirteenth century, or of fifth-century Athens, lacked unity of style, perhaps unity of purpose. For the nineteenth century was a time of extraordinary diversity of thought, an age of multanimity. Its extremes were great extremes, its tensions clearly marked—tradition against innovation, authority against liberty, faith in God against faith in the machine, loyalty to the nation against loyalty to humanity—the list could be very long indeed. Somehow the nineteenth century managed to keep these warring human aspirations, these basically conflicting ideals of the good life, in uneasy balance. Our century has seen this balance upset. Two great wars and a great depression are the witnesses of this upset. We are now attempting, among ideals quite as conflicting as those of the nineteenth century—they are indeed essentially the same ideals—to establish a balance of our own.

CHAPTER SEVEN

THE TWENTIETH CENTURY

THE ANTI-INTELLECTUAL ATTACK

Our Continuing Multanimity

The extremists, at least, of the eighteenth-century Enlightenment be-lieved that human beings were very shortly to begin to live in a perfect society, a society in which what all men consider evil would not exist and only what all men consider good would exist. This attitude is for our analysis a sort of base line. Or rather, the reflection of this attitude in the ordinary Western man's more modest hopes of personal improve-ment in his own lot, of visible social progress in his own lifetime, should be our base line. Now this general optimism has had to hold out against the mere passage of nearly two centuries at the end of which evil seems as lively and as prevalent as ever; and it has had to survive two great crises of world war, with their attendant sufferings from death, disease, scarcity, and all the long catalogue of man's inhumanity to man. The first of these crises, the thirty-year struggle of the wars of the French Revolution and Napoleon, we have seen helped make the revision of earlier optimism we have called the Victorian compromise. The second—the half-century of World Wars I and II, the cold war, the welfare state—we can already see has brought a second flood of pessimistic feeling and criticism, and is now actively at work in further modification of the heritage of the eighteenth century, the democratic dream. We are still too near the process to see it clearly. Perhaps by 2000 A.D. critics will find that there was a characteristic twentieth-century faith, culture, *Weltan-schauung*.

But already it is clear that the dream has survived the second crisis; we are in the West still children of the Enlightenment. Do not believe the prophets of doom who tell you otherwise. They may be right—most of the cluster of ideas and values we call democracy may go down in the years to come—but we cannot yet foresee the future in matters of this sort. As for the present, the fact of the survival of the basic optimism of the eighteenth century is evident from any newspaper, any periodical, any

lecture platform, especially in the United States. Alterations in this fundamental pattern are still for the *common man* in the West of much
less importance than the pattern itself.

It is true that there have been among *intellectuals* complex tides of
fashion; there have been phases of despair, of cynicism, of earnest pursuit
of still greater perfection. Even before the war of 1914 there had been
the celebrated decade of the nineties, with its self-conscious wit, its rather
energetic effort to seem tired and sophisticated, its discovery that decadence is a possibility of history. But the Western world at the turn of
the last century was not merely the world of Oscar Wilde and the *Yellow
Book;* it was the world of the Fabians as well, of Teddy Roosevelt and
the Progressives, of the revived France of the Dreyfus case, a world still
full of hopeful conflict. The war of 1914 brought among many intellectuals the feeling of horror and disgust tempered with hope in a really
radical Leftist movement that comes out in the war novels of the time,
Henri Barbusse's *Le Feu,* Remarque's *All Quiet on the Western Front,*
Ernest Hemingway's *Farewell to Arms*—the last, contrary to stereotypes
about American optimism, at least as pessimistic as the French or the
German novels. By the nineteen-twenties, we seemed settled down to
something like the old life once more. Harding's "normalcy," though the
term offended the high-minded, was a faithful reflection of what most
people wanted.

There are still other tides of intellectual fashion. One of the most obvious—though its real importance is difficult to judge at this date—is for
the ambitious historical systems we must still call philosophies of history.
From Spengler of yesterday to Sorokin and Toynbee of today through
many less-read prophets, intellectuals in the West have been seeking a
sign from the past, a sign of what lies ahead, not just for the few decades
an adult can hope to live, but for centuries ahead when no man now
alive can ever check up, in the flesh, on these prophets. Most of these
writers are prophets of impending doom. The favorite parallel is between the last period of the declining Roman Empire and our own day,
but there are at hand for historians like Toynbee many other examples
of civilizations that failed to meet a challenge like that of "parochial
nationalism" he finds we are facing. These philosophers of history are
not, however, altogether without hope for the race. They think that in
the form of traditional Western culture our present civilization *may* be
doomed, but that a new culture is bound to rise on its ruins. Theirs is
a philosophy of cycles that turn out to be spirals, of erratic nonlinear
evolution (but still evolution), of darkness to be followed by the Great
Dawn. There is a tendency to place us now in some materialist abyss,
but about to rise to some spiritual height. Thus Gerald Heard's "super-
consciousness," Arnold Toynbee's "etherialization," and Pitirim Sorokin's "ideational" culture all seem to have something in common. All

three terms attempt to describe—and invite us into—a state of immaterial bliss.

These twentieth-century philosophers of history may or may not prove to be more accurate in their predictions than was Marx; their methods are not the methods of science, and their work is not a part of cumulative knowledge. For us, the important thing to note is that, like Marx, they use history as a cosmology. This use of history is a development from the modern repudiation of the supernatural, and the modern retention of the desire for omniscience and certitude that the supernatural, perhaps only the supernatural, can supply. The Newtonian world-machine supplied this certitude for the eighteenth century, but failed to account satisfactorily for the obvious facts of organic life, growth, change on this earth. Such an explanation was in the nineteenth century very neatly supplied by Darwinian notions of organic evolution. Now we could not only understand how the planetary system worked; we could understand how men and mice and coral reefs came to grow as they do. The key to knowing what is and what will be is for the historicist a knowledge of what has been. The curve can always be plotted in time past— and then, so to speak, it extrapolates itself into the future. If you know how societies and cultures have evolved—that is, if you know their histories—you know what they are going to be, a knowledge some people find comforting.

Now there are many human beings who seem temperamentally unable to accept this kind of historicism; they must transcend mere experience of space-time, they must find God and truth in pure Being freed of vulgar Becoming. If, however, you accept the general validity of the attitudes and approaches of modern science, you will have to agree that *in its basic assumptions* this historicism is consonant with modern science. None the less the gap between men like Sorokin and Toynbee and the natural scientist is very great indeed, certainly in performance, and probably also in method and aims. In the first place, natural science *as science* simply does not attempt to set up a cosmology. (Scientists are *as full human beings* believers in a whole range of cosmologies; many of them are still innocent "materialists" in the direct tradition of the Enlightenment, others good Christians, even good Catholics, still others, like Eddington and Jeans, inventors of rather weird and unsatisfactory cosmologies of their own which they fondly attach somehow to their science.) In the second place, we do not know at present nearly enough about the history of man in society to be able to make even the kind of generalized long-term predictions the meteorologist can make. Moreover, the variables involved are too numerous for our present comprehension in scientific terms. In short, you cannot really plot the curve in the past as the scientist would plot his curve; you can only guess at it, only sketch it in freehand, very dashingly. Patient generations of labor will be needed before we can get much further. Moreover, the curve does *not* extrapolate itself. For there is, in the third place, always the possibility of new variables, of genuine novelty, of the unforeseeable. We have noted already that Marx, by temperament one of the most absolutist of these philosophers of history, proved on the whole a bad prophet, and notably failed to guess at a number of new factors—including whatever brought about his revolution in Russia instead of in Great Britain. We do not know nearly enough about the disease that kills civilizations (if there is such a disease) to recognize it in ourselves. Skilled historians like Toynbee can certainly point out alarming symptoms, much the same in late Roman culture and in our culture; but we don't really know what the symptoms mean. At any rate, worry over such symptoms as the parallel between our rate of divorce and the Roman rate of divorce is rather on the edge of hypochondria.

The determinism that goes with most philosophies of history is in our time balanced by a form of indeterminism that also—such is the preoccupation of our time with *process*—is much concerned with ideas of flow, change, growth. This is the voluntarism that crops up in many otherwise disparate formal philosophies of the last fifty years—in Nietzsche, in the Frenchman Bergson, in the Americans William James and John Dewey. Bergson's philosophy was not so long ago the fashion among cultivated Westerners, who found in his *élan vital,* his "creative evolution," and his other phrases a most agreeable philosophy of change and flow. Bergson was in the direct romantic line of protest against something the romantics have always found disagreeable, unacceptable, in the tradition of the Enlightenment. It is difficult to put one's defining finger on that something—it is something the romantics think of as dead, finished, cerebral, stuffy, rote-and-formula, dryasdust, unimaginative. We have earlier somewhat apologetically tried to sum up the cluster of ideas the romantics hated under "head," what they loved under "heart."

At any rate, most determinisms are matters of the head, most voluntarisms matters of the heart. But Bergson, as a modern and a sophisticate, could not take refuge in a simple reversion to the native, the primitive, in a rejection of the complex inheritance of modern thought. So he tried to keep the best of both worlds, the freshness of emotion and the nice, logical ruts and grooves of thought. Indeed, this effort to give to thought itself—to an activity the nonintellectual usually associates with safety and armchairs—a quality of danger and adventure is one of the central themes of the most distinguished of twentieth-century philosophers, the late Alfred North Whitehead. The pragmatism of James and Dewey—the most distinguished American contribution to formal philosophic thought—is also in revolt against the certainties and the static quality of systematic thought. James held thought to be an instrument of the will; good thinking was thinking that got you what you wanted. He was not, of course, cynical or anarchistic or logical enough to hold that all wanting was good wanting, at least from the point of view of the individual wanter. For James, the good was what a sensitive, tolerant, kindly but basically respectable New England intellectual of his day would find good. He liked or at least sympathized with, as a good psychiatrist should, the odd and the troubled, and he agreed with John Mill that the good, the useful, the profitably new may come from the most unlikely sources. For James variety, conflict, and multanimity really are practical; they work—or did in 1900.

Finally, the twentieth century, like other recent centuries, did not fail to find a great natural scientist from whose work philosophers and essayists and men of ideas in general could apparently take the kind of lead the eighteenth century took from Newton. This was the physicist Albert Einstein, whose work as a physicist was beyond the understanding of all but a few fellow scientists. But for the general public Einstein was not merely the tribal magician of our times; he was the man who stood for relativity, for the notion that things look different to observers at different places and different times, that truth depends on the point of view of the seeker for truth, that a man moving at one rate of speed sees everything quite differently from a man moving at another rate, that, in short, there is no absolute Truth, but only relative truths.

Einstein's name also sums up in the public mind the great scientific revolution of the first half of this century. With the more detailed history of modern science we have not concerned ourselves in recent chapters. Everyone knows that the natural sciences have continued in our day their fruitful alliance with technology and business enterprise, that they have continued to be cumulative. The work of physicists and mathematicians like Einstein, Planck, and Bohr, however, bore fruit early in the twentieth century in great new master-theorems about the physical universe, so that it became fashionable among popularizers of science to say that Newtonian physics had been "overthrown." It is fairer to say that relativity, quantum mechanics, the further study of the bewildering, complicated atom (the old Greek philosopher Democritus would never recognize his simple philosophical atom) have made emendations in, additions to, Newtonian physics. The fact that a clear element of unpredictability in the behavior of a single atom is recognized in quantum mechanics does not mean that statistically, in masses of atoms, the old predictability has ceased to exist. Newton's physics, in fact, are still good for a lot of important everyday rough work. The real importance of the new physics for us is that they helped put the finishing touch on the destruction of the simple nineteenth-century notions of scientific causation, notions that conceived all relations in the universe on a neat mechanical model, and that were associated with very innocent notions about scientific induction. Modern scientific theories about the methods of science are very subtle and complicated, and have recognized that the creative scientist is in a sense a creative artist, that the report his theorems give of the universe is in part the work of his own mind, and no mere mechanical replica of reality. Indeed, good physicists will say that they do not discover, but invent, their laws or uniformities. Even more important, the modern scientist knows, or should know, that his laws or uniformities are not absolute truths, *not truths in the tradition of religion and of most Western philosophy.*

For the moment, however, we need merely to record that from the point of view of the historian of ideas, the persistent elements, especially of the last two or three centuries, seem more conspicuous and more important than the elements of novelty. The atom bomb is in a sense a new thing; it explodes in a new way, and of course with a new force and intensity. But the feeling that the atom bomb may bring about the destruction of humanity, the "end of the world," is new only in its relation to the atom bomb; as a *human feeling,* as a part of human experience even in the relatively limited sphere of Western cultural history, the fear of an end to the world is a recurrent one. At times—in the earliest days of Christianity, and rather less so in the year 1000—it has been epidemic; at all times among cranks and the odder sects it has been endemic. The splitting of the atom should have no new horrors for the faithful reader of the Apocalypse.

So far, at least, most of what we have attempted to analyze in the last few chapters still exists among us. It would be difficult not to recognize as living in the contemporary world most of the ideas that have come before us in the course of this book. Cumulative knowledge, that of natural science, has continued without serious relapse. Indeed, wars, hot and cold, stimulate some phases of scientific achievement. The tender-minded who maintain that only the vulgar application to practical matters goes on in wartime, and that the creative work of "pure" science must have peace, may be right. The truth is that among the many things we are ignorant about are the social and cultural conditions necessary to the optimum flourishing of natural science. The fact remains that in the West both pure and applied science have unquestionably added to their cumulative achievement in the course of the war-torn first half of the twentieth century.

As for noncumulative knowledge, our culture is an almost incredible palimpsest in which nothing is ever suddenly or *wholly* blotted out. There are shifts in the proportionate success or fashionableness of different attitudes and ideas, but very few are eliminated. Go over the materials of the last few chapters. Christianity most certainly persists in what to an outsider remains its rich diversity and its basic tension between this world and the next. Our century has seen no new great sect of Christians, and it has seen the kind of frittering away of the faithful

into the indifference that each generation of preachers of a certain temperament regards—or feigns for preaching purposes to regard—as new.
But it has also seen revivals of spiritual energy in all sorts of sects and in
all sorts of places—including perhaps the Soviet Russia that tried so hard
to destroy Christianity. There has been an intellectual religious revival markedly parallel to that of the years after the crisis of the French
Revolution. Berdyaev, the Russian exile, was in many ways, at least in
his feeling for the sins of the godless generation that brought on the
crisis of our time, a kind of modern Joseph de Maistre. Two of the pro-
foundest and most influential of attempts to correct by Christian vision
what they regard as the shallow optimism on which our democratic
Western cosmology is based have been made by Karl Barth in Germany
and Reinhold Niebuhr in the United States. Roman Catholicism has
continued to assert its claim to a greater wisdom than the Enlightenment
ever found, and at least an equal concern with the lot of the common
man on earth. In Jacques Maritain the Catholics have shown that they
can still produce the thoughtful, sensitive, orthodox but undogmatic
politique et moraliste.

And the anti-Christians persist. The successors of Tom Paine and
Herbert Spencer, the piously and dogmatically liberal agnostics, humanists, secularists, positivists, materialists, followers of Ethical Culture and
the like, though they begin to look a little old-fashioned and quaint, still
exist. They may, like the bustle and the slit skirt, suddenly become fashionable again, though like these feminine fashions of Victorian and Ed-
wardian days, in a somewhat chastened form. Indeed, some were apparent
in their new costumes in the mid-century vogue of existentialism, which
spread into cultivated circles at the end of the war of 1939-1945. Existentialism centered in France, with its best-known figure the writer Jean-
Paul Sartre. The existentialists did not believe in God—certainly not in
a good God—and they found the world a very unpleasant place in which
man is clearly born to trouble from which he can never emerge. The
doctrine of progress seemed to these determined pessimists great nonsense. Yet they would fight the good fight as preachers always have, they
would lead a substantially moral life (not a prudishly Victorian moral
life, of course, but an artistic moral life), they would, in short, exist since
existence is human.

It is easy to see in existentialism merely a symptom of the exhaustion
of western Europe at the end of a great war. Yet the prophets of the
movement, Nietzsche and Kierkegaard, are men of the nineteenth century. From one point of view, existentialism is the pessimistic and disillusioned inversion of nineteenth-century hopeful materialistic faiths.
Existentialism and other defiantly anti-Christian philosophies have not,
however, gone very far into our Western society. Moreover, there are
Christian existentialists, heretical though the combination would seem

to be. It seems likely that in the Western world the ordinary educated man—*l'homme moyen intellectuel*—is still, as he was in the nineteenth century, a somewhat inconsistent mixture of Christian conformity and eighteenth-century optimistic naturalism, though larded with twentieth-century indifferentism.

The Marxists are far from dead. In Russia their faith has suffered the fate that comes to most reforming faiths when they get themselves established. The process of turning Marxism in Russia from an explosive—or at any rate a stimulant—into a sedative has been going on for several decades. It has gone so far that the good citizen of Soviet Russia is apparently no longer disturbed by the contrast between the old Marxist slogan "from each according to his abilities, to each according to his needs" and the existence within the Soviet Union of very great differences in individual income and status. Any fair appraisal of just what Marxism means within Russia, and indeed within the states now under Russian influence, is beyond the powers of a Westerner. We have not the necessary conditions for a reasonable degree of detachment. Marxism is still in many parts of the world a growing and a fighting faith, one we must not dismiss as simply a perverse and wicked thing, but must consider, at the very least, as a grave symptom of our failure to recover even the degree of social stability the West achieved in the nineteenth century.

As for nationalism, it still seems in mid-twentieth century the strongest single factor in the existing networks of interests, sentiments, and ideas binding men into territorially based political groups. Itself a complex blending of almost everything that goes into Western cultural life, nationalism has been a kind of backlog for all the more abstract political forms we have been dealing with in the last few chapters—for Russian Communism (this despite the theoretical cosmopolitan and antinationalistic principles of original Marxism), for German Nazism, for American democracy. The units that fought the last war were *national* units. The new Asian and African states that have come out of the struggle against colonialism are *national* states. Those who hate war and hope to abolish it on this earth are nowadays mostly convinced of the need for a world-state or at least a small number of regional states eliminating the nation-state as we know it. To us, two hundred years after the innocent environmentalism of the eighteenth century, it must seem that, even if nationalism is produced by environment, the product is the result of so many centuries of history, is so firm and solid a product that in any given generation it cannot be greatly altered by new and planned environmental pressures—such as a nice world constitution on paper, or even regional economic associations.

Nationalism is a fact of modern life, one of those observed facts no scientist can neglect. It is not identical in any two nation-states, since it is but one element in the complex of culture. It can be transcended, as in a sense the active minority of world federationists have transcended it—though there is nothing so "nationally" American as the optimism, the faith in the magic of written constitutions, the pious intoxication with high ethical abstractions, displayed by most American proponents of world government. But for most people nationalism is a sentiment deeply rooted in their whole lives. It is most usefully studied by the social psychologist, who is as yet no more than at the beginning of his scientific work of building cumulative knowledge. He can already make tentative statements such as that nationalism is likely to take its most aggressive forms in national groups that feel themselves oppressed, put upon, and treated as inferior; and that it seems least aggressive, most like that agreeable cultural variation of life's flavor Mazzini thought it could be, in small, relatively prosperous, but politically independent groups like the Swiss or the Norwegians or, nowadays, the Irish. Moreover, the many independent states freed from their colonial status since 1947 surely display the usual symptoms of Western-style nationalism.

The nineteenth-century patterns of ideals, altered by our own experience, are, then, still with us. We still have our democratic center, and it is still attacked from Right and Left. One more survival from the nineteenth century must be noted. Our intellectuals are still alienated from ordinary people, still in revolt, still not agreed on what that revolt should lead to. Those who write and paint and act and preach are still a group apart. In America, indeed, there was a brief time during the Great Depression and the war of 1939-1945 when the writers rejoiced that they, like Sinclair Lewis's George Babbitt, believed in democracy, individual initiative, the common man, and the American Way. But this was a brief, if not an altogether illusory, honeymoon. Nowadays the intellectual writers and other artists are once more in revolt, writing nasty things about this world as it is, and about each other. Some of them are Marxists, of all the sects from Soviet orthodoxy to the latest variety of revisionism; others continue to cultivate the subtler and less vulgar kinds of antidemocratic ideas, from those of the critic Irving Babbitt to those of really intellectual fascists like Ezra Pound. And all of them continue to bellyache, so that whether you open the *Partisan Review* or the *Atlantic* or even the *Reader's Digest* you will not read far before you find an article that could be entitled "What's the Matter with. . . ."

Finally, we may revert to the great variety of architectural styles we took as a symbol of the multanimity of contemporary Western society. No one can argue that in the mid-twentieth century we have come back to mankind's earlier habit of building in one style at one given time. It is true there has grown up in the twentieth century a reasonably unified style (in spite of some individual variants), a style called "functional" by many of its practitioners, and known to the layman as "modernistic."

This style has its suitable concomitants in interior decoration and in the plastic arts, so that it is possible to build and furnich a house that will belong to the mid-twentieth century and to no other part of space-time. Actually this possibility has merely added another ingredient to the hash. Many people are infuriated by the modernistic style; many more cannot afford it. By the 1960's a definite reaction has already set in, relaxing and adorning the rigor of functionalism.

The mid-twentieth-century intellectual is in the West likely to be well aware that the multanimity of the modern world on all questions, big and little, is new, relatively speaking, in the history of mankind, and he is more than a little afraid that we can't take it. He is asking for a new synthesis, a new faith, a common basis of agreement on the Big Questions. In fact, a distinguished American psychologist, Henry A. Murray, has proposed that the right people get together and select from the stock of world literature a *new* Bible, a really effective secularist New Testament. But for such proposals there would not seem to exist the necessary conditions; there are no clear beginnings of a new spiritual synthesis, not even of something very new and modern that can at least be added to the mixture as the modernistic building was added to the others. This is not to say that our time has not its own spirit of the age, its own flavor, its own little touches of style by which it will be known to later historians. It is rather to say that we are so far no more than a variant in a fairly consistent cultural pattern that grew out of the Middle Ages and that became distinct in the seventeenth and eighteenth centuries. Indeed, the newest thing in our intellectual lives is probably nothing aesthetic, in spite of the vogue of modernism, but rather a tendency in the study of men and of human relations that may be the beginnings in fact of what we have long had in a phrase—the social sciences.

Anti-Intellectualism—A Definition

Yet this tendency is in many of its concrete manifestations a very old one—you can find traces of it in the *Politics* of Aristotle—and it may be wrong to consider it an earnest of the beginnings of a formal scientific study of human relations. Perhaps what we here call anti-intellectualism will to the future historian be no more than one of the strands of our twentieth-century culture, part of the spirit of the age, part of the whole of our attitudes toward life and the universe that is so much more than cumulative knowledge, or science. It seems safer here to treat anti-intellectualism, especially in its bearings on the study of men in society, as simply one of the characteristic manifestations of the spirit of our age.

The name is an unfortunate one, especially in its emphasis on negation or opposition, yet there seems at the moment no other that will do as well. For, as should be clear in a moment, any attempt to indicate by a name

that this tendency positively values, say, emotion as higher than thinking, the heart as superior to the head, drives, urges, impulses, or, if you
wish to be Freudian, the "libido" or the "id" as better than the intellect,
would be a bad misrepresentation of its nature. Basically the anti-intellectual, in the sense we here use the term, does not regard the instrument
of thought as *bad,* but among most men most of the time as *weak.* The
romantic agrees with Thomas Hardy that "thought is a disease of the
flesh"; the anti-intellectual notes merely that thought seems often at the
mercy of appetites, passions, prejudices, habits, conditioned reflexes, and
of a good deal else in human life that is not thinking. There is unfortunately no agreed-upon nomenclature in this matter. In this book we
shall use the term *anti-intellectualism* to describe the attempt to arrive
rationally at a just appreciation of the actual roles of rationality and of
nonrationality in human affairs. The term is widely used, however, to
describe something quite different—the *praise* of nonrationality, the exaltation of nonrationality as the really desirable human activity, the
denigration of rationality. Such an attitude of dislike for rationality and
love for nonrationality we prefer to call *romanticism,* the romanticism
of Goethe's "feeling is all." Wordsworth has put this hatred for reasoning very firmly:

> One impulse from a vernal wood
>   May teach you more of man,
> Of moral evil and of good,
>   Than all the sages can.
>
> Enough of science and of art;
>   Close up these barren leaves;
> Come forth, and bring with you a heart
>   That watches and receives.

The modern lover of the nonrational, like many of the apologists for
Nazism, goes far beyond these first romanticists. Perhaps the extreme
was set by a twentieth-century Spaniard with the cry: "Down with intelligence and long live death!" Still, the root of the concept is in romanticism. It is most unfortunate that there is such confusion in a very
important problem of terminology. We shall, however, attempt to use
the term *anti-intellectual* without praise or blame, to describe the attempt to ascertain the place of rationality in actual human behavior.

Now the anti-intellectual tends to distrust a certain kind of abstract,
deductive thinking about the Big Questions of the kind we have encountered frequently in this book, and nowhere more clearly, perhaps,
than in Hegel. But the anti-intellectual *is in a sense a true heir
of the Enlightenment:* He is at bottom a believer in the power of
thought to make man's life here on earth a better one. Freud himself,

whom some tender-minded people quite wrongly regard as the apostle of deep, dark, instinctual self-indulgence, believed as firmly as any eighteenth-century *philosophe* in the power of the truth—scientific truth duly established—to promote good conduct on the part of the individual who had succeeded in learning the truth; but—and this is a difference of major importance—the *philosophe* thought that all that stood between the individual and the learning of truth was a rotten shell of decayed institutions, the Catholic Church and the French monarchy; whereas Freud thought that not only a very strong set of institutions but also a strong set of "natural" human drives and a strong set of habits established in early infancy stood between the individual and the learning of the truth. Freud, even before his old age of exile and unhappiness, had no hopes that *many* men could win their way through to this sort of truth in a short time.

The tempered hopes for the slow improvement in human relations— an improvement that even the Leftishly inclined among the anti-intellectuals put well short of Utopian perfectibility—comes out in a quotation from Graham Wallas, an English Fabian of the days of Wells, Shaw, and the Webbs, a Progressive member of the London County Council, and the author of a book called *Human Nature in Politics* (London, 1908). Wallas had made a mildly anti-intellectualist and "realistic" study of British politics in which he pointed out that voters did not coldly and logically reason things out, did not even very often exercise intelligent self-interest, but were influenced by flattery, by appeals to their prejudices, by the goods looks of the candidate, and above all by a candidate's paying them attention as persons, by so small a thing as calling them by name. Wallas was grieved when some of his fellow workers in the Labour party accused him of selling out to the enemy by this anti-intellectualism, and he wrote:

> Thought may be late in evolution, it may be deplorably weak in driving power, but without its guidance no man or organization can find a safe path amid the vast impersonal complexities of the universe as we have learned to see it.

The anti-intellectual insists that man is a complex creature whose behavior must be studied as far as possible without preconceptions concerning the goodness and badness of that behavior. Just as with the place of logical thinking in human life, so with the place of good behavior; the anti-intellectual does not deny the difference between good and bad, does not hesitate to prefer goodness to badness. What he does insist is that, to judge by the evidence to be obtained by observation of what men have done and are doing, there is a great deal of badness around and—this is the important thing—there seems to be no direct and simple causal relation between men's moral ideas and their actions. Therefore the anti-intellectual repeats Bacon's praise of Machiavelli, himself in many ways an early anti-intellectual: "We are much beholden to Machiavel and others that wrote what men do, and not what they ought to do."

To sum up: Most anti-intellectuals accept, by and large, the goals of order, happiness, individual freedom, and all the rest we associate with the Enlightenment, but they hold these goals as only imperfectly and only very slowly attainable on earth; and they believe the best way to attain them is not to preach that they must be attained, *not to pretend they have been attained* (a not uncommon claim among American educators, editors, and preachers with aspirations to mass audiences), but to work patiently at building up a true social science based on the long-tried methods of cumulative knowledge and to hope that this knowledge will be used by men to promote the good rather than the bad. They are in more complete agreement on what is good than youthful cynics, fresh in the discovery that human ideas of the beautiful and the good are not quite the same in New Guinea as in New York, are likely to think. They differ more in their hopes. Pareto, whom we are going to meet shortly, apparently had at his death in 1923 very little hope that men would use better knowledge of social science to promote the good on earth; contemporary American social scientists influenced by anti-intellectualism (and there are many of them, though they would usually dislike the label of anti-intellectual), are likely, in the good American tradition, to believe that on the whole the new knowledge will be put to good ends— that social science will be used to promote the good working, the health, of society, just as medical science has been used to promote the health of the body.

Contemporary Anti-Intellectualism

We have already noted how such natural scientists as Newton and Darwin gave leads in the social sciences. In our own times the great leads have come from biology and psychology. Probably the two most commanding figures in this respect of influence on the social studies are Pavlov and Freud, both psychologists trained in physiology and the other biological sciences. Note once more that, as with Newton, we are here considering, not the meaning of their professional studies within their own nowadays very specialized professions, but their influence on the much more general currents of thought among men of various training concerned with human affairs.

Pavlov's is the simpler case. What reached the outside world from the laboratories of this Russian scientist whose independence was respected by both Tsarist and Soviet governments was the well-known phrase "conditioned reflexes." Pavlov's dogs are as familiar as any laboratory animals have ever been. Most of us know how, after being repeatedly fed at a certain signal, such as a bell, they came to water at the mouth in anticipation of food at a mere signal. The natural—that is, the untrained—response of watering at the mouth would ordinarily come only when the dog had actual food before him; Pavlov got the same response artificially by a signal that certainly didn't smell or look like food to the dog. The upshot was clear evidence that training (conditioning) could produce automatic responses in the animal that were essentially similar to the kind of automatic responses the animal is born with, or to what some modern biologists call "species-specific behavior." Conditioned reflexes like watering at the mouth at a signal are the same as natural reflexes like watering at the mouth when a fine red beefsteak is held before the animal.

What this meant in broad lines for the social scientist is this: In a way, eighteenth-century notions about the power of environment (training, education) of the kind Robert Owen expressed so clearly were confirmed, in the sense that environment can be manipulated to give organisms new responses; but—and this is a bitter blow to eighteenth-century optimism—once such training has taken hold the organism has, so to speak, incorporated the results almost as if they had been the product of heredity, not environment, and further change becomes very difficult, in some instances impossible. Pavlov, after having trained some of his dogs, tried mixing his signals, frustrating and confusing the dogs by withholding food at the signal that had always produced food for them, and so on until he succeeded in producing symptoms of a kind close to what in human beings would be neurosis, or even psychosis.

Now the cautious social scientist does not, of course, take over Pavlov's conditioned reflexes and apply them uncritically to all human behavior. He does not assume, for instance, that the Vermonter voting the straight Republican ticket is behaving quite like the dog watering at the mouth as an accustomed bell is rung. Even in Vermont, voting Republican is probably not quite a conditioned reflex. But the cautious social scientist will hold that concepts like that of the conditioned reflexes do throw light on a great deal of habit-determined human conduct. For the anti-intellectual, Pavlov's work was further demonstration that a very great deal of our behavior is not determined—nor even greatly influenced—by what goes on in the cerebral cortex.

Freud is a much more complex figure than Pavlov—indeed one of the most complex figures in the intellectual history of the West. He was a nonreligious Jew, a scientist brought up in the simple craftsman's belief in a material universe from which the supernatural was ruled out, and with the scientist's contempt for all metaphysical ideas but the unavowed, positivist metaphysics of conventional modern science. In a book of this scope we cannot properly examine Freud's complexities; moreover, his work, like that of all great system-making thinkers, looks quite different to outsiders and to true believers. He has created a method of dealing with certain kinds of human disability usually thought of as mental—nervous breakdown, neurosis, and the like. This method is called psychoanalysis, and must be distinguished from conventional handling of mental disease, usually by physicians with special training as neurologists, which is called psychiatry. Freudian psychoanalysis, though as a part of medical science it is in the 1960's vastly more reputable among conventional physicians than one would have thought possible only a few decades ago, is still mostly heretical, the belief of an ardent sect. This is especially true when the ideas Freud developed in the treatment of mental disease are extended, as Freud himself extended them in later life, to most of the fields of the social sciences. Moreover, the work of Freud is for the "advanced," for the young, beginning to look old-fashioned; and yet we are not far enough away from it to judge it without reference to mere fashion.

Freud gave leads in the study of human behavior to many who knew nothing, or very little, about psychoanalysis and its metaphysical superstructure. Our century is indeed a century in which psychology is the fashionable science, and in which the chatter of the educated makes use of psychological terms much as the habitués of the eighteenth-century salons chattered about the laws of physics and astronomy discovered by Newton. Many of these modern smooth coins of conversation were once sharply minted by Freud himself—libido, Oedipus complex, infantile sexuality, sublimation. Perhaps the smoothest coin of all—inferiority complex—was minted by a disciple, Adler, who later quarreled with the master and set up his own psychological shop.

Here, as has been our practice in this book, we are concerned rather with this phase of Freud's ideas as they circulated among the intellectual classes than with their professional significance in psychology and medicine. For this purpose, a very schematic outline of his basic ideas as of about 1920 should suffice. To Freud, what makes people go is a whole set of "drives" he first called *libido* and associated very closely with sexual desires and later called the *id,* and made a little less clearly sexual; but note that for Freud the sexual relation was never a simple matter of sensual satisfaction, but a very complex set of mixed elements, some of which less determined "materialists" than Freud would call "spiritual." Now the id in the human being is part of the unconscious; it wishes, pushes the individual into action. But the whole behavior of the human being involves two other parts of the human psyche, the *ego* and the *super-ego.* Conventional natural scientists are greatly annoyed by the fact that there is no way of locating the id, the ego, and the super-ego in the human brain or anywhere else in the human anatomy; nobody ever "saw" a part of the id, even under a microscope; actually Freud was not in this respect at least sinning against true science—the test of these concepts is not whether they can be apprehended as a part of human receptor experiences aided by instruments, but whether they work, whether their use enables us to understand human behavior better.

The *ego* is wholly—or almost wholly—part of a man's conscious mental life, but it is not pure logical activity; it is an umpire, or governor, the guardian of the interests of the organism as a whole and the arbitrator of conflicting desires rising out of the id into consciousness. Some of these desires, especially if they seem to the ego of the kind to discredit the person, are suppressed by the ego, but continue hard at work in the unconscious id; some of them are "sublimated," turned from a sexual goal, for instance, into art or poetry or governing men. The *super-ego* involves some of the elements that go into the conditioned reflexes. In the super-ego the notions taught the individual about right and wrong, the "proper" way to behave, the "proper" ideas to hold, come to play on the individual's actions. In part, the super-ego is unconscious, its dictates inculcated from infancy on so that they do not go through the logical process, do not present him with problems of alternative action. The ego is like a somewhat un-Christian individual conscience; the super-ego is like a social or collective conscience working on and in the individual. The ego mediates between the id and the external world of material *reality;* the super-ego mediates between the id and the external world of ideals, of "higher things," which last Freud rather begrudgingly granted a kind of objective reality.

In a healthy individual the id, the ego, and the super-ego cooperate to keep him aware of the realities of his environment and to enable him to adjust his conduct in accord with these realities so that he is on the whole a happy man and a good citizen. In the neurotic individual desires balked by the negative of the ego or the super-ego or by both are thereby driven back into the unconscious, where they continue to live and push on as desires must. They make the stuff of a man's dreams. They crop up in disguised (but not genuinely sublimated) form in all sorts of acts that are clearly not in the line of normal, sensible conduct—in obsessive fears, in withdrawal from ordinary responsibilities, in worrying and fretting, in all the great variety of conduct we nowadays label "neurotic." These balked desires are, be it noted, in the unconscious; the neurotic individual does not really know what he wants.

Freud's basic notions of therapy—and it is these that caused us to classify him as a child of the Enlightenment—can be summed up as an elaborate, difficult (and very expensive) way of teaching the patient to know what he really wants or as a more innocent moralist would say, *ought to want.* More particularly, Freud held that the original repression, the original driving back into the id of certain desires, was the source of the evil, the *trauma* or wound inflicted in the individual's psyche. Usually, he thought, this trauma went back to infancy and was tied up

with the fact that the infant's very early sexual desires are strongly dis-
approved in our culture, that both his ego and his super-ego are taught
rather harshly that they must not allow such conduct. Even if there
were no simple single incident of infancy that seemed the origin of a
difficulty in later life, Freud believed that the very early years were always of major importance. But how could these forgotten things be dug
up by the individual? Only by a long process of "free association," of
letting the individual roam back in memory day after day, with the psy-
choanalyst at his side noting the tiny clues as they came into the flow
of memories, and by aid from dreams, recent and recalled.

We cannot of course attempt a detailed account of Freud's methods of
therapy. The point should be clear: Freud held that the individual was
a bundle of confused thoughts and desires that could only with the greatest difficulty be brought to make sense; but that when after long investigation the analyst could show the individual just *why* he behaved as he
did, then the individual would cease to behave badly, unprofitably for
himself and for his fellows. Note particularly that Freud did *not* take
the old, innocent, Rousseauistic position that since all the trouble came
from the original suppression the way to avoid difficulty is to have everybody from infancy on follow all his desires, let the id dictate all his acts.
Freud and the Freudians do indeed tend to be "permissive" in child
training, tend to sympathize with the ideal of as much individual freedom in society as can be attained. Freud himself seems never to have
liked the contents of most of our super-egos, the "higher things" of Western tradition. But the Freudians do not advocate an orgy of lust, they
do not want man to be the slave of his cruder appetites, they are not—
for the most part—antinomian cranks. They are trained physicians trying to be true to the standards of an exacting profession, trying to see
men as they really are.

Freud's contribution to contemporary anti-intellectualism was very
great. His work, taken with that of Pavlov and many other psychologists
and physiologists, put great emphasis on the proportion of human
actions in which the traditional instrument of thought—Aristotle's
phronesis, Christian *ratio,* the reason of Locke and the Encyclopedists,
even the illative sense of Newman—had no part, or little part. Action
came to the anti-intellectual to be the result of automatic responses,
natural or conditioned, of all sorts of unconscious drives and urges, of
traditions, social habits, even theological and metaphysical principles
made by early training and conditioning part of the individual's way of
responding to the need to make a decision. To the anti-intellectual actual
ratiocinative thought in an individual is to the rest of his living even
less than the small part of the iceberg visible above water is to the whole
mass of the iceberg. The *amount* of reasoning in human life, then, and
not the *existence* of reasoning, is the point over which the anti-intellec-

tual and those who oppose anti-intellectualism really differ. The tradition of American moral and political thinking is *not* anti-intellectualist in content. The practice of a good deal of American politics, and of much of American life—advertising is a clear example—*is* anti-intellectualist in content.

The roots and ramifications of this view that the actual, functional, place of the instrument of thought in the sum total of human activity on earth is small—and remember it is not either rejoicing over or bemoaning the smallness of this place—can be traced in many fields of modern thought. Important roots lie in what social thinkers made of Darwin; for it became pretty clear that, if in general one could hold that what gave man such good results in the struggle for life was his brain, in most concrete cases it was by no means the intellectual, the "pure" thinker, who did best in the struggle for life.

One of the first, and one of the most interesting of nineteenth-century writers on man as *politique et moraliste* to take up this theme was the Englishman Walter Bagehot, whose *Physics and Politics* (1869) is one of the earliest attempts to follow up Darwinian leads in the study of human affairs. The book should have been entitled *Biology and Politics;* Bagehot was merely using *physics* to stand for *natural science*. Bagehot held that the first stage in building civilization from mere savagery was a state of totalitarian rigidity of law and order—not a personal dictatorship, but the dictatorship of what Bagehot called the "cake of custom." In competition among groups, that group wins, by and large, which has the best discipline, the firmest cake of custom. But in the next stage the inventive mind comes more into play; new ideas are produced that enable one group to cope better than another with the environment; and finally there comes the "government by discussion" that is a mark of the modern age.

All this may sound like the conventional Victorian view of unilinear progress. But Bagehot is careful to insist that even after the breaking of the cake of custom by the new ideas, the successful society will still have a lot of the old nonintellectual traits, or it will go under. Indeed, he found what for his age was a paradoxical, and for us a typical anti-intellectualist, explanation for the success of parliamentary democracy: The great trouble with a civilization made up of *Homo sapiens* is that human beings are impatient, unrestrained animals, always wanting to *do something;* the great virtue of government by discussion is that it *postpones* action, takes up time in debate and palaver and so allows time for the healing work of nature. In much the same way, Bagehot decided that the trouble with the French is that they are too intellectual, too interested in ideas to achieve adequate political stability; he found that the English people, on the whole, are able to withstand the temptation to indulge in abstract thinking, that they have the necessary stupidity to make democracy work.

The same Nietzsche who in one mood appealed to the Superman and wrote in pseudo-Biblical prose about the prophet Zarathustra was in another mood an early anti-intellectualist. Nietzsche attempted what he called a "natural history of morals"—that is, a rapid survey of how men actually did behave in relation to how they thought they ought to behave. Like many of the school, he was perhaps too much tempted to paradox by his opposition to the general belief of mankind that their acts follow logically from their beliefs. He was, moreover, unable to carry out his study in a systematic way; all his work is a series of aphorisms, a long and uncommon commonplace book. Nevertheless, Nietzsche hit clearly upon another of the main points the anti-intellectualist makes, a point Machiavelli himself had already made. That is the observation that men often gain ends useful to themselves and to society by acting on erroneous ideas.

> The falseness of an opinion is not for us any objection to it: it is here, perhaps, that our new language sounds most strangely. The question is, how far an opinion is life-furthering, life-preserving, species-preserving; perhaps species-rearing; and we are fundamentally inclined to maintain that the falsest opinions (to which synthetic judgments *a priori* belong) are the most indispensable to us; that without a recognition of logical fictions, without a comparison of reality with the purely *imagined* world of the absolute and immutable . . . man could not live—that the renunciation of false opinion would be a renunciation of life, a negation of life. *To recognize untruth as a condition of life:* that is certainly to impugn the traditional ideas of value in a dangerous manner, and a philosophy which ventures to do so, has thereby alone placed itself beyond good and evil.

By the twentieth century some of anti-intellectualism had begun to catch on with the intellectual classes, and in less obvious forms had begun to seep down into popular consciousness. In its origins a good deal of the point of view we here call anti-intellectualism is that of a self-conscious "superior," a man wise enough to know how little wisdom prevails in the world. It is a point of view that turns easily into a kind of snobbery, the feeling that the masses are the herd and we wise few are, or should be, the masters. This runs all through Nietzsche, who is the clearest example of this strain in the attitude of modern anti-intellectualism. Yet there is also a strain, clear ultimately in Freud, that emphasizes the possibility that ordinary men may learn the truth about themselves, a truth far more complex than the eighteenth-century view of man, and that once having learned it they can themselves make the necessary adjustments to this newly seen reality. Once men realize the really grave difficulties of thinking straight, they will, according to this more democratic view, be well on the road to straight thinking.

The most familiar phase of contemporary anti-intellectualism brings out this aspect clearly. From obscure and difficult philosophical writers like Alfred Korzybski through more graceful literary figures like I. A.

Richards to frank popularizers like Stuart Chase, the word *semantics* has gone far, especially in the English-speaking countries. Semantics is the science of meaning, the study of the way in which human beings communicate with one another. The semanticist will point out, for example, that three different observers may refer to the actions of a fourth person, the first as "pig-headed," the second as "obstinate," and the third as "firm." The actions are the same; the words the observers use to describe the actions are by no means the same; they indicate certain feelings of the observer, and they communicate these feelings, rather than an objective report. Words are, then, charged with emotional overtones and are not mere signs like the *x* and *y* of algebra. *Pig-headed* carries with it strong disapproval, *obstinate* rather less strong disapproval, and *firm* is slightly approving. *Persevering* would in our culture be still more approving.

Again, there are the great big words that draw into themselves all sorts of confusing human hopes and fears, so that even on close analysis it is very hard—the ardent semantic reformer says impossible—to find for them a concrete meaning. In the language of semantics, terms like *liberty, equality, fraternity* have no *referent;* you cannot perform the "operation" of proving them as a mathematician proves a theorem, or of checking their truth as the scientist checks the truth of his laws or uniformities by experiment or by observation; they are "meaningless." Stuart Chase suggests in his *Tyranny of Words* that whenever we are tempted to use great big vague phrases like *the democratic way of life* or *Western individualism* we should simply substitute *blah-blah* and let it go at that. Of course at this extreme we have merely come to the current form of the nominalist position. We are ready for the reflection of this anti-intellectualism in formal philosophy.

That reflection takes on a paradoxical form: a philosophy that would eliminate most philosophy from our studies. The exponents of this philosophy, the "logical positivists" or "linguistic philosophers" or "neo-positivists," developed their position, not from the simple belief of some nineteenth-century positivists in the induction and natural science of Herbert Spencer's time, but from syllogistic logics and mathematics *and* the modern conceptions of scientific method. Very briefly, logical positivism asserts that the only valid kind of knowledge is cumulative knowledge, the kind one finds in natural science. For this kind of knowledge there exists a process, the process gradually worked out in Western culture by our scientists, through which one can test the truth of any statement that is claimed to be knowledge. In Bridgman's term, you can perform an operation on the statement—sometimes a long and difficult operation involving laboratory and field research, much mathematics and hard logical thinking—but an operation that will enable you to test the truth or falsity of the statement.

Mostly the logical positivists take their illustrations of the legitimate kind of knowledge from the natural sciences. We may vary their procedure and bring the legitimate and illegitimate kinds of knowledge (as they maintain) to bear on at least the same topic. If you make the statement "All men believe in God," you can test that statement by the methods of the public-opinion pollsters. You can send out men to ask everyone they meet the question, "Do you believe in God?" As soon as one of the interviewed says no, you will have an operational proof that the statement is false. But if you make the statement "All men really believe in God deep down within themselves, no matter what they say," you have gone beyond any pollster's tests, beyond the possibility of the logical positivist's tests. If you say "God exists," you are making the kind of statement the logical positivist says cannot be classified as being within the scope of "knowledge." You are making a metaphysical answer to a metaphysical question; you are doing the same thing men have been doing since the Greeks. You are still getting answers that will by no means be accepted by everyone—and especially not by those with expert training in philosophy.

The logical positivists are themselves highly abstract thinkers, whose positive interest is chiefly the modern extension of the mathematician's way of going at things that is called symbolic logic. Some of the more innocent of them hoped that once they had worked out symbolic logic to perfection all communications in symbolic logic would be perfectly understandable by all human beings, who would thenceforth never quarrel, since they would never suffer from ignorance and misunderstanding. One of them, a parent, is said to have wished for a manual on child-rearing written in symbolic logic! But mostly the logical positivists simply pushed aside these questions of moral and aesthetic standards (value-judgments) as to them "meaningless." They did not really believe that just because no scientific answer to these questions could be found there were in fact as many answers as there were human beings on earth. They were not, in their practice, moral cynics or nihilists. They simply took values as not to be thought about profitably, a point of view annoying to those brought up in prevailing Western traditions, which have tended to hold that some judgments about morals and aesthetics are truer, or at least make more sense, than other such judgments.

Yet since from its more innocent to its more sophisticated forms anti-intellectualism emphasizes the immense role of the irrational in men's lives, there is a constant temptation for the anti-intellectualist to see only the clear-cut triumph of the objective thinking we call natural science. Heir to the long Western tradition of tough-mindedness, he is afraid of the kind of thinking Newman defended as the work of the illative sense. He sees that *all* sane men of sufficient education can be convinced of the truth of certain propositions in physics; he sees that *all* sane men of sufficient education simply cannot be convinced of any propositions in English literature—beyond simple statements of fact, such as that William Shakespeare wrote a play called *Romeo and Juliet*. And, at that, there are those who maintain that Francis Bacon or someone else wrote that play! The really cautious true statement would therefore be: the authorship of *Romeo and Juliet* is now commonly attributed to a man whose name is now commonly called Shakespeare. Yet, of course, the position that on any statement save simple statements of verifiable fact and statements of scientifically established uniformities one man's opinion is just as good as another's, the position that, as Bentham once declared, "push-pin is as good as poetry," is one that most men—even anti-intellectuals—find displeasing.

One way out for them we have seen already suggested by Machiavelli and Nietzsche: The truth of these value-judgments may not be rationally establishable, but their importance in the social life of a given culture *can* be established. A society that believes in the efficacy of certain religious rites wholly incapable of scientific justification may yet gain strength from such belief. Pareto cites as an example a Greek crew in ancient times sacrificing to Poseidon, god of the sea, before they set sail on a dangerous voyage; we today should be willing to accept regarding Poseidon the logical positivist's verdict that there is no possible proof of his existence; yet, says Pareto, it is clear that if under the influence of the belief that they had put themselves right with Poseidon the crew rowed more heartily, maintained better discipline, stuck together better under pressure of danger, then clearly belief in Poseidon was useful to them, and in a sense, true.

We have come with Pareto to a most representative twentieth-century anti-intellectual, a trained engineer, a mathematician who turned first to economics and then to sociology in an effort to build up a social science that would stand comparison with a natural science. Pareto was an Italian who did most of his creative work in Switzerland; but in his last years he accepted a post under Mussolini, and for this and for many of his doctrines as expressed in his *The Mind and Society* he has been labeled a reactionary, a Rightist, the "Karl Marx of the bourgeoisie." He was—like most articulate anti-intellectuals—a confirmed scholar and intellectual. Emotionally attached to the sort of ideal John Mill brings out in *On Liberty*, Pareto saw his world moving apparently farther and farther from individual liberty and toleration of great variety of human behavior, farther from international peace and free circulation of men and ideas. He was in some senses the disillusioned liberal, trying to explain why liberalism hadn't worked, not rejoicing that it hadn't. Of course, for the traditional reforming liberal all wrapped up in words and faith, the mere admission that liberalism wasn't working, the insistence that the facts of life were not entirely what the liberal thought and hoped they were, was a treason on Pareto's part. Moreover, Pareto is profoundly irritating to many readers because he insists too vehemently that he is in effect the first person to study human relations with the cool detachment of the scientist, keeping his value-judgments outside his work, or actually, insisting that he never makes value-judgments. Of course he comes nowhere near living up to these professions; his likes and dislikes, somewhat different in many ways from those of the reforming liberal, come out on every page. His great hatred is for the people he calls the "virtueists," the crusading reformers who wish by legislation, policing, and perhaps some education to wipe off the face of the earth sexual irregularities, alcoholic drinks, gambling, and the other lesser vices.

Pareto prefaces *The Mind and Society* with a somewhat tedious but by no means superfluous essay on just what the scientific method is. This method he calls the *logico-experimental;* other kinds of conscious human mental activity he calls *non-logico-experimental.* Note that he does not use simply the word *logical;* that is because he holds that logical thinking is merely a set of rules for using the mind in a certain way, a way that can be applied to problems like the existence of the Trinity or the Aristotelian entelechy as well as to problems like that of the chemical composition of a given protein.

Pareto as a sociologist is concerned chiefly with the problem of separating out in human action the rational (logico-experimental) from the nonrational (non-logico-experimental). In our social behavior, he found a part to be the expression of certain sentiments he called "residues," and another part the expression of other sentiments he called "derivations." Note that neither residues nor derivations are for Pareto drives, urges, appetites, libidos, or whatever else the psychologist tries to analyze in human behavior as a sort of underlying animal push to action. Pareto is willing to assume this push, and leave its study to the psychologist; what interests him as sociologist is action that is expressed in words, ritual, symbolism of some kind. Buying wool socks for cold weather is one such action. If they are bought deliberately to get good socks at a price the buyer can afford, this is rational, or logico-experimental action in accord with the doer's interests. If, however, they are bought without regard for price by a sentimental lover of England who buys imported English socks in order to do his bit to help England, then clearly something else, something the economist has to disregard in his price statistics, has come into play. This something else is the substance of Pareto's study.

The part of the action of our Greek sailors sacrificing to Poseidon that explained Poseidon as ruler of the seas, maker and quieter of tempests, is for Pareto a *derivation,* a theory or explanation usually logical in form, but *not logico-experimental,* not capable of verification by the methods of natural science. The derivations are close to what Bacon called the "Idols" and to what we all know nowadays as "rationalizations." Pareto gives them a much more complex and useful classification than did Bacon. Indeed, his is for the purposes of semantics one of the very best analyses of the commonest way the human mind has gone to work in social and ethical theory. He is clear in his own mind that these derivations have very little effect on the general behavior of men in society, very little effect on social change. What we have in this book called cosmologies Pareto would have held were mostly tissues of derivations; he maintained that they have little or no effect on the behavior of those who hold them. Yet in his own emotional life he was clearly unable to treat one cosmology as no better or no worse than another. He hated socialism, and medieval Christianity as well; he was himself a good nineteenth-century bourgeois.

What does move men in society, and keeps them together in society, says Pareto, is the residues. These have extraordinarily little intellectual in them, though they are usually put in logical form. They are expressions of relatively permanent, abiding sentiments in men, expressions that usually have to be separated from the part that is actually a derivation, which latter may change greatly and even quickly. He used the term "residue" to indicate that these sentiments are "left over" after the derivations are analyzed out by the sociologist. Let us revert to our pagan Greek sailors, and compare them with a group of Christian Greek sailors a few centuries later praying, lighting candles, and making vows to the Virgin Mary just before sailing. The *derivations* are the explanations of what Poseidon and the Virgin respectively do. They vary. The believer in the Virgin thinks his pagan predecessor was dead wrong. The *residues* are the needs to secure divine aid and comfort in a difficult undertaking, and to perform certain ritual acts that give the performer assurance of such aid and comfort. The residues are nearly the same for our two sets of sailors. Both the pagans and the Christians have the same social and psychological needs and satisfy them in much the same ways, though with very different rational (intellectual) explanations of what they are doing.

Pareto's conception of the residues was much more original than that of the derivations, and much more difficult to work out. His actual classification of the residues and the detailed analysis of the way they work in human society are by no means as good as that of his derivations. But two of the major classes of residues he distinguishes stand out, and help form what we must call—non-logico-experimental though it may be—his philosophy of history, his limited but genuine cosmology. These are first the residues of *persistent aggregates,* the sentiments that mark men who like regular ways, solid discipline, tradition and habit, men like the Spartans, the lions; and second there are the residues of the *instinct for combinations,* the sentiments that mark men who like novelty and adventure, who invent new ways of doing things, who like to cut loose from the old, the tried, men not easily shocked, men who hate discipline, men like the Athenians, the foxes. Now men as individuals hold all sorts of logically quite inconsistent mixtures of these two and the other (and to Pareto less important) residues. But in societies of many individual members, men influenced largely by one *or* the other of these major residues tend to predominate, and to characterize that society. Like most philosophers of history, Pareto is far from clear on just how a conservative society where the residues of persistent aggregates predominate changes into another kind of society. But he does have this conception of a pendulum swing, a Yin and Yang—even, though the comparison would have angered Pareto—a struggle of thesis and antithesis.

The nineteenth century in the West was in Pareto's mind a society in which the residues of instinct for combinations played perhaps the maximum part they can in a human society. The nineteenth century was a century of competition among individuals full of new ideas, inventions, enterprises, convinced that the old ways were bad, that novelty was the great thing to strive for at the expense of everything else. It was a society notably out of equilibrium. It had to turn toward the other kind of residues, toward the persistent aggregates, toward a society with more security and less competition, more discipline and less freedom, more uniformity and less variety. It had to go the way Pareto thought we were going to go, toward a totalitarian society.

Pareto's final general conception is this one of an equilibrium in a society, an equilibrium constantly disturbed at least in Western society, but constantly renewed by a sort of *vis medicatrix naturae* not to be supplanted by any social physician or planner. Pareto does not entirely rule out the possibility that human beings by taking thought may in little ways here and there change social arrangements in such a way that what they plan turns out to be a reality. But the overwhelming emphasis of his work is that in human affairs change in human conduct as a whole must be distinguished from change in human ideas and ideals. Man being what he is, and in our Western culture the residue of instinct for combinations being so widespread, there is bound to be change in many fields of human interest. Fashion and all its commercial dependents can almost be said to be change for change's sake. But for Pareto there was also—and more important for him to point out just because the reformers, the liberals, the virtueists, the optimistic planners would not see it—a level of human conduct where change is very slow indeed, almost as slow as the kind of change the geologist and the evolutionist study.

This level of human conduct where change is very slow indeed is the level of the residues. At most, Pareto held, the skilled political leader can manipulate the derivations in such a way that some residues are made relatively inactive, and others are activated. He cannot possibly produce new residues or destroy old ones. He will get effective governmental inspection of meats, for instance, not just by an appeal to men's sense of civic responsibility, not just by a rational argument of the eighteenth-century sort, but also by propaganda, by literary work like Upton Sinclair's *The Jungle,* making as many people as possible *feel fear* that they will eat uninspected dirty meat and die of food poisoning unless the government does inspect. Obviously, the men who direct American advertising are Paretans without knowing it.

The wise leader according to Pareto will read Bacon's famous aphorism, "nature is not to be commanded save by obeying her" (*natura non vincitur nisi parendo*), as "*human* nature is not to be commanded save by obeying it"—or at least taking it into account! You must not expect human beings to be consistently unselfish, sensible, devoted to the common good, kindly, wise. Above all, you must not expect that any institution, any law, any constitution, any treaty or pact, will make them so. But Pareto goes a bit beyond this position. Planning, except for limited and always very concrete ends, is dangerous. Pareto, starting from mathematics and engineering, and with actual hostility to Christianity, comes on this specific question very close to the Christian Burke. Not only is it very likely that a big, ambitious, legislated change will not achieve the results the planners planned; it is likely to produce unpredictable and perhaps unfortunate results. Pareto would have gloated a bit, one suspects, over the fate of the Eighteenth Amendment, which did not promote temperance in the United States, but helped produce newer and in many ways less desirable habits of drinking—helped, for instance, to make alcoholic beverages a respectable drink for middle-class women. Until we know more of social science, the best thing to do is to trust to what the upstart intellectual arrogantly condemns as the *irrational* side of human nature; we must believe that the ingrained habits of the human race are, even by evolutionary standards, more useful to survival than the impertinent logic of the reformers.

Much of modern anti-intellectualism, unpalatable though it is to optimistic democratic taste, is actually widespread in Western culture today. Even semantics has spread into popular consciousness, to be sure in forms Korzybski would hardly recognize. We have all heard about rationalization, propaganda, the ambiguities and other inadequacies of language; we are all reminded daily that to get ahead in this world you must exercise your skill in handling other people, you must deliberately win friends and influence people by arts other than logic. The experts in propaganda know that one of the factors they must reckon with is public awareness and distrust of propaganda, of the not so well hidden "hidden persuaders" which the French call expressively— and cynically—*bourrage de crâne,* "brain-stuffing."

We are brought squarely up against the problem of the relation of anti-intellectualism to our democratic tradition, way of life, cosmology. Democracy as it ripened in the eighteenth century held out hope of rapid and thorough social change toward universal happiness on earth to be achieved by educating all men to use their natural reason—or at least by entrusting power to an enlightened group of political planners who could devise and run institutions under which all men would be happy. Anti-intellectualism maintains against these democratic beliefs the belief that men are not and cannot under the best educational system be guided by their reason, that the drives, the id, the residues, the habits, the conditioned reflexes that mostly do guide them cannot be changed rapidly, that, in short, there is something in the nature of man that makes him and will continue to make him behave in the immediate future not very differently from the way he has behaved in the past. These two sets of beliefs, the democratic and the anti-intellectual, seem mutually incompatible. Many of the Leftist and Rightist attacks we discussed in the last chapter seem in comparison relatively close to democracy, mere extensions or modifications of it. But Pareto's position, for instance, seems in some ways as much a polar opposite of democracy as Maistre's, and of as little use to us today.

Yet Graham Wallas, as we noted, was in sympathy with what we call democracy, and went part way with the anti-intellectuals. So good a defender of all sorts of democratic causes as Stuart Chase has been greatly influenced by anti-intellectualism. All but the very softest and most idealistic of social scientists in our culture have had to retreat from eighteenth-century rationalism and learn from the anti-intellectuals. And it is difficult for most of us to read Pareto—and Machiavelli, Bacon, La Rochefoucauld, and the other "realists" about human nature and human affairs—without feeling that much of what they say is quite true.

We are back, of course, to the eternal contrast, the eternal tension, so strong in Western culture, between this world and the next, the real and the ideal, the practical and the desirable. The anti-intellectuals are pulling democracy over toward the first of these pairs. Yet to emphasize the facts of life, the "spotted actuality," is not necessarily to adopt the conclusion that no improvement in actual conditions is possible. Indeed, in Western tradition the realists (in our modern sense, which is confusingly different from the medieval sense of philosophical "realism") have more often been ethical meliorists, even optimists, than cynics. They rarely gloat with pleasure over the bad conditions they insist are there, are real. The real and the ideal are not, we have insisted throughout this book, by nature enemies. They belong together. It is only when they are divorced that each, pursued in neglect of the other, is a danger to society. One of the great questions we now face is whether good democrats can accept the reality the anti-intellectuals have brought to their attention without losing their belief in the possibility of improving that reality.

CHAPTER EIGHT

MID-TWENTIETH CENTURY

SOME UNFINISHED BUSINESS

The West and Other Cultures

We have hitherto, and quite deliberately, treated the intellectual history of the West with but incidental mention of any other culture. For we have focused on the attitude of Western men and women toward the Big Questions, toward cosmologies. And it is a fact that on the whole the West has not been greatly influenced by the cosmological, nor even by the ethical and aesthetic, ideas of other cultures. There is unquestionably a great deal in the first form of Western culture we have here studied, the Greek, which comes out of the cultures of the Eastern Mediterranean region in the millennia before Homer and the Ionians. But in many ways these early cultures are simply the ancestors of our own Western culture; and at any rate, save for the Hebraic and other Near Eastern elements in Christianity, they had mostly done their work before the rise of the great Greek culture.

A detailed study of Western culture would, of course, have to take into account many kinds of contacts with other cultures, especially in India, China, and Japan, and note many ways in which our inheritance would be different had these contacts never taken place. There is first the familiar interchange of material goods, the kind that even the pre-historian can trace through archaeological remains. The West has usually been willing enough to accept strange wares, to experiment gingerly with strange foods. Western man is not quite the complete devotee of newness, invention, experiment he seemed to the nineteenth-century progressive to be: There have been neophobes even in our culture. Nevertheless, any modern Western language bears the traces of these borrowings from all over the globe—*sugar, alcohol, curry, tomato, tobacco, pajama, kowtow, bungalow,* and many more.

Sometimes the borrowings involved inventions and ideas, a very typical example of this sort of external influence on Western culture being the sign for zero, which is of Hindu origin and was borrowed through the Arabs. This and many other borrowings are important; without some of them at least we could not have Western culture as it now is. The eighteenth-century intellectuals admired the Chinese very much indeed. In part, as we shall see, they used the wise Confucian Chinese as sticks with which to beat their Christian opponents. But they also brought Chinese art into Western art—Chinese Chippendale, for instance. The vogue of *chinoiserie* is the beginning of that modern eclecticism out of which may yet come a real style. The French physiocrats were much influenced by the Chinese.

With the discoveries of the fifteenth century and the beginnings of the expansion of Europe the study of non-European lands and peoples of all sorts began to take an important part in Western learning. Yet the growth of most of the formal sciences was very slow in these early centuries. Anthropology is in origin a nineteenth-century science; even comparative linguistics, the serious study of India and of China, are no later than the Enlightenment. Still, by the nineteenth century it is true that the very careful study of all phases of the lives and cultures of peoples outside the Western tradition was a commonplace among scholars and students. The popular press, books, and the lecture platform had spread among many millions of Westerners at least some information about other peoples. This knowledge was by no means broad or deep; and it is probable that few Westerners actually thought they could learn anything from the heathen. Perhaps the typical Britisher or Frenchman was not quite so "culture-bound," not quite so narcissistic in his admiration of the West as he was thought to be by the intellectuals who wanted us to be really cosmopolitan, really human, and absorb the best of the universe. Yet the familiar quotation from Tennyson can stand as a fair sample of the value the nineteenth-century West set upon the East: "Better fifty years of Europe than a cycle of Cathay"—that is, China.

There is another phase of the interrelation of cultures that comes out at its best in the eighteenth-century Enlightenment. This is the use of bits of information—actually more often misinformation—about one culture to further a policy you are pushing in your own culture. In the eighteenth century, the *philosophes* loved to invent wise Persians, Chinese, Hindus, Hurons, and South Sea Islanders who, coming in contact with European ways, brought to the criticism of Europe the wisdom of their own points of view. The trouble is that all these yellow, black, brown, and red men, bringing to bear on European problems their own supposedly native wisdom, turn out to be themselves European *philosophes,* with exactly the same ideas about right and wrong, beautiful and ugly, reason and superstition, nature and convention the other enlightened had. These non-Europeans are no more than fictions, straw men, sticks with which to beat something Western, and no proof at all that we Westerners have really learned at high ethical and metaphysical levels from other peoples. With nineteenth-century improvement in sciences like geography and anthropology, this rather innocent game could not go on in quite the same way. Too much was known about the primitive peoples. It is still played, however, though much more skillfully, as witness Ruth Benedict's quietly co-operative Zuñi in *Patterns of Culture* and Margaret Mead's sexually blissful maidens in *Coming of Age in Samoa*.

We return to our point. For the historian of the clusters of ideas about the Big Questions which have prevailed hitherto in the West, it is hardly necessary to devote much attention to other cultures than the Western. This statement is not provincial or otherwise wicked; it is simply a recognition of a fact. Indeed, the marginal and sectarian nature of influences at this level from outside the West is clear from the fate of the little modern groups that appeal to Eastern wisdom, from Bahaism or Theosophy of Madame Blavatsky's kind to learned admiration for the wisdom of Confucius, Lao-tzu, or Buddha. These exotic cults are all outside the main current of Western thought and feeling, however intense and real some individual conversions to them may be.

It is quite possible that this spiritual self-sufficiency of the West may be changing, and that in the next century or so there will arise in the West and indeed all over the world a great syncretic religion and philosophy into which will pour the ancient wisdom of the East. F. S. C. Northrop's recent *Meeting of East and West* is perhaps a prophetic as well as a symptomatic book. There may be One World of the spirit to make possible One World of the flesh. Already it is clear that somehow or other a very large number of Western men and women must learn to understand the cultures of non-Western people, even though understanding prove to be not quite conversion. But we cannot be sure of what lies so far ahead, nor of what will go into the cosmologies of the twenty-first or twenty-second centuries. Even the most high-minded of cosmopolitans should not shut from his mind the possibility that the rest of the world may in the next few generations be won over at least to Western material wants, that the Ford, air conditioning, and the comic strips may conquer Confucius, Lao-tzu, *and* Buddha.

The Shaping of Modern Thought—A Summary

What can be said to be really persistent notes or traits or characteristics of Western culture? Obviously, at this high level of abstraction, there is nothing that can satisfy the type of mind that refuses to accept the validity of our analogies with the spectrum or with the normal distribution curve. It is probable that somewhere in the two or three thousand years of our culture you can dig up at least one Westerner in almost every possible category of human experience. There is not even agreement on the continuity of Western culture. A man like Spengler holds that what appears to be a continuous stream is in fact three, none of which communicates in any way with the others—the Apollonian or Graeco-Roman, the Magian or Arabic, and the Faustian or European, each of roughly one thousand years' duration. Even if you find Spengler an oversoulful German, you will recall that there are many, both lovers and haters of the Middle Ages, who regard medieval culture as just about the antithesis (in the common, not the Hegelian, sense) of ours today.

Still, certain big generalizations about the intellectual climate of the West can be made. First of all, we must note that in no other culture have the natural sciences flourished as they have in the West. Increasingly, it is true, men from other cultures have practiced the study of science with great success; science is in many ways the most successful of human efforts to break through the bounds of the modern territorial in-group, or nation-state, more successful in this respect than commerce, more successful than religion. But science in its modern form bears plainly the mark of the West in which it was developed. It could hardly have developed save in the Western atmosphere of tension between the real and the ideal, between this world and the next. Complete absorption of the mind, at least, in another world, complete devotion to inner logic, would have made science impossible; but so too would complete preoccupation with the world as it is, so too would mere unsystematic ingenuity in concrete worldly problems. Science needed not merely an interest in material things; it needed the intellectual apparatus to devise the incredibly complex ordering of things we call science; it needed above all the long training in the use of reason afforded by the Greek and medieval philosophy and theology our innocent logical positivists scorn.

But natural science, as we have insisted, does not in itself provide a cosmology. It has congruence or consonance with modern Western cosmologies; it has not to the same degree consonance with others. If, for instance, you are an Eastern mystic for whom the body is a complete illusion, you will no doubt have to feed that illusion with a minimum of food and drink (which is also an illusion) but you will not make yourself an expert on human physiology. You cannot, however, get from science an answer to the question, Is the human body an illusion (which is meaningless in scientific terms), nor even to the question, Is it better, as most of us do in the West, to consider the human body a real thing or is it better to consider it an illusion (which is also a meaningless question for science). In brief, the pursuit of scientific knowledge may well be a *part* of our Western values; it cannot possibly *make* our Western values.

Let us take a concrete case for illustration. That branch of biology that studies heredity, genetics, though it will if it follows precedent improve its command over its material, is already good enough so that it is possible to learn from the geneticist much about the biological possibilities of eugenics, breeding human beings well. From the social sciences, still in their infancy, and often denied the status of science, it is none the less possible to learn something about how to persuade people to accept the recommendations of the biologist, about the kinds of social groups that would probably be produced if certain types of human being were bred, and about many other pertinent social problems. There is indeed an immense area of ignorance in all these fields, especially where they converge; we do not really know, for instance, what is the relation between human body types and human personality. Still, let us assume we know or can know enough to breed human beings.

What kind shall we breed? Shall we specialize on types—the artist, the football player, the manager, the salesman, a graded series of intelligences from the Alphas or intellectuals to the Epsilons or low-caste workers, as in Aldous Huxley's grim *Brave New World*? Or shall we try to breed the all-around man who can turn his hand and brain to anything? Or, since we are looking well ahead, shall we try to breed the body away, so to speak, or at least to a minimum as in Shaw's *Back to Methuselah* and thus paradoxically rejoin the Platonists? Science cannot answer these questions. The human mind, at least in the old simple sense of the logical, ratiocinative mind, does not in fact answer them. They are answered by what is still best called the human will, by the whole force of the personality. In a democracy they are in fact answered by what there is no harm in calling the general will, by a sort of rough adjustment among competing but not antithetical groups pursuing different but not wholly different ends. In the Western tradition the leaders, the *aristoi,* the elite, the ruling classes do much to shape these ends, and to persuade the masses to accept them. But they do not wholly make these ends, or purposes, or values—at least, not in the traditional attitude of the West.

For the first of the generalizations we can make about the non-cumulative body of Western thought is that it displays from the Greeks and the medieval Christians down to the enlightened of yesterday and today a belief that men's sense of values is a groping awareness of the organization of the universe, an organization not evident to unreflective men, not provable by scientific methods, never wholly plain to the best and wisest of men, but an *organization,* not a chaos. Over the ages, the clearest common indication of this feeling is the term *natural law,* which to be sure did not mean exactly the same thing to a Stoic, a Scholastic, or an eighteenth-century philosopher, but did to all three mean a faith in the substance of things hoped for. Or, to put it another way, the very concept of *natural law* means that those who hold it believe that the gap between the real and the ideal, between what we have and what we want, is no abyss, not actually a gap, *but a relation*. It is summed up in the Epistle to the Hebrews: "For here have we no continuing city, but we seek one to come."

Second, there is throughout Western intellectual history a feeling for what is commonly called the "dignity of man." The area, the group, to which is applied the irreducible notion that men may not be treated as things, or animals, has varied. For the early Greeks this group was limited in some ways to the in-group of the Hellenes; it was clearly so confined to the in-group among the early Hebrews. Greek Stoics and Hebrew prophets extended this idea to the human race. To the Christian all men are equal in the possession of immortal souls. The basic democratic "liberty, equality, fraternity" is, once more, part of the heavenly city of the eighteenth century; it is in our modern cosmology the direct reflection, the direct successor of the Christian conception of the equality of souls before God. One may add as a footnote that the main Western tradition has very firmly separated man from the rest of nature, to which it refuses to give the special status of sharing in the moral struggle. Animals in the West do not have souls. Pantheism, and most certainly metempsychosis, are not normal Western doctrines. Indeed the Hindu, who finds so much coarse about us, thinks we are most inconsiderate of our fellow animals.

Third, there is a striking continuity of Western ideas of the good life here on earth. Once more, we must use the figure of the spectrum. Central in this spectrum is the way of life that was the ideal of the aristocratic culture of Greece—the ideal of nothing too much, of the Golden Mean. This statement will not be acceptable to those who hold that the central Christian ideal, almost realized in the thirteenth century, is ascetic, other-worldly, ineffable; nor will it be acceptable to those who find the central point of Western culture in some kind of manic drive for the heights—any heights. Since indeed we could make as a fourth generalization that Western culture shows, save perhaps for the interval of the Dark Ages, an amazing variety of views and practices moral and aesthetic, since even at its most stable, Western society has rarely even approximated the Spartan model of uniformity and discipline, it is obvious that both the ascetic and the manic (Faustian?) ways of life are present in our tradition. Nevertheless, as a kind of recurring resolution of the complex tensions between Western striving for the ideal, the unattainable perfection, and Western pleasure and interest in the world at hand, the Golden Mean of the old Greeks keeps its hold—sometimes, as in Aquinas or Chaucer, or even John Mill or William James, in forms Pericles might not have recognized. How far this aristocratic code of conduct can be approximated in the masses of society is one of the most acute of modern problems. The basic belief of the eighteenth-century philosophers who formulated the democratic ideal was that the common man can lead this form of the good life now that the material basis lacking to the Greek masses is potentially available to all.

Beyond these generalizations, which will disappoint the adepts of the philosophy of history, it is hardly safe to go. We cannot pretend to answer the fascinating problem of why our Western society has, at least by our own not wholly subjective standard of evolutionary survival, been the most "successful" of societies so far in human history. The answer will lie in many variables we cannot isolate and therefore cannot assemble into anything like a formula. There probably is not even any central taproot, any determining factor of the sort the Marxist sets up in the mode of production. Of course, the Marxist gives us no really satisfactory account of why the development of Western economic life from the simplicities of the hunt to the complexities of modern industrial life was so different from the development of modes of production elsewhere on this globe. Our generation distrusts simple environmental explanations, such as the favorite one that the soil and climate of the small European peninsula off the great Asiatic land mass were particularly favorable to whatever virtues seem most needed to explain the success of Western society—energy, inventiveness, imagination, love of competition, and so on. Most of us distrust the simple—and even the complex—forms of explanation that assign an innate superiority, god-given or evolution-given, to certain groups or races. We cannot believe that there is really any kind of *Homo occidentalis,* Aryan, Nordic, Caucasian, or what you will, with hereditary biological equipment different enough from that of non-Westerners to explain the recent success of ours in competition with other societies. Most of us would also distrust any form of idealistic explanation, any form of explanation that attributed to the *mind* of Western man the shape our culture has taken. Indeed, many readers will probably reject the mildly intellectualist notion just advanced in this book, that in part the growth of cumulative knowledge (which surely is the means by which we Westerners acquired the weapons to defeat the rest of the world and the material abundance to tempt them) is due to the happy balance our major cosmological systems have maintained between this world (experience) and the other (logic, planning, the *esprit de système*).

Yet all these explanations, which we rightly reject when they are claimed to be sole explanations, are probably ingredients in that most unstable compound we call Western culture. Take away any one of them, and any one of many others we have not analyzed, and you do not have the Western culture we know. Take coal, iron, water-power, banks, and capital away from western Europe, and of course you do not have the Industrial Revolution as we know it; take St. Paul and St. Augustine, Calvin and Karl Marx away, and you do not have our Western view of life.

Our Present Discontents

In the perspective of Western intellectual history, we can see that many of the problems that seem to our alarmists so new, so demanding, so imperative of solution, are in fact very old problems that men and women of Western culture have managed to survive without solving. Notably, those prophets of doom who hold that modern Western man must agree on the Big Questions, that we must somehow escape from our present multanimity into a new Age of Faith, have against them several thousand years of Western history in which men have disagreed over these fundamental questions. But beyond this problem of agreement on the Big Questions there lies a more specific cosmological question that is concretely a problem for our times: Can we continue to hold even those modified eighteenth-century ideas of progress, of the possibility of closing here and now, or very shortly, that gap between "is" and "ought to be" which as historians we have to note Western man has never come very close to closing, and yet has never, for very long, given up trying to close?

There is always the possibility that the next few generations will see almost no change in Western cosmology, that we shall continue on the whole to accept as answers to the Big Questions those we accept now, in all their bewildering and mutually contradictory variety. Such a persistence of existing states of mind is, of course, possible, and to certain temperaments, even probable. We certainly do not know clinically how much variation in attitudes toward fundamental problems of value and conduct a society can stand. Yet it does not seem likely that those prophets who keep talking of crisis, crossroads, and the little time left are *wholly* wrong. Some further emendations in our inheritance from the Enlightenment we shall almost certainly have to make. For the gap between our ideals and our behavior, between the world we think desirable—indeed, morally right, necessary—and the world we have to live in has been since the Enlightenment a gap of very different psychological character from the gap the traditional Christian knew and felt.

The gap between what ought to be and what is probably exists in all men's minds, certainly in all civilized men's minds. But ordinary men and their leaders *must not be constantly, naggingly aware of this gap*. Most of the time, they must—though the outside observer may think their position hypocrisy—somehow persuade themselves that the gap really isn't there. There are many ways of filling it. On one's own private account, there are personal relationships, ritual practices, conviction of belonging to a body of the elect, mystic submission to some greater will, all of which will help close the gap. For those who have to take humanity as a whole into view, there is the more difficult way of the optimistic reformer just about to close the gap with one last law, one last sermon. There is also the Christian attitude toward the gap—that it can never be wholly closed here on earh, but that those who work honestly, justly, considerately toward closing it on earth will find it fully closed in heaven, that those who do not will find it fully closed in hell.

But to many of the heirs of the Enlightenment the gap is still painfully there, yawning as wide as ever. They cannot take the Christian way out, for they cannot believe in any other world than this often rather unpleasant one. They have a firm notion of what is on the other, the ideal side of the gap—peace, plenty, happiness in all its range from lazy comfort to the leap of the heart. They believe we human beings should have what we want, and that we cannot successfully fill in the gap between what we want and what we have with words, ritual, or any other consoling illusion. This last is, from a naturalistic-historical point of view, one reason why the Victorian compromise did not hold, why the lower classes refused to stay put, why socialism preached the need for economic democracy after political democracy had been attained. Men wanted economic equality, not just spiritual equality. No ritual could satisfy the desire of the poor to be materially richer. The material ideals of the eighteenth century are deceptively simple; just because they are so simple and so material it has been very hard to pretend we have attained them when we have not. The last generation has seen this same kind of dilemma spread into relations between Westerners and "colonial" peoples. Asians and Africans too have repudiated the Victorian compromise doctrine of the "white man's burden." They too want real, not symbolic, equality.

Now it may be possible to lessen the gap between the real and the ideal by bringing the ideal a long way back toward reality, by setting small, modest goals all along the line—not "temperance" but less criminal alcoholism; not perfect sexual life on earth but fewer divorces; not the elimination of "soap operas" and Westerns but better-balanced radio and television programs; not complete economic security but less disastrous depressions with less widespread unemployment; not a world government that will forever guarantee peace, but a United Nations that will help us stave off war and perhaps make it less barbarous when it comes. The list could be prolonged indefinitely. The moderate realist asks that democracy give up some of its eighteenth-century optimism about the natural goodness and reasonableness of man, about the magic effect of a readily changeable social and political environment (laws, constitutions, treaties, new educational institutions and curricula), about the nearness of the approaching millennium. He asks that democracy accept some of the pessimism of traditional Christianity as embodied in the doctrine of original sin, some of the tragic sense of human limitations that has inspired great literature, some of the doubts about the universal capacity of all men to think straight that come out of modern psychology, some of the practical, common-sense awareness of the impossibility of perfection that most of us have in those fields of activity where we act under the burden of responsibility.

Western democrats may be able to shake off the burden of excessive optimism about human perfectibility that they have inherited from the Enlightenment, and adapt their ideals to this harsh world. Many of them are increasingly aware that something must be done to close the gap between promise and performance the years have opened up in the Western democracies and indeed throughout the world. They cannot go along with the self-deluded idealists who seem to think that all that is necessary is to reaffirm the promise more firmly than ever. For one thing, they begin to detect a touch of bitterness in the affirmation which shows that even the idealists can look about them. You will find the case for a democracy willing to face the facts of life very cogently put by Arthur M. Schlesinger, Jr., in his *The Vital Center.* It is not at all unlikely that in the next few years this point of view will make real gains in the West.

But is such a pessimistic democracy likely or even possible—a democracy that resolutely refuses to promise heaven on earth and still does not return to the older heaven in another world? One very strong element in the democratic cosmology, we have insisted, has been a denial of the supernatural, a denial of an afterlife. We have indeed seen that much of the democratic cosmology has been after a fashion reconciled with formal churchgoing Christianity; but we have also noted that, especially in the liberal Protestant groups, very little indeed of the divine, the miraculous, the transcendental has been left in a formal, rationalistic faith. Finally, of course, there remain in all the Western democracies millions of men and women who range all the way from violent positivists and anticlericals to the completely worldly and indifferent, millions who are simply not Christians. Can these men and women find the spiritual resources needed to face hardship, frustration, struggle, and unhappiness—all the evils they have been taught to believe would be banished shortly from human life?

Though there have persisted through these last three centuries many Christian groups who held to the spirit and the letter of the traditional faith, there have also grown up certain surrogates for the Christian faith that many had lost, or that had been altered into pseudo-Christian optimistic rationalism. These surrogates are democracy, nationalism, socialism, communism, totalitarianism, and their many variant creeds and sects.

Most of these surrogates have in common a belief in the perfectibility of men here on earth—provided the proper measures are taken. Most of them deny the existence of any supernatural being capable of interfering in the affairs of this earth, though many do indeed retain the notion of some sort of guiding principle of goodness—a kind of impersonal God—and all believe that the universe can be made a comfortable place for man to live in. Back of them all lies the very general attitude or cosmology of the Enlightenment, which perhaps takes on its most representative form in the kind of liberal, democratic system of values you find in John Mill. But the actual institutional form, the Church for this faith, has been the territorial nation-state, so that in practice democracy and nationalism have been united in complex and varying fashion. Socialism is originally an heretical development of earlier democratic thought—or if you prefer, a deepening of democratic aims—which also, wherever it has been successful, has got itself tied up with the nation-state and with nationalism.

Now we have deliberately used of these impersonal faiths—these formally nontheistic religions in which abstractions, like virtue or liberty, groups like the national in-group, are hypostasized—the term *surrogate,* with all its connotations of a somewhat synthetic and not quite adequate *substitute.* The inadequacy of the impersonal faiths in comparison with Christianity is especially evident in relation to the problems of the individual in trouble. These impersonal faiths are weak in their cure of souls. It is true that in their fighting and crusading stages—socialism before it comes to power, for instance—they are able to enlist the full spiritual ardor of many of the faithful, give them a sense of belonging to something very great indeed, melt away their petty selfishnesses in emotional self-surrender. But once they are established, once they are faced with this routine world, these impersonal faiths have little to offer the unhappy, the maladjusted, the suffering.

Nationalism is probably the strongest of these faiths. It bulwarks the weak and the inadequate with their membership in the great whole, their share of the "pooled self-esteem" of patriotism. It has in times of crisis been able to rely on both human patience and human daring. But it does not take the place of a consoling God. Marianne, the symbol of the French Republic, is a heroic figure of the barricades. But it is hard to pray to Marianne, as generations have prayed to the Virgin Mary. Socialism would seem to have even less of the consoling touch. It is no doubt encouraging to the faithful Marxist to know that Dialectical Materialism is hard at work making things better for the oppressed. But the really unhappy need something more human, something more aware of *them,* not as temporary victims of the mode of production, but as important, unique, sovereign human beings deserving the immediate attention of God or his agents.

Moreover, there is another psychological weakness in modern surrogates for older theistic faiths. These new lay religions find it very hard to permit repentance. In the numerous trials for treason (heresy) that have gone on in Soviet Russia, though the accused have usually broken down and made most complete confessions of their errors, they were by no means forgiven and taken back into the fold. The United States government tends apparently in these days to the opinion that "once a Communist, always a Communist," especially in the case of Englishmen and other West Europeans. A French intellectual who admits to having joined the Communist party in the dark days of the thirties but has since declared his repentance is apparently still a Communist to the State Department. But the phenomenon is obvious in any study of modern social and political movements. In the great French Revolution, for instance, it was very difficult, indeed almost impossible, for a man who had voted conspicuously with the Moderates in 1790 to excuse himself in 1793 with the then triumphant Extremists by pleading his error, by claiming that he had repented and seen the light. He commonly ended on the guillotine. It is hard to repent effectively in these impersonal religions.

Yet the forgiving of the repentant sinner has been one of the great strengths of Christianity, one of the ways wise Christian leadership has tempered the wind to the shorn lamb. Now it may be that the rigid attitude toward repentance displayed by the newer impersonal faiths is related to the abstract and perfect ideal—*an ideal improperly separated from the real*—that they hold for human behavior in the Utopia they were designed to achieve on earth. Those who hold these ideals desire so passionately that man be perfect that they cannot forgive him the slightest imperfection. A wholly this-worldly idealist can hardly avoid trying to eliminate those who do not behave according to his ideals. No doubt the riper democracies, like the English, are much less exacting than the Communists, much more willing to put up with human weaknesses. Still, none of them seems to offer to their leaders the chance for effective and not at all shaming compromise that the Christian requirement (note that it *is* a requirement) of forgiveness to the penitent affords; nor do they offer to the faithful the spiritual security, the flexible discipline, that the Christian doctrine of sin and repentance offers.

Finally, these abstract faiths are a grave danger for the modern intellectual, since they make easy, indeed they seem to ennoble, his ready assumption that he knows just what is wrong with the world, and how to right it. These faiths encourage the separation of the ideal from the real, as we have noted, for they oversimplify human nature. But the modern intellectual, already separated from the mass of his fellows by a rift that has surely not narrowed since it developed its modern form early in the nineteenth century, needed rather to be called back to the close and realistic study of the whole range of human behavior than to be allowed to develop in fine moral indignation his notions of "ought to be." Indeed, even when these notions take on the appearance of realism, of hard-boiled acceptance of things-as-they-are, they are a very evident form of that "inverted idealism" some writers have already found in Machiavelli. Balance, a sane resolution of the tension between the ideal and the real, is the heart of the matter. Certainly, the balance can be tipped, as many a modern intellectual like Pareto has tipped it, much too far away from the ideal. But at this moment in history, tipping toward the ideal, the *over-simple* ideal, is a grave danger encountered by the rawness and simplicities of our surrogate faiths.

In summary, then, these newer faiths do not have the richness and depth of awareness of what human beings are really like that the older religions have; they are therefore not as able as the older religions to cope with the problem of human relations in a time of troubles. Democracy and socialism have hitherto, in a sense, had relatively comfortable going in a world where most of the material indices really were going up in a steady curve. They have not yet had to face from too many unhappy men and women for whom this is not even remotely heaven on earth the menacing and very natural cry of "put up or shut up." Perhaps they will not. It may be that the great masses in the West can take the attitude, hitherto confined to aristocracies like the Stoic, that this is a tough world in which nobody is always happy, in which everybody has got to keep coping with his troubles, and in which there is no reward beyond the grave. But this seems most unlikely. The mass of mankind, even in the West, have never been able to take the tragic view without the help of a personal religion, a religion hitherto always transcendental, supernatural, other-worldly. Somehow, democracy, if it is not to return wholeheartedly to Christianity (which many today would have it do), must take on the cure of souls.

There is still another, and more definitely intellectual, difficulty in the way of a pessimistic, realistic democracy without belief in the supernatural. This democracy would have to extend to all our activities the tentativeness, the willingness to experiment, the patience, the acceptance of slowness, the recognition of the limits set on human effort by those two words *impossible* and *insoluble* which characterizes the work of the scientist as scientist and which, in part at least, all of us attain in the specific tasks we must fulfill. In such a democracy a very large number of people indeed would have to forgo the delights of certitude, the assurance that comes from knowing in advance that certain absolutes are true, that there is something that never changes, something not part of history but still part of ourselves. But it is clear that we humans cling to certitude; those who lost Christian certitude promptly tried to find scientific certitude, historical certitude, certitude anywhere they could turn it up. And we cling to omniscience as the companion of certitude—

an omniscient force, if we cannot have an omniscient God. If a thorough-going relativism (not of course nihilism) in values is to be asked of our new citizens of a pessimist democracy—and it would seem that only such a relativism could effectively sustain their pessimism and keep them from hoping at least for some new kind of pie in the sky—then such a democracy will be very difficult indeed to set up in our time. It would ask too much of poor human nature, more actually than optimistic democracy asked, since the average citizen of the old optimistic democracy was allowed his bit of the old consoling religion.

Moreover, we come in the mid-twentieth century to the difficulty that was encountered in ancient Athens: Just what is the relation beween the attitudes taken toward the Big Questions by the intellectuals and the whole structure, the whole equilibrium, of a society? The slightest attention to what is going on among Western intellectuals—existentialists in France and elsewhere, followers of Barth and Niebuhr in Germany and America, the bright young Catholic converts in England, Western adherents of Zen Buddhism, even the "new conservatives"—makes it plain that the intellectuals are tightening their spiritual belts, getting set for a long spell of hard going, growing very scornful of such cheerful democrats as Benjamin Franklin, or such shallow democrats as Thomas Jefferson. The Enlightenment may well be due for even more bitter attacks than those it received from the romanticists of Wordsworth's day. Yet one finds it very hard to imagine the average American—or indeed the average European—in quite the mood of sensitive, high-minded, world-embracing despair that has come over the vanguard of Western intellectuals. There is a certain coarseness, like that that wells up from the *fabliaux* in the midst of the high-minded thirteenth century, that one suspects will keep the fleshpots boiling for a while even in our tragic world.

It will not do, then, to conclude that our Western culture is about to make some sort of *volte-face* into another Age of Faith. The democratic cosmology is almost certain in the West to receive another revision even more thorough than the revision the nineteenth century gave to its original heritage from the Enlightenment. One cannot be at all sure at present what form that revision will take. A very great deal will depend on the result of the struggle between the United States and Soviet Russia, a struggle in which the whole cosmology is at stake. The very necessities of the struggle may drive the West into a much more regimented society than our tradition holds good. For it is one of the unpleasant facts of human relations—one of the kinds of facts that the new realistic democrats have got to face—that in war, cold or hot, you have to have more authority and less liberty than in quieter times.

Very roughly, and with all sorts of specific twistings and turnings in each that contradict the generalization, it would seem that in the United States and in Russia are temporarily embodied a number of the sets of opposites that in some kind of union have hitherto maintained that tension which is so characteristic of the West. We are not, of course, pure Liberty, and they pure Authority. We do not stand for the individualism of the great cats, nor they for the collectivism of the beehive or anthill. We are not variety, and they are not uniformity. Neither of us lives up to the extremes of our own systems of values. Still, the opposition is there, and is very real, in spite of recent competition in similar kinds of technology and sharing of "culture." We do, on the whole, stand for the series of values that in this book have been treated as the central values of Western culture—a feeling for the irreducible something in each human being still best suggested by that worn old word *liberty,* a feeling which, though it will pause a little and turn on itself when confronted with the very real problems suggested by such phrases as "force a man to be free" or "you are free when you do right, but a slave when you do wrong" or "liberty, not license," is nevertheless deep down defiantly unconvinced that these paradoxes are necessary. The Western tradition of which we are now the chief defenders is not dogmatically, not even idealistically, but all the more firmly *individualist.*

Our chances of maintaining the traditions of the West, and of preserving them in a form not unfairly described as democratic, are greater than our prophets of doom will admit. For if the anti-intellectualism of the last few decades has been corrosive of the more naive hopes of a heaven on earth through the perfecting of human nature, or simply by the release of human nature from its bad environment, it has given us reason to believe that if our democratic way of life really is anchored in our habits, traditions, sentiments, conditioned reflexes, and super-egos it may well survive even a very harsh reality. What to our grandfathers seemed the strength of democracy, its dependence on the rationality of men, now indeed seems its weakness; but perhaps after all democracy does not depend on the rationality of men. The democratic West has now withstood two wars in which it was supposed, with its addiction to variety, indiscipline, spiritual multanimity, and even comfort, to go down before the superior discipline, toughness, and unanimity of its antidemocratic foes. It did not go down, but won through to victory in spite of, or more likely because of, what looked to certain critics like weaknesses.

For what looks in purely intellectual analysis like disintegration, squabbling, rank inability to agree on anything at all may well be no more than disagreement on matters we Westerners have been disagreeing on publicly and violently most of the time since Socrates played the gadfly in Athens. If you think of the full logical implications of their creeds, it is really astonishing that Catholics, Protestants, Jews, and Marxist materialists fought side by side in the American forces in the two world wars. You may say that they did not really believe so much in their respective formal faiths as in the United States, but this would be much too logical a position to be true. You may say that they "believed in" religious toleration as a positive good, and that would no doubt be true in part of many of them. But the truest thing you could say would be that they never thought at all about the general problem of religious toleration, that most of them simply accepted the existence of Catholics, Jews, Protestants, and all varieties of materialists as one of the facts of life, one of the things you take, like the weather. A very great deal of the Western way of life is thus embedded somewhere in quite ordinary Americans, not in their cerebral cortexes, probably, but in a much safer place which the physiologist hasn't quite located—we used to say, in the heart.

We come back, then, to the proposition that for all we yet know in terms of a cumulative social science, the relation between the strength of a given society and the degree of agreement on matters cosmological among its members cannot be determined. There seems to be excellent evidence that very considerable multanimity in matters of theology, metaphysics, art, literature, and even ethics can persist if the existence of such disagreement is taken, not as a lofty ideal of toleration, of progress through variation (though for many intellectuals it is just that) but as something given, something normal for human beings. If democracy really means anything so unnatural to Western intellectuals as intellectual agreement, then it is all up with democracy. But the whole course of our intellectual history would indicate that in some perverse, obstinate way Western intellectuals have always thrived on their differences, and that somehow these differences have not really disturbed the nonintellectuals enough to upset the social equilibrium. Even today, there is no good evidence that the intellectual alarums of our age of philosophical worries have really gone beyond that small section of the population that possesses high verbal aptitudes. We are not even quite sure that social psychologists like Erich Fromm are right in declaring that nervous instability, even neurosis, is so far common in all parts of our society as to threaten our traditional democratic way of life. Maybe the flight from freedom has been exaggerated.

There is a further grave intellectual difficulty no thinking democrat can avoid facing. We have granted, in accordance with the current of modern anti-intellectualism, and probably also of common sense, that there is a deep energy and toughness in the human race no intellectual system can contain, that our culture has sources of strength not greatly affected by our philosophy—or lack of one. Yet even Pareto lists as one of his strongest residues the *residue to make derivations*—that is, to make sense. The need for satisfying our desire to understand, to have our experience hold together logically, not to be shockingly, patently, inconsistent, not to be hypocrites in our own or in others' eyes—this is a very strong need among human beings. It is safe to say that no civilization has been led by an intellectual class persuaded that their world of values, their explanation of why they were there, was pretense, hypocrisy, pure fake. In a democracy there cannot be for long an unbelieving intellectual class and a believing nonintellectual class; nor can a skeptical or cynical intellectual class devise a religion for the masses.

Now our intellectual classes are by no means today in such a plight. But many of them are puzzled, and they are likely to be more puzzled until they come more successfully to grips with the problem of modifying our eighteenth-century heritage from the Enlightenment. Let us make a final brief summary of that problem.

The democratic world-view was formulated in the eighteenth century at the end of three centuries of change that had culminated in the great triumph of natural science in the work of Newton and his fellows. Whatever may have been the philosophical and theological opinions of these working scientists as private persons—and to this day many of them are sincere Christians—as scientists they had to make use of an intellectual method of arriving at generalizations, a method that was wholly at the mercy of observed facts. These facts were ultimately, no matter how much more subtle than human senses the instruments by which they were recorded, statements about the world of sense experience, this world—and no other. Briefly, a proposition made in accordance with the methods of natural science has to accord with the facts of this world; it may not transcend them and it may not contradict them.

Now two of the master generalizations of the democratic faith as it emerged in the eighteenth and nineteenth centuries, the doctrine of the natural goodness and reasonableness of men and the doctrine of inevitable unilinear progress toward human perfectibility on earth, either transcend the scientific attitude toward truth or contradict it. You have only to follow down through the ages from Thucydides to Machiavelli to the ablest of modern social scientists to note that the tradition among those who really observe carefully the behavior of human beings is one of conviction that men are born to trouble, and that in recorded time, at least, human nature has not greatly changed. If you study the recorded behavior of *Homo sapiens* from the earliest times right down to the mid-twentieth century in the spirit and with the methods of the natural scientist (as far as the inadequacies of the historical record will permit such study) you will be unable to take anything like the attitude of Condorcet, for instance, or even that of Paine and Jefferson. You will be unable to accept as even rough scientific generalizations the concepts of the natural goodness and reasonableness of man and of the increasing perfection, in human terms, of our life on earth.

Nor, again, will you be able to follow completely those other heirs of the Enlightenment and its "enlightened despots," our modern technocrats or cultural engineers. You will not believe that the engineer can devise, *and get accepted,* any institutional device that, while accepting

men as they are, yet transforms their actual behavior into Utopian perfection. You will have to give up Robert Owen, Fourier, and their modern successors (mostly hopeful professional psychologists). You will not
accept the doctrine of the infinite or even very great pliability of human
nature.

Democracy, in short, is *in part* a system of judgments inconsistent with
what the scientist holds to be true. This inconsistency would not create
difficulties—or at least would not create some of the difficulties it now
creates—were the democrat able to say that his kingdom is not of this
world, able to say that his truth is not the kind that is in the least tested
by the scientist, any more than the truth of the Catholic doctrine of the
Eucharist is tested by the chemical analysis of the bread and wine. Such
a solution of the democrat's intellectual quandary is not a happy one,
but is not altogether inconceivable. Democracy may become a genuinely
transcendental faith, in which belief is not weakened by lack of correspondence between the propositions it lays down and the facts of life on
this earth. There are cynics who say that when an American boasts about
the lack of class distinctions in his country he never bothers his mind
with the facts, the facts of our class structure, the facts about Negroes,
Jews, Puerto Ricans, or Mexicans. We Americans have no trouble in
recognizing that the basic principles of that democratic heresy, Marxism,
are contradicted by almost every principle of the actual structure of present-day Russian social life; we recognize that Russian "democracy" is defined quite differently from ours. In short, democracy may be able to take
its promised heaven out of this world, and put it in the world of ritual
performed, of transcendental belief, of vicarious satisfactions of human
wants, may keep it an ideal not too much sullied by the contrast with
the spotted reality.

Or we may see the working out of a democratic attitude toward the
world which accepts the limitations of ordinary human nature, which
accepts a pessimistic view of this world, a democracy with no pie in the
sky and no really ineffable, no all-satisfying pie in the larder. Its enemies
have long said that democracy is a fair-weather thing, that even in its
incomplete realization of liberty, equality, fraternity it sets for human
nature standards that can be approximated in human conduct only in
times of ease and prosperity. In a time of troubles, they say, we shall
need discipline, leadership, solidarity not to be achieved by letting men
even in theory, even in fantasy, follow their own private wills. Such discipline men do indeed accept in times of crisis, as the Western democracies showed well in this last war. Most European peoples took with
amazingly little apparent psychic damage the bombing of cities which
put all civilians on no mere metaphorical battle line. Even more striking in a way was the spirit with which most Americans went into this
last war. To the horror of the tender-minded idealist, they went into it

with very little apparent belief that they were going to make a much better world, with very little of the crusading spirit of the war of 1914-1918. They went into it as into a disagreeable but necessary task that they were able to do very well indeed, but which they saw no reason to pretend to enjoy, or to ennoble. *They went into it as realists, not as cynics.* So far, and in spite of the horrid forebodings of many intellectuals, Western peoples seem not yet driven to mass psychosis by the prospect of atomic or nuclear warfare.

And here we may well conclude, as far as a book of this sort can conclude. An *idealistic* democracy, a *believing* democracy (in the old transcendental sense of religious belief) is perhaps possible, though such a democracy would find it hard to accommodate its this-worldly and scientific heritage to an other-worldly faith. Its God would at the very least need to make some difficult compromises with the psychiatrist. A *realistic,* pessimistic democracy—a democracy in which ordinary citizens approach morals and politics with the willingness to cope with imperfection that characterizes the good farmer, the good physician, the good holder of the cure of souls, be he priest, clergyman, counselor, or psychiatrist—such a democracy would demand more of its citizens than any human culture has ever demanded. Were its demands met, it might well be the most successful of cultures. Finally, a *cynical* democracy, a democracy whose citizens profess in this world one set of beliefs and live another, is wholly impossible. No such society can long endure anywhere. The tension between the ideal and the real may be resolved in many ways in a healthy society; but it can never be taken as nonexistent.